THE

COUNTRY PARISH

Also by Anthony Russell
The Clerical Profession (SPCK 1980, 1984)
Groups and Teams in the Countryside, ed. (SPCK, 1975).

THE

COUNTRY
PARISH

Anthony Russell

First published in Great Britain 1986
SPCK
Holy Trinity Church
Marylebone Road
London NW1 4DU

British Library Cataloguing in Publication Data
Russell, Anthony, *1943–*
    The country parish.
    1. Church of England   2. Church and social
    problems—England   3. Rural churches—England
    I. Title
    261.1′0942   HN39.G7

ISBN 0-281-04214-4

Typeset by Pioneer Associates, Perthshire
Printed in Great Britain at
The University Press, Oxford

Contents

To Sheila

Preface

On many occasions I have had cause to recall a former Archbishop's dictum that writing a book is a hazardous undertaking for a parochial clergyman. Undoubtedly this book has suffered from the piecemeal fashion in which it has been written, amidst the many demands of a country clergyman's life. It would not have been written at all without the patience and skill of Mrs Phyllis Singer who typed the manuscript and to whom I owe a deep debt of gratitude.

Whilst writing the book I have been constantly aware of my gratitude to those who have written about the countryside in recent years, and to those who work in the principal rural organizations. I am indebted to my colleagues at the National Agricultural Centre; to the staff of the Arthur Rank Centre for their encouragement and support, and particularly to the Revd John Clarke, Chaplain of the Arthur Rank Centre, whose comments and criticisms have improved this book in many places. I am indebted to the Management Committee of the Arthur Rank Centre for its support and encouragement, and to the Rank Foundation for the support which it gives to the Centre. To the people of the parishes of Preston-on-Stour, Atherstone-on-Stour and Whitchurch, I also owe a great debt for their stimulation and encouragement over many years which is reflected in the book.

Whitchurch Rectory
September 1985   Anthony Russell

The Country Parish —
An Introduction

In recent years so much has been written about the countryside, that any new book would seem to demand an apology if not an excuse. Any bookshop will witness to the growth of interest in conservation, landscape protection, historic buildings, the protection of flora and fauna, rural crafts and the village in the pre-industrial period. However, there are still relatively few books on the social aspects of the contemporary village, and almost none on the contemporary village church. This latter omission is particularly surprising, as the Church is the most ubiquitous rural organization and its clergy are the last professional group which can still be found in relatively large numbers in rural areas. The job of a country clergyman gives him a particular vantage point from which to observe the changes which are transforming the village at the present time.

A Church report ('Putting Our House in Order'), published during the last war, spoke of the rural church as 'the true nursery of the religious life of the nation'. While such language could not be used today, there remains a sense in which the countryside may be regarded as the heartland of the Church of England. Not only does the Church receive its strongest support in proportional terms for its country churches, but the Church of England remains, at many levels, a rural church or at least a church whose dominant understandings and ethos are more congruent with rural society than with the city centre. Yet, for too long the country church has been regarded as peripheral, and rural ministry has been rather contemptuously seen as the Church's 'second eleven'. This book seeks to make the point that ministering to the contemporary rural community is a highly skilled and demanding role which requires particular insights, skills and understandings. Unless the Church develops these understandings more widely, there will be little to stop its drift towards becoming an urban sect and severing all connection with its roots in what for generations has been the heartland of the Church of England.

At another level, the book seeks to be a phenomenological study of the contemporary village. Amidst the growing literature of the countryside, there are relatively few books which seek to describe the changes which have transformed villages in recent years. Such books as there are, are written by those who are principally concerned with the specific aspects of the countryside and convey little of what it feels like to live in a contemporary village. In the post-war period, much of what was written about the countryside centred on the problems of the depopulation. Within a relatively short period of time depopulation became repopulation as people moved out of the cities and towns: a process sometimes referred to as 'counter-urbanization'. The 1960s and 1970s, in particular, saw what has been called 'the quiet revolution' of the countryside as a result of the impact of population migration and the subsequent 'embourgeoisement' of village life. The influence of the new villagers has profoundly altered the nature of many rural settlements and the interaction between the new villagers and the old villagers is considered in this book from both the point of view of the village and of its church. For generations what seemed like a deeply rooted inferiority complex seemed to grip the countryside, but recent years have seen the emergence of a new movement of 'rural conscientiousness' both in this country and the United States. After a long period, in which rural matters were of no national consequence, suddenly they are enjoying a period of considerable prominence. However, the nature of the debate is no longer that of a traditional confrontation between urban and rural but between the different elements of the contemporary rural community. This book seeks to sensitize the Church both to the dimensions and significance of the debate and to the part which it can play as the most ubiquitous organization within the contemporary countryside.

All generalizations about the countryside need to be approached with some caution. A large part of the attraction of the English countryside lies in its variety: there are forty-four different geological strata in Great Britain, varying from the great wedges of chalk, carboniferous limestone, granite and weald clay, to isolated fragments of rock and strips of magnesium limestone. Traditionally, the nature of the geological strata determined not only the nature of flora and fauna, but also the type of farming that was possible and the dominant form of architecture. However, today, the determining factor in shaping rural life tends to be proximity to the nearest metropolitan centre rather than the nature of the geological strata.

At a very simple level, it is possible to suggest that there are four countrysides in England which form concentric rings around the principal metropolitan areas. *The urban shadow countryside* can be found in the immediate vicinity of urban areas. In this countryside, commuters tend to be predominant, and the villages often have the feel of a discontinuous suburb. The farming community, though present, is not particularly evident, and, because of the proximity of an urban centre, the facilities and services in the village are often minimal. *The accessible countryside* frequently has better facilities as the urban centre is at a great distance. Commuters and the retired live in considerable numbers in these villages, but the farming community and the local resident group are more evident. By definition, communications to the nearest metropolitan centres, either by rail or by car, are good. *The less accessible countryside* (sometimes defined as that area beyond a travelling distance of one hour from a metropolitan centre) is characterized, in some areas, by de-population. Commuters are less evident, though there are significant numbers of retired people in such villages. The farming and local resident community is much more evident than in the previous two types, but services and facilities are seriously affected by the spiral of decline in village life. In *the remote or marginal countryside,* the local resident community and the farmers form a majority of the year-round population, although there are some retired people. Second homes and occasional holiday residents play an important role in many areas. Services and facilities in the remoter countryside have been seriously contracted in recent decades. Before any assertion about the contemporary countryside can be evaluated, it is necessary to determine which of the four dominant types of English countryside is being referred to, as social and economic patterns in these areas are significantly different.

However, behind all the issues and questions which face the contemporary countryside today lies the problem of definition.

The definition of what is 'rural' in modern English society is both varied and complex. At the physical level, it is difficult to distinguish between urban and rural areas, not least because any attempt to devise a continuum between extreme rural and extreme urban leaves most of the English countryside in the intermediate categories. Some social geographers have developed indices of rurality, and planners and administrators (since the demise of the rural district council) have found it necessary to devise arbitrary delineations between urban and rural areas. Estimates of the size of the contemporary rural population vary considerably; various yardsticks have been used based on the degree of remoteness from urban centres, the density of population and the size of settlement. The Scott Committee on Land Utilization in Rural Areas (1942) suggested that any compacted grouping of over 1,500 people was a town. At about the same time, Professor Dudley Stamp suggested that 500 was about the minimum size for a village. More recently, R. J. Green has suggested that a population of 5,000 marks the watershed between rural and urban. In 1977 it was suggested that the rural population could be defined as those who live outside the radius of five miles from an urban centre of 20,000 and ten miles from a metropolitan centre of 100,000. By this estimate, the rural population in 1977 totalled 6.4 million. However, for the purposes of this study the rural population may be defined as those who live in market towns and villages up to 10,000, of which there are approximately 13,000 such settlements in England and Wales, in which very nearly 20 per cent of the population live. Of these settlements, 9,000 have a population of less than 1,000 and 80 per cent have no more than 500 people. In Warwickshire, where the total population in the 1977 mini-census was 474,000, 165,000 people lived outside the urban structure plan areas, i.e. about 35 per cent of the population.

In the 1930s it became common to use the terms urban and rural, not to denote location but to indicate different lifestyles. Commentators suggested that while the distinctions between urban and rural areas were, in many places, difficult to maintain, nevertheless it was possible to speak of a rural culture, which was significantly different from the dominant urban culture. However, it is hard to see in what sense such a distinction can be maintained in England in the last quarter of the twentieth century: everyone lives in an urban and industrial mass culture, and people are exposed to the same media influences. Particularly in the younger age groups all acknowledge the same culture symbols, receive similar education, dress alike, watch television, and share common, or at least related, aspirations and goals. This is not to deny that there are attitudinal patterns, values, dispositions and modes of behaviour that are characteristic of those who live in the countryside (what the Americans call 'the rural mind-set'). But the degree to which the term 'rural' can be used in this sense is extremely problematic.

If it is difficult to define the term 'rural', it is equally difficult to define the word 'village'. For the average Englishman the word village is like a telegram in code; at its mention his mind is flooded with a series of pictures, impressions and beliefs which have been reinforced in every generation by, among other things, the idealistic way in which the countryside and its people are treated in children's books. The village has become, in contemporary Britain, a symbol of that lost community and that lost sense of belonging, that disappeared when society became more sophisticated and affluent. There is a real sense in which the village is the paradise from which the Englishman has been thrust out. Perhaps it is hardly surprising that one of the most industrialized and densely populated of countries should possess a deep sense of arcadianism and pastoral nostalgia. The dream of human innocence in a garden has deep roots. It is hard not to believe that some part of this nostalgia, this homelessness and this rootlessness, is not itself part of a wider search for faith. Certainly, for some, the countryside in modern Britain has become an object of faith and is protected and venerated with what might be regarded as an almost religious intensity.

In one sense, the oddest thing about an English village is that it is called by a French name. Left to ourselves, English people would have spoken of 'boroughs' and 'towns'. Chaucer used the word 'village' only once, but the word 'town' repeatedly. It seems to have been about the time of Shakespeare, and the translators of the Authorized Version of the Bible, that the word 'village' became popular as something distinct from, and smaller than, a town. Definitions of a village are many and varied, and what constitutes a village is far from clear. The *Oxford Shorter English Dictionary* defines a village as a settlement 'larger than a hamlet and smaller than a town', which seems to leave almost every question unanswered. Statistical thresholds, in the literature of rural sociology, vary enormously, some choosing figures as high as 12,000, as the threshold between a town and a village, others as low as 1,500 (as in the Scott Report). One definition speaks of a village as 'a nucleated rural settlement of twenty or more homesteads; a large village being distinguished from a small market town by the paucity of its services'. Another speaks of a village as 'a community of families in a compact collection of houses'. Other commentators have sought to draw up typologies of villages based on the open—closed continuum; whether they are integrated or disintegrated communities, or of the dominant resident type or the principal economic activity (fishing, tourist, farming, commuter, etc). Attempts at statistical and objective categorizations of villages have proved both hazardous and not very illuminating. Clearly, when people talk about a village in English society, (and the term village is sometimes used of urban areas as well as rural) they are speaking of a small-scale community, in which a person can know, at least to recognize, the vast majority of those who live there. Some social analysts have suggested that a village community is one in which a person can at least recognize 80 per cent of the people who live there (or as one local resident has said, 'big enough for a fair amount to happen; and small enough so we don't miss any of it'). Characteristically, villages are small-scale rural communities which have identifiable boundaries and which have complicated and complex internal dynamics.

Generalizations about villages tend to affront the belief that all villages are totally different; a difference which is both real and symbolic. Certainly, all villages have a life of their own; their own character and nature, much of it obscured and not easily accessible. And the church is often the custodian of the village's identity and of its past. Nor is the tradition of the English village restricted to this country, for many people left the villages in the late nineteenth century and settled in the United States, Canada, Australia, New Zealand and many other places. Much of what they loved they took with them, and much of what they found oppressive they left behind.

In another sense, a village is defined by its past, for a village is a community in time and the product of its history which in part makes it what it is today. A consciousness of the past hangs heavily in many villages and there is a real sense in which the contemporary village is the product of its past. At another level, it can be maintained that the people who move into villages today do so partly because they wish to be surrounded by the symbols of the past — the parish church, the village green, the black and white cottages, the old pub. Because both the village and the parish church are so often seen in terms of their past, it is important to achieve an accurate understanding of the past and its influence on the present. For this reason this book is concerned both with the village today and with its distant and immediate past. Accurate historical knowledge checks the growth of arcadian fantasies about the village's past. Those who have recently moved into a village may be tempted to view the nineteenth century in a nostalgic and romantic manner, yet within the village there will be older residents for whom the past is inextricably linked with the period of poverty, deprivation, dependence and deference. By the same token, the country church has to learn how to develop, and live with its tradition, without becoming imprisoned by it, in an age of very different social circumstances and ecclesiastical realities. In many country churches the past can be a burden which prevents the Church of today from growing towards the future. As Lord Acton wrote: 'If the past has been an obstacle and a burden, knowledge of the past is the safest and surest emancipation.'

Much of what has been written in recent years about the Church of England has carried the implication that the Church is drifting loose from its roots and traditional understandings. If this is true, it is perhaps even more important that we should study more closely what may be regarded as the heartland of the Church of England — the country parish. But the country parish has also changed radically in recent years, and this book seeks both to account for that change and to offer ways in which the ministry of the Church may develop in the future. The countryside has changed dramatically and if the Church is not to become an urban sect it must develop new ways of ministering in rural areas with much reduced levels of stipendiary clergy. Those who have written or spoken about rural ministry recently have tended to advocate either radical and far reaching changes or steadfast adherence to ancient patterns. This study seeks to commend neither alternative but to show that with an understanding both of the village's history and of the contemporary changes which are reshaping the rural community, there are ways in which the historic parish system can be adapted and modified so that it continues to fulfil its ancient function in a time of changed social and ecclesiastical circumstances.

This book, therefore, is at one level an attempt to describe the contemporary village both in terms of those aspects of its history which have given it its present shape, and the impact of more recent changes on the rural community. At another level, at a time when much has been written about the urban church, it is an analytical attempt to describe contemporary rural ministry and the changes which are transforming the country parish. Clearly, such changes call for a reinterpretation of the Church's ministry in the countryside and a re-emphasis on those skills and understandings which are specific to the Church's task in rural areas. At such a time the Church is called to new developments in ministry but these must be congruent with its historic understandings of the place of the Church in the country village, for it is only by changing and adapting inherited practices that we are able to fulfil ancient intentions in changed circumstances. A Norfolk parish decided to hang a framed list of former incumbents in the church. When it was hung, the list contained forty-seven names, ending with that of the present incumbent. There was no space for adding to the list. By our actions we demonstrate that the parish ministry in country villages has a long and honourable past; but our respect for that past but must never be so great that it sets limits on the future.

Recently, some voices within the Church have suggested that it may be necessary to withdraw almost entirely from certain areas of the countryside and concentrate on those areas where there is likely to be the largest numerical response. The rural community will never be significant in statistical terms in our society, but villages remain important because they say things about the nature of society and the nature of man in community that need to be said. It is easier in a village, for a number of reasons, to act out some of those basic beliefs we hold to be true about the nature of man in community. This is in part because villages are small and human in their dimensions, and in part because they have a past, the consciousness of which tends to confer both stability and perspective. In the village is found among other things that supreme human virtue which is merely called 'neighbourliness', that subtle combination of love, care, tolerance, support, sacrifice and respect for the individual. This is a powerful combination of deeply Christian values which alone can make a community human in the fullest sense of that word. This is not to deny that these virtues do not occur in abundance elsewhere, or to suggest that they may be sought in every village, but merely to say that villages in social terms, like monasteries in religious terms, are the repositories of values that are of importance to the wider society. This may in part explain the powerful hold that villages have on the English mind and the desire of many to live in them. It may be that in this period of profound turbulence in our society and its institutions, villages, like the monasteries in the Dark Ages (or, rather, the values and symbols they enshrined), will reassert themselves and be accorded a complimentary significance.

2

Changing Attitudes to the Village
and the Countryside

It is necessary to preface a study of the contemporary village with a brief account of the changes in attitude to the countryside which have shaped the way in which the contemporary village is widely regarded. This chapter is concerned to demonstrate that the way in which many people think about the village has been coloured, consciously or subconsciously, by ideas about the countryside which have their origin in the picturesque and romantic movements of the eighteenth and nineteenth centuries. Some examination of the development of these understandings of the countryside which are such a powerful force in contemporary English society, is necessary before the reality of the contemporary rural community can be studied.

In the period before the Industrial Revolution it was possible to speak of England as a society composed of thousands of small rural communities which shared a common and agrarian culture to which there were relatively few urban exceptions. In the late eighteenth century many industrial enterprises, such as the naval dockyards at Portsmouth, stopped work for a period at harvest time, so closely were town and country interrelated. Commercial centres were also cattle markets and cities depended obviously and immediately upon the surrounding rural hinterland. Indeed, the notion of town and country, as separate environments and social systems, was not well developed in pre-industrial society. It was the impact of the Industrial Revolution and the development of the specialist manufacturing cities, such as Sheffield, which led to an accelerating division between urban and rural. When 'the condition of England' came to be discussed in the third and fourth decades of the nineteenth century, the Victorians were chiefly concerned to discover a new urban population which, in many of its essential features, was totally unlike traditional rural society. Though Disraeli's famous 'two nations' referred to the rich and poor in Victorian England, it could equally have been applied to urban and rural society, so distinctive had they become in a relatively short time. Horace Mann's religious census of 1851 merely confirmed, in statistical terms, facts of which the mid-Victorian clergyman was becoming increasingly aware, namely that the Industrial Revolution had created a new urban secular culture. This culture was, in many respects, totally distinct from rural patterns in which religion, and particularly the Church of England, had been so inextricably a part.

During the latter part of the nineteenth century there was a rapid acceleration in this process of differentiation, and today England is predominantly an urban and metropolitan society in which at least 85 per cent of the population live in large cities. Urban and metropolitan values and norms dominate English society, and whether people actually live in country villages or in the city, they are the products of a broadly similar educational system; they dress alike; they read the same newspapers and watch the same television programmes. In brief, unlike many other countries of the world, it is increasingly difficult in England to speak of a rural culture which is distinctive in significant ways from the mainstream urban and metropolitan culture of our society. Nevertheless, there lingers in many rural areas a constellation of values, dispositions, and understandings and modes of thought, reinforced in every suceeding generation, which may be regarded as characteristically rural and are the remnant of the old rural culture (sometimes called the 'prior' or 'residual' culture) which, in many areas, has been almost totally eclipsed.

Most villages in England were already established on their present sites by the time of the Norman conquest. Then, as now, the village was a group of dwellings clustered round the church and the green which were both its social and architectural focus. The Saxon farmers who developed these settlements regarded the countryside as unfriendly and hostile, and unlike modern country dwellers who site their houses so that they can enjoy the best view, the Saxons built their dwellings in a defensive ring facing inwards, with the backs of the houses to the hostile and threatening countryside. For them, the church was not just the centre of religious and social life for the community, but also a strongpoint and place of defence from whose roof or tower a watch could be

11

kept on the surrounding countryside. In pre-industrial society the countryside was predominantly seen as hostile, primitive, violent and barbaric; the word 'pagan' literally means 'dweller in the countryside'. For the Saxons, the first month of the year was the month of the wolf, the cold and hungry month in which the wolves were most conspicuous around the village. The wolf was a potent symbol of the wildness, brutality and unpredictability of the countryside, and in the forest areas of the Midlands many Saxon place names are associated with the wolf (Wolford, Wolvey, Wolverton).

The village farmer of the early Middle Ages would have found in the poetic accounts of the creation in Genesis 1 and 3 an account of man's relationship with the natural world which was meaningful within the terms of his own experience. In the Garden of Eden man is portrayed as living in a state of primitive harmony with the natural world; this is broken as a result of his disobedience. The punishment of man takes the form of the cleavage of this relationship between man and the earth. Nature is now seen as hostile and threatening, a place of 'thorns also and thistles' (Genesis 3.18). Man has become alienated from the earth in which he was formed and this alienation is expressed in the dogged and relentless struggle of primitive farming. It is as if a spell had been cast on the earth which somehow denies man easy access to its fertility and abundance. The natural world is seen as malevolent, unpredictable and unfriendly, and farming as a constant struggle of unending physical work.

As the early European cities developed, so their walls were built not only to defend their inhabitants against attack but also against the encroachment of rural barbarism. Within the confines of those walls slowly emerged the intellectual, religious, artistic and commercial life to which the word 'civilization' was given. There was an inclination everywhere to regard the countryside as the least desirable place in which to live and men shared the 'Dick Whittington' myth that, in the city alone, refinement, wealth and culture could be found. The pre-industrial countryside was not the sunlit Arcadia of received opinion, but a place of poverty, disease, sickness in animals, fire and flood, and frequent starvation. Whenever the opportunity arose people left the harshness, poverty, uncertainty and the social and physical confines of rural life either for the developing industrial cities or to join the steady stream of settlers in the colonies overseas.

If the Renaissance had its origins in the city states of northern Italy, then the Age of Enlightenment had its roots in the countryside and in the formative influence of the concept of nature on religion, philosophy, ethics and law in the early eighteenth century. Nature had been an important concept in western thought since the classical period, but it was in the eighteenth century that nature, as an alternative to all that was made by man, came to be seen as the dominant theme in European thought. One of the central motifs of eighteenth-century classicalism was that of the pastoral idyll and the notion that life consisted of an eternal return to this primitive archetype. Philosophers and theologians, lawyers and economists, artists and scientists, all attempted to discover the natural (the divine and archetypal) laws which governed their disciplines: laws that were clear, authoritative and universal and which could be regarded as the outworking of the mind of God the Creator. If theologians in the Renaissance and post-Reformation period had been preoccupied with the word of God, the eighteenth century saw a new concern for the works of God. As Bacon had written (and Sir Thomas More before him), science was the study of the works of God and this should be almost, if not quite, as pious a pursuit as the study of his word. Thus, this interaction between theology and science played an important part in producing one of the dominant concepts of the eighteenth century, the divinization of nature. Such a materialistic perspective did not dispense with the idea of God himself (at least in the eighteenth century), for the great machine presupposed the divine mechanic.

This new emphasis in theology found expression in the writing of George Herbert's brother, Lord Edward Herbert of Cherbury (1583—1648) who aroused considerable interest by his writing on the 'religion of nature' published in Paris in 1624. After the complexities and mysteries of medieval thought and the theological controversies of the seventeenth century, men everywhere turned to nature as a source of authority and inspiration. The divinization of nature, which began in the Renaissance, proceeded during the eighteenth century and culminated in the works of William Wordsworth. The painter Turner, by all accounts a man almost without religious belief, proclaimed on his deathbed: 'The Sun is

God.' Scientific, philosophical and social writers all saw in nature the divine hand and the place where a true understanding of the world, in both a physical and a moral sense, could be found. European thought was profoundly influenced by the experience of Rousseau on his island refuge on the lake of Bienne. In his total absorption in the natural world he became aware not only of the beauty and innocence of nature, but of its moral order. Philosophers and missionaries praised the virtues of the unspoilt natural man whose physique and morals, it seemed to them, put Europeans to shame. A number of black men appeared in the capitals of Europe as examples of prelapsian innocence.

Partly because of the influence of these ideas and partly because the wealthy in early eighteenth-century England, at the end of the European wars, were able to travel more extensively in Europe, there emerged a changed attitude towards the countryside. Such travellers brought home to the shire counties of England not only paintings by Claude, Lorrain, Poussin, and Salvator Rosa, but also new ideas about landscape, scenery and the countryside. If in the medieval period the countryside in a painting was seen through a window or over a garden wall and separated from the foreground, in the seventeenth century the countryside was recognized as a proper subject for painting in its own right. For now it was seen as a place of beauty and innocence, eloquent of the divine wisdom. Pastoral literature (which goes back to Theocritus who, in his *Idylls,* adapted the popular songs and ballads of Sicilian peasant culture) enjoyed wide popularity, and by the early eighteenth century Virgil's *Georgics* appeared in a flood of translations for a public eager to reclaim the pastoral tradition.

The medieval farmer had seen the countryside in simple terms; good land was easy to cultivate and yielded well and bad land did neither. While his attitude to the land was pragmatic and functional, the new concepts of landscape and scenery seemed to imply separation, observation and a lack of close involvement with the actual working of the land. Repton claimed that 'a ploughed field was no fit sight for a gentleman's elegant mansion'. Influenced by such ideas, the returning travellers commissioned the Palladian country houses of Burlington and his protégé Flutecroft in styles of approved good taste and decorous elegance, and created with Repton and Capability Brown's help many fine examples of neoclassical pastoral landscape. (The eighteenth-century gentleman, standing in his library with a book of poetry in his hand and gazing out over his park and estate, came to be regarded as the embodiment of the Age of Enlightenment.) Possibly the most celebrated example of landscaping is that of Stourhead with its temples and grotto grouped around a lake in the centre of the garden. It was principally the work of Henry Hoare the younger (1705–85) who had inherited the estate in 1741. He sought to create a real landscape which would imitate the idealized Virgilian scenes painted in Rome in the previous century by Lorrain and Poussin. However, for his poorer neighbours, these new understandings of the countryside which manifested themselves in enclosures and parks served only to further increase their distress. For them the countryside was a far cry from the sunlit Arcadia filled with shepherds and shepherdesses wearing garlands and playing recorders and hautbois, as portrayed in Watteau's paintings. The new concept of landscape and scenery brought great changes to the mid eighteenth-century countryside (as we shall note in the following chapter) and their impact is graphically recorded in Oliver Goldsmith's poem 'The Deserted Village' (1770). The title page was illustrated in the first edition by a drawing of an old villager shown recounting the destruction of her village and pointing to the crumbling cottages which can be seen in the background. Goldsmith is often thought to have been inspired by the case of Nuneham in Oxfordshire which was rebuilt as Nuneham Courtenay after the emparking of the original village.

However, it was in the writing of William Wordsworth that this process of the divinization of nature reached its zenith. In some senses England was the first European society in which widespread adherence to the Christian faith ceased, and it is no coincidence that the belief in the divinity of nature took a strong hold in this country. That ease of heart which Bunyan had found at the foot of the cross, Wordsworth found in contemplating the fields, mountains and the natural world. He came to see that only total absorption in nature could heal and restore his spirits which were distracted by the realization of man's inhumanity as revealed in the French Revolution. But neither Wordsworth nor his followers would have lifted up their eyes to the hills for such help if the eighteenth century had not unfalteringly directed them towards the visible universe as the clearest evidence of God. This new religion was a religion of feeling and response to the natural world, rather than one of learning and intellectual quest. In a relatively short period, in both poetry and art, there was a change from the grand and heroic to a concern for images drawn from the familiar, the homespun and the ordinary. Artistic and cultural life, which had been associated from the beginning with urban lifestyles and values, came to be dominated by images of the countryside. Constable's much admired painting, 'Willows by a Stream', portrayed an undistinguished section of muddy Suffolk riverbank, with a distant view of a village, but it spoke eloquently then, as it does now, of the beauty and the melancholy of the natural world. If plain thinking and high living were the characteristics of this new religion, then country walks were its liturgy, for generations of English people have recognized the Wordsworthian insight that a country walk is a spiritual experience as well as physical exercise. As Lord Clark has commented, the countryside where Wordsworth himself walked in solitude is now almost as crowded with pilgrims as are Lourdes and Benares. John Burroughs wrote in 1912 (quoted by J. A. Walter): 'Every walk in the wood is a religious rite . . . If we do not go to church as much as did our fathers, we go to the woods much more, and . . . we now use the word nature very much as our fathers used the word God.'

In the late eighteenth century, stimulated by Thomas West's guidebook of 1778 and cut off from Italy by the European wars, many people made their way to the Lake District, where a number of classical villas were built. 'Morning amongst the Coniston Fells', Turner's painting of 1798, shows a man and a woman with some sheep alone in the vast lakeland landscape. A quotation from *Paradise Lost* identifies them as Adam and Eve calling on the elements of the natural world to praise their Creator. It is no exaggeration to say that Wordsworth's book *Description of the Scenery in the Lakes in the North of England* (1822) changed the way in which people looked at landscape and scenery. Without doubt his influence had a lasting effect on the English view of the countryside, but his name should be linked with that of Ruskin, whose successor in part he was. (In 1844 they co-operated in a campaign which attempted to prevent the construction of a railway line between Oxenholme and Kendal.) Ruskin saw the natural world as a direct revelation of God's glory, designed for the edification of man and to be read like a holy book, which it was his privilege to interpret as nature's priest. While he rejected the implicit pantheism of Wordsworth, nevertheless he saw the natural world in a similar light, as evidenced by his enthusiasm for the paintings of Turner who he believed was alone among modern painters in his capacity to see the revelation of the divine in the natural world. Ruskin and Wordsworth shared the widely held belief that the spread of urban and industrial areas in the late eighteenth and early nineteenth centuries was to be regarded as the social equivalent of 'the fall of man'. When William Cowper wrote 'God made the countryside and man made the town', he was articulating the widespread belief that the countryside was the place of virtue, morality and religion, and that the town was characterized by lawlessness, greed, violence and atheism. Anti-urbanism became a prominent feature of mid-Victorian society and Ruskin denounced the 'great foul city, pouring out poison at every pore'. This polarity between town and country, and its association with moral values, remains a vein in the English understanding of the countryside and is discernible in some modern writing which tends to regard industrialization and the loss of the pre-industrial countryside as the cause and origin of contemporary social disorders.

The rural romanticism which owed so much to Ruskin and was so strong a feature of nineteenth-century literature and art, appears to have arisen as the compensatory shadow to the overcrowded offices and noisy factories of an increasingly urbanized and industrialized society. The popular Victorian landscape painters suggested in their work a timelessness which was in its own way an implicit protest against the rapid transformation of both urban and rural areas in the late nineteenth century. Like Thomas Hardy, Myles Birkett Foster (1825—99) portrayed a landscape which was being speedily transformed by factory-made products and by new means of communication, particularly the railways. Such men were the voice of the old rural culture with all its picturesqueness and poverty, its touching gentleness and its brutal violence. Helen Allingham's cottage scenes portrayed in drowsy, warm, unnaturally still weather (which some people still call 'Tennyson weather'), the English virtues of rural domesticity, continuity and repose.

However, at the same time, they were an accurate reflection of the living conditions of the rural poor in the late nineteenth century and the poverty, the mud and the effects of poor diet and hard labour are clearly visible. It is part of the paradox of the Victorian treatment of the countryside that the idealization of the happy cottagers and tenantry, supported by honest toil, appeared side by side with an awareness of the poverty and squalor of their homes, and the melancholy and violent nature of much village life. Thomas Hardy, who was born near Tolpuddle only a few years after the deportation of the 'martyrs', portrayed the countryside as changeless and timeless but also as a struggling and developing community. He particularly identified new means of communication — the railways and cheap newspapers — as the destroyers of the old rural culture.

From the mid eighteenth century to the late nineteenth century, England was slowly changing from being a wholly rural to a predominantly urban society. Increasingly the countryside came to be seen no longer as intimidating and hostile, and village life as brutal and boorish, but both were viewed with a wistful sense of loss by those now living in urban and industrial areas. On the walls of their new houses such pictures as Millet's 'The Angelus', with its aura of pious humility, honest toil and the dreamy calm of an evening landscape, spoke eloquently of community, continuity and contact with nature to those constrained by the pressures of urban and industrial life. Rural romanticism and nostalgia were one of the dominant themes of Victorian society, and artists and craftsmen sought to bring indoors by means of carving, wrought iron, stained glass and painting, the trees, foliage, flowers and fruits of the countryside. Others took their easels out into the fields to record the life and ways of a countryside which was rapidly changing. The gothic revival was in part an attempt to recreate the lost world of pre-industrial society and to emphasize the social harmony, community and simple piety which, it was thought, had been eroded and destroyed by urbanization and industrialization. Some sought to recreate the medieval countryside and, following William Morris, C. R. Ashby brought 150 men, women and children from London to Chipping Campden to form the Guild of Handicrafts in 1902 in the old silk mill in Sheep Street.

A more common response was that of the typical Victorian who sought refuge in the rural world of his imagination and of his childhood. None touched this vein in Victorian life more deftly than Kate Greenaway, whose 'Gleaners Going Home' depicts the rural poor struggling half-asleep through the sunset, wearing immaculate peasant costumes and clasping posies of corn and flowers. She herself was a working-class girl who grew up in the slums of Hoxton; she had stumbled upon this folk ideal of the countryside by chance, on holiday at Rolleston near Newark. Away from the dirt and squalor of the slums she painted cowslips and appleblossom and created what was, in effect, a toy landscape to delight a child. Her pictures became a symbol of the countryside for many urban Victorians. Her first book of pictures and verses, *Under the Window,* sold 20,000 copies in the weeks before Christmas 1897, and within two years she had created a small industry of books, clothes, greetings cards and wallpaper, all illustrated with her pastel-shaded drawings of an imagined pre-industrial countryside. Ruskin, while he was Slade Professor of Fine Art at Oxford, said that her vision of flowers and children might save England from the sordid effects of industrialization.

Beatrix Potter's *Peter Rabbit* was first published in 1902 and sold 27,000 copies in the first year. Several generations of children grew up with books by such authors as Kenneth Graham, E. Nesbit, J. M. Barrie, Richard Jefferies, Frances Hodgson Burnett and Arthur Ransome, all of whom saw the countryside as a place of escape. It seems that for many Victorians and Edwardians the old order of the countryside had become inseparable from their childhood; the lost countryside was regarded as a symbol of purity and moral order, and its disappearance became associated with their own loss of youth and of childhood innocence.

It seems that whenever English society experiences a period of disturbance or turbulence, it seeks to reaffirm its rural origins and roots (what Americans call 'the Jeffersonian values'). It is as if there is a turning for spiritual nourishment to the heartland of our society, those lanes which, as H. J. Massingham wrote, 'lead to what the world calls nowhere, namely, the hamlets, villages and farms which are the cornerstone of England'. In the years before the First World War, perhaps on account of an unconscious sense of impending change, the seemingly eternal changelessness of the English countryside was widely celebrated in poetry and a genre of literature known as the 'Norfolk jacket' school of writing. Poets such as Thomas Hardy, Edmund Blunden and Edward Thomas wrote what were, in a sense, elegies for the passing of the immemorial rural order. Their work was edited and published in five anthologies of 'Georgian poetry' between 1912 and 1922 by Edward Marsh. Edward Thomas, who did much to popularize the works of Richard Jefferies and was a friend of Arthur Ransome wrote a series of topographical books at this time: *The Heart of England, The South Country, The Icknield Way* and *The Pursuit of Spring.* Perhaps no writer since Wordsworth can have walked so many miles through England and Wales and, like Wordsworth, Thomas saw himself as a recorder of the slow destruction of rural society and its culture. It is interesting to note that these books by Thomas and the works of the 'Georgian poets', which have long been out of print, have recently reappeared in popular editions. At the same time, the emergence of similar themes and sources of inspiration can be seen among musicians, for after the German influence of Handel and Mendelssohn, there emerged around the turn of the century a new era of English music. Elgar and Vaughan Williams, Holst, Delius, Walton and Britten all drew on the countryside as a major source of inspiration, to form what modernists dismissed as the 'cowpat' school of music. Elgar in particular echoed Victorian literature in using the theme of the countryside as a bridge back to his village childhood.

During both World Wars there was a flood of nostalgic and sentimental books about the English countryside. Sheila Kaye-Smith's *Little England* (1918) is typical of those books which appeared during wartime and which combined a particular blend of the rural and the patriotic. In the book's opening chapter she has a character who looks down from a hillside footpath across the Sussex countryside as far as the coast, seeing the England for which they are all fighting. At a stile, he pauses to read a letter from his soldier son and listens to the guns in France. There is much contemporary evidence to indicate that the England for which many fought was the England of the countryside and the village: the countryside — as recorded by Siegfried Sassoon in the first volume of his trilogy — which was radically changed as a result of the 1914—18 war.

Although such landmarks as *The Shell Guide to the Flowers of the Countryside* by Roland Hilders (first published in 1955) and Nikolaus Pevsner's first volume of *The Buildings of England* (1951), appeared in the 1950s, nevertheless the thrust of this period was essentially urban. The 1960s may be regarded as the zenith of confidence in the urban future of man, marked in theology by the publication of Harvey Cox's *The Secular City*. However, the 1970s saw a dramatic resurgence of concern for, and interest in, the countryside. Just as in mid-Victorian England interest in the countryside and the village appeared to arise as a response to the threat of social and cultural change, so in the 1970s a similar awareness appeared to prompt a similar reaction. Gradually the excitement and the confidence which had been widely felt in the urban future of man gave way to an uneasy weariness and a growing pessimism. The awareness of increasing levels of violence, privatization and alienation, drove people back to the countryside in search of certainties and values, away from the corruption and violence of the cities. The 'Golden Country' of George Orwell's *1984* was sought by many who were disenchanted with urban lifestyles and were seeking a route back to the simplicity, moral goodness and paradisal innocence of the countryside and the village. As we shall note in Chapter 5, an increasing number of people sought a surrogate involvement in the countryside through television, for apart from the programmes on wildlife, country crafts and sheepdog trials, serials and plays were increasingly located in the countryside, and particularly in the period before the First World War. *The Forsyte Saga* demonstrated what an excellent medium television was for conveying nostalgia, precisely because it could dwell on the visual manifestations of the past and thus make them real and almost graspable.

In a sense the countryside has become the dominant symbol for genuineness, integrity, authority, meaning and value in a society dominated by the instant, the expendable and the superficial. As people revolted against the technical standardization and the commercialization of life in the 1970s, so they developed a taste for dairymaid and peasant dresses (with their suggestion of rural values and pleasures, without any hint of rural toil), cottage-style scrubbed furniture and coffee-table books about the countryside. Advertisers used the countryside as a symbol of homespun goodness and simple virtues, to market their products. In a world of change and profound insecurity there is a deep desire for the predictable, slow-moving world of the pre-industrial countryside. This collective nostalgia for rural simplicity is reflected in any bookshop where the memoirs, reprints and books that accompany television serials evoke the untroubled world of the pre-industrial countryside. Just as *Common Objects in the Countryside* by the Revd J. C. Woods was the publishing phenomenon of the late Victorian period, with 100,000 copies sold in a week in 1881, so *The Country Diary of an Edwardian Lady* (1977), which has sold two and a quarter million copies in hardback and has been translated into thirteen languages, has become a contemporary publishing phenomenon. It is ironic that Flora Thompson's account of Juniper Hill in the 1880s should have given rise to a merchandising promotion which was given a £250,000 launch by a major chain of stores; it is a poignant comment on the poverty of late nineteenth-century rural England that Flora Thompson's sole descendant missed this event, because she lives in Australia (where the family emigrated).

As Peter Berger has commented, modern man suffers from a sense of 'homelessness', of futility, insecurity, moral confusion and loneliness. In one generation man has progressed from horse-drawn transport to space travel, and it is not surprising that he is left with a feeling of rootlessness and uncertainty. Such rootlessness makes people both hanker for the past and see the countryside in terms of pre-industrial patterns and lifestyles. In short, rural nostalgia is the medicine that modern man takes for the side effects of living in the age of the computer and the silicon chip. However, the coffee-table books about the countryside and the guidebooks to English villages all portray the countryside not as a dynamic and modern community but in a static and fixed way, as if it were something which was not the product of human labour but had been dropped at our feet from the distant past as a remembrance from a simple and uncorrupt time. The 'picturesque' attitude towards the countryside, which replaced the more vigorous and robust attitude of medieval man, sees the countryside literally 'as a picture', devoid of its economic, political and social reality. The townsmen, and many who now live in the countryside, do not wish to know about those things which make the modern countryside what it is; council houses, combine harvesters, rural poverty, declining services, capital intensive agriculture have no place in the countryside of their imagination. But such a view conceals and obscures the reality of modern life in the village, and many of those seeking to develop and relate to the social and economic aspects of modern rural life frequently find that they have to contend against such attitudes.

The Village in the
Distant Past

This book is about the contemporary village, but the way in which
the village is regarded today is conditioned not only by attitudes
towards the countryside and the rural aspects of English life which
have been explored in the previous chapter, but also by our
understanding of the history of the village. The contemporary
village speaks to many people in terms of the past, and it is seen as
a refuge from the pressures of contemporary living and the
repository of essential Englishness. At one level, the problem of
our history is that there is too much of it and as a consequence we
tend to accept stereotyped versions of the past which in their own
way are significant distortions. The history of the English
countryside has attracted little attention until recent years, but
modern historians have demonstrated the need to question many
of the old assumptions about the development of the village. For
instance, it is now appreciated that England was never a peasant
society which was destroyed by the Enclosure Acts; nor was the so-
called Agrarian Revolution a sudden transformation of the
countryside in the way that urban areas were transformed by the
Industrial Revolution. The next two chapters seek to place in
perspective the two dominant stereotypes of English rural history:
first, England as a country of peasants and small-scale yeoman
farmers, the 'Merrie England' of Robin Hood, celebrated in
primary-school May Day pageants, morris dancing and folklore
societies; and second, the rural England of the mid nineteenth
century which is represented on innumerable Christmas cards
portraying stagecoaches and peaceful hamlets of cottages and
country houses. Both these stereotypes have had a powerful
influence on the way in which people think about the contemporary
village, particularly those who move into the countryside from
urban areas. It can be seen that much of the opposition to change
in the village today relates to static views of the countryside which

24

appear to imply that it should still conform to the patterns of previous centuries. However, it is historically illiterate to idolize the rural past and to fail to perceive that the countryside today is the result of many centuries of gradual change and development, a process which has left marks at every stage on the contemporary village.

By the time the semi-literate Norman clerks attempted to take down, in Latinized form, the unspellable Anglo-Saxon names of the two and a half million inhabitants of England in the Domesday Book of 1086, most English villages had already been established on their present sites for many generations. Historians have commonly regarded the prehistoric and British people as having farmed higher land because they lacked the equipment to farm the heavier valley soil. However, recent research has indicated that much of the English native forest was removed in the Bronze and Iron ages, and that in the latter period villages were located close together in many areas, such as the chalk downs of Hampshire. On the eve of the Roman conquest, England was already an old country in the sense that much of the land had been farmed for many centuries and the settlement pattern had been established as a result of the decisions of prehistoric villagers. If early English agriculture was essentially self-sufficient farming, this was in marked contrast to the Roman latifundia, which were large farms producing grain for export. (It was the inability of the Roman farms in the provinces to provide sufficient grain to feed the legions, which in part led to the decline of the Roman Empire.) It is suggested by some authorities that the population of Roman Britain may have reached as high as 10 million, a figure which did not reappear until the sixteenth century.

The final withdrawal of the Romans in AD 410 left England vulnerable to invaders from the continent. Initially they came as raiders, but by the mid ninth century they wintered on the western side of the North Sea, in 850 on the Isle of Thanet and in 854 on the Isle of Sheppey. Gradually raiders became settlers: Saxons in Essex and Wessex; Angles in Norfolk and Suffolk; and Jutes in Kent and the Isle of Wight, who brought with them superior tools which accelerated the clearing of the forests and larger ploughs with which they were able to bring these areas and the fens into cultivation. In some places the Anglo-Saxons made use of the

Roman road system but they were essentially a farming people who avoided the towns which the Romans had established. They chose gravel terraces for their settlements where drinking water was available from shallow wells, and an indicator of their distribution is afforded by place names. Many Anglo-Saxon place names have the suffix -ing, -ington, -ingham, -ton, or -ham. Other Anglo-Saxon place names, which are an outstanding feature of the Midlands, are related to topographical features: for example, the cluster of names ending in -ley or -hurst referring to the woodlands or clearings of which Stoneleigh is one of the most southern examples in the Forest of Arden which once covered that part of the Midlands. In other places the Anglo-Saxons used more ancient names which they already found, such as Bre (meaning a hill).

After the Anglo-Saxons came the Scandinavian tribes who, when they decided to settle rather than raid this country, established villages with place names frequently ending with -by, -thorpe (meaning a piece of ground), or -thwaite (meaning an isolated plot of land). However, a Scandinavian place name need not imply a large Viking population, for a village might simply be renamed after its new Scandinavian lord without any significant substantial change in the local population. There is still controversy about the number of Scandinavians who actually settled in Britain. The surviving evidence can be given many interpretations, and the presence of Scandinavian personal names in eastern England in the late eleventh century may reflect widespread adoption by the local population of the Scandinavian names of the new land owners just as northern French names became popular in the generation after the Norman conquest. During the period up to the Norman invasion settlements gradually expanded either by sub-division, which accounts for the frequent occurrence of 'upper and lower', 'great and little' as prefixes to English village names, or by clearing waste or woodland, where villages had the suffix -holt, -fold, or -stock. The overall effect of these various waves of colonization was that by the time of the Norman invasion the spatial distribution of rural settlements in this country had been established in its recognizably modern form.

A typical area of heavy population density at this time was the Feldon (or open field) area of south Warwickshire. The Vale of the Red Horse (named after the equine figure cut out of the red marlstone rock on the side of Edge Hill), with its string of gravel banks and low hillocks, attracted considerable settlement in the Anglo-Saxon period. In many ways such an area could be recognized already as having a human geography not so very different from our own. Many accounts of their development reduce villages to two stereotypes: 'the green village' and 'the street village'. However, in reality, villages defy such a crude dichotomy. Many villages were formed by a cluster of homesteads around an open area in the centre, which was used as a place of safety for keeping stock at night. 'Green villages' almost always have Anglo-Saxon origins; that is why their greatest concentration is to be found in the south east and along the eastern side of the country. The green itself was essentially a stockade and place of safety for animals; the pond was not infrequently the remains of an old clay pit. By contrast, 'street villages' were built either along the side of a road or a river, or on the edge of a hillside. Preferred sites in both cases were those that were well drained, with adequate supplies of fresh water and access to a variety of soils as well as woodland, and which often were places that had obvious defensive advantages. Each village was surrounded by a large unfenced field, divided into strips for cultivation. The common grazing land for sheep and cattle lay beyond the cultivated area, and beyond that lay the woodland and forest.

On 14 October 1066 the Anglo-Saxon kingdom came to an end with the defeat of Earl Harold by William, Duke of Normandy. While in many instances the major political events in English history have had only a minimal impact on village life, it is clear that the Norman conquest marked a decisive break with the Anglo-Saxon past and its impact was felt immediately in the village. After the Battle of Hastings William of Normandy met resistance, principally from London, but was able to subdue the rural areas with little devastation except in the south. Many influential Englishmen assisted the invaders including Aethelwig, Abbot of Evesham until 1077, who was given oversight of the seven western Mercian shires. The Normans did not invent feudalism but they did extend and regularize it by imposing on the village a close legal relationship between the lord of the manor and the inhabitants of the village. The manorial system was based on the obligation of the lord of the manor to supply trained soldiers for the king's army, and the new Norman landlords were granted a number of manors, not in a contiguous block, but scattered in various counties. The manor did not necessarily coincide with the parish, and its affairs were governed by a manorial court which met in the hall of the manor house, customarily at six-week intervals, with the lord of the manor as the arbiter of justice. So complete was the subjugation of the Anglo-Saxon culture that French became the language of court until the fourteenth century. Many place names with prefixes such as Abbots, Kings, Temple, Priors, or a prefix which is the surname of a family, indicate the presence of the Normans. At this time a number of buildings in the village would have been of stone, including the church, one or more of the manor houses and possibly the manorial water-mill. Thus, when the Domesday Book was collated in 1086, it presented a picture of a country in which most modern villages had existed for generations and all the best, well-drained land was cultivated.

By the end of the eleventh century a period of economic expansion in the English countryside was well under way, and this had a profound effect on the nature of village life. Between the end of the eleventh century and the middle of the twelfth century there was a marked expansion in population from 2 million to 6.7 million in 1347. This was particularly apparent in counties such as Lincolnshire where much previously uncultivated land existed, and in the forest areas of the Midlands where clearance continued apace as a result of the pressure of increased population. The early mouldboard ploughs (often made of cherrywood to which the earth did not stick so firmly), date from this period; often only a single plough was possessed by a parish and was kept in the parish church. Individual villagers who farmed about twenty acres would only have been able to support, at most, two oxen, so the formation of a plough team might have required the resources of three or four families. Although people collaborated in the village, ownership of land and animals was by individuals and only the plough itself was owned by the community as a whole. Further indications of the advancement of new settlements can be seen in the reclamation of marshland in Somerset, Sussex, Holderness and on the Romney marshes, and in the advancement of settlements in upland areas, especially on Dartmoor and Exmoor.

The nature of village life and the rural economy in the period before the Black Death is impossible to describe in any detail, for the picture is only partial and there must have been considerable local and regional variations. In those areas where arable cultivation was possible on a relatively large scale, much of the land was arranged and managed in open or sub-divided fields on the basis of strips, as in parts of the south and east Midlands. The ridges and furrows of the open field, particularly in the south Midlands, often form an 'S' pattern, probably as a result of the team swinging as it approached the headland. However, in other areas such as the south west, much of the land was enclosed, often in small square fields, and the settlement pattern tended to be more dispersed. In areas with heavier soils the ploughing-up of substantial cultivation ridges was necessary in order to allow some of the water to drain down the furrows. The most mature form of field system was the two- or three-field system found in a broad belt of territory running from north east England through the Midlands to south central England, which involved the sub-division of two or three major arable fields into furlongs and the division of the arable area usually into three cropping zones, one of which was left fallow each year. However, in the mainly upland and marshland areas, following the ancient Celtic pattern, there was minimal cropping and the economy was essentially pastoral. In all areas surrounding forests and wilderness provided fuel as well as grazing for domestic and wild animals, although rabbits were not introduced into this country until the early Middle Ages. An important feature of the landscape in this period was the royal forest and its diminutive form, the deer park. When William I carved out his vast hunting ground in Hampshire, the New Forest, approximately thirty villages and hamlets were completely destroyed and many others partially so. Already it can be noted that changes were taking place in the settlement pattern, and it is possible at this early stage to distinguish between the pastoral west and the relatively larger villages of the arable areas of the east Midlands and East Anglia. In this region farming practice dictated that relatively large numbers of people should live in the same settlement in order to provide a sufficient work force for what was still essentially manual farming, supplemented by oxen. By contrast, pastoral farming did not need a concentrated labour force and, as a result, upland and western England is characterized by scattered isolated hamlets and farmsteads.

The increase in the monastic orders in Britain after the Norman conquest was a significant feature of contemporary rural life. It is estimated that in 1066 there were 280 religious houses in England and Wales, a figure that had increased to over 1,300 by the end of the twelfth century. The majority of these houses of monks, nuns, regular canons and hospitals were in rural areas. Many of the early religious houses also established villages: for example, Bushey and Cassio, established by St Albans Abbey. The monasteries played an important role in the development of the cultural and educational life of the countryside but, increasingly, it was their contribution to farming which had the most far-reaching effects. In the twelfth century most new monasteries were Augustinian, such as those at Northampton, Cirencester, Kenilworth and Osney. But this century also saw the beginning of the Cistercian movement, whose houses — Fountains, Rievaulx, Tintern and Melrose — were associated with the cultivation of marginal land and the new sheep-based rural economy. However, these areas were not unpopulated when the monasteries were established, and later the monasteries themselves cleared villages in order to develop their new estates.

By the end of the twelfth century villages would have looked significantly different from the period of the Norman conquest. The population expansion and the increasing wealth of the previous two centuries was reflected in the growing number of stone buildings. In this period barns, particularly those of the manor, and the manor house itself, would have been built of stone. Even some cottages had stone footings. However, the countryside was still predominantly seen by most people as alien, hostile and unfriendly. The houses of the village huddled together for protection and security, for the countryside, particularly during the nineteen winters of Stephen's reign (1135—54), was still a place of constant danger. The havoc wrought by the regular and irregular troops of the barons, particularly during the struggle between Matilda and Stephen, was no doubt exaggerated, but the taxation accounts for 1156 record that nearly two-thirds of Warwickshire and two-fifths of Oxfordshire were declared to be 'waste'. Whatever the truth of this, there is little doubt that the widespread civil disorder of this time did not constitute a climate that was conducive to economic expansion and development.

The period between 1200 and 1381 (the year of the Peasants' Revolt) is often portrayed as the high noon of English feudalism. The received picture of rural life in this period is of a peasant society, broadly similar to that of the rest of Europe, which was ultimately transformed into a form of rural society which was markedly different from that of France, Ireland or Spain. Some historians have regarded the Industrial Revolution as providing the decisive break with peasant society; others have instanced the first enclosure movement, in the fifteenth century and early sixteenth century, as destroying medieval society; others have pointed to the Puritan crisis of the seventeenth century and the rise of capitalism. Increasingly, contemporary historians have sought to question the existence of this dramatic break and are now inclined to see English rural society as having always been fundamentally different from the classic peasant societies of Europe and Asia. Certainly, by the late eighteenth and the early nineteenth century, European visitors to rural England were struck by the unique spectacle of a rural society without peasants or serfs. However, in much late nineteenth and early twentieth-century writing, the loss of the English peasantry is regarded as one of the principal causes of the decline of rural life; the enclosures and the rise of capitalist farming are usually blamed for this occurrence. Such views can still be found in contemporary books and doubtless have done much to influence our view of the countryside. It is important to make the point that such views now appear to need substantial modification. In short, England never was a peasant society in the way in which this term is usually employed.

This brief chapter is no place in which to review extensively the contemporary debate about this subject. However, local historians in recent years have been able to show that the English countryside was as capitalist a society in 1250 as it was in 1550 or 1850. Even at that early date (and before) markets were well developed, there was considerable mobility of labour, land was treated as a commodity, and individual ownership of property was well established. At the same time there was a degree of general and social mobility and, perhaps most important of all, the distinction between the farm and the family, as an economic and social unit, already existed. It is suggested by some that the notion of England as a classic peasant society, from the Norman conquest until well into the eighteenth century, has been read into English rural history by a former generation of historians who had observed at first hand nineteenth- and early twentieth-century rural societies in Poland, Italy and Ireland. In effect, they assumed that traditional medieval England must have been similar in its essential features to the rural social systems they observed in these countries. However, historians such as Alan McFarlane have shown that the central and basic feature of English social structure has always been the rights and privileges of the individual as against the wider group or the state. By contrast, the term 'peasant' is used to describe a form of society in which the extended family forms the primary and basic social and economic unit and in which the individual is of markedly less significance and customarily without property rights.

The principal features of the classic peasant societies are sufficiently similar for it to be possible to draw up a model of peasant society. The main feature of this model is the fact that the ownership of the farm is corporate rather than individual and that the farm is owned by the extended family, who are also the labour force. The roots of the destruction of peasant society have been identified as the development of the concept of private ownership, allied to the need for cash to pay taxes and wages and to make purchases. However, in England it is clear that individual ownership dates from an early period. In a classic peasant society there is almost no market in land; but, by contrast, in the period 1200 to 1349, local historians have recorded considerable evidence of land sales and a sharp decline in subsistence farming linked to the need for cash for rent, taxes, tithes and wages. From the early twelfth century there is evidence of land belonging to an individual and that property was left to the eldest son (primogeniture) and not divided between the children as in a classic peasant joint ownership unit. In true peasant societies women have a markedly inferior role and cannot own land, but local historians have discovered instances of women owning land in their own right in the thirteenth century, and it is clear that they took part in local economic life in their own right. In classic peasant societies girls married at an early age in order to contribute to the household labour force by giving birth to sons. However, there is evidence of late marriage (and of a proportion never marrying) in early medieval England. There is also evidence of children being put out as servants in other people's houses at this time, a practice not found in peasant society.

The picture of English society that has emerged from recent historical studies is that of parishes populated by nuclear families of farmers and craftsmen who were mobile both in the geographical and the social sense. Alongside them lived a number of small landowners and a significant number of wage labourers (not found in peasant societies). The farms were individual economic enterprises owned by the farmer, whose activities were aimed at maximizing profits in order to have commodities or cash with which to pay rent, tithes and wages and to purchase needs not supplied by the farm on the open market. There is much evidence to suggest that English rural life at an early stage was a mobile market-oriented form of rural society, which differed in many essential points from traditional peasant societies in which there was no labour or land market, in which the institution of servanthood hardly existed and where the family, as a unit, formed the labour force.

It is suggested by some that the attraction of the 'from peasant to industrial' theory of social development is closely related to nineteenth-century evolutionary social thinking. However, there is no evidence that the twelfth- or thirteenth-century villager thought of himself in ways which are similar to classic peasant societies, or that capitalist and market-oriented understandings suddenly emerged in the sixteenth century. Historians have used the word 'peasant' very freely and have invented such terms as 'the Peasants' Revolt' (a phrase not used at the time). The term is essentially a French one, and in English it is used only of other countries (and frequently in a derogatory way). Thus it can be seen that a view of the development of the village from a basically peasant tradition which was overthrown by the Enclosure Acts and the Agrarian Revolution, and was transformed into one of capitalist farming in a short period of time, should be abandoned. The roots of modern rural society go much deeper than frequently is realized and there was no abrupt change but rather a process of gradual development. As W. G. Hoskins has said, modern practices are much older than we realize.

The 300-year period between the middle of the eleventh century and the middle of the fourteenth century was a period of unparalleled development and expansion in the village. By the middle of the fourteenth century the population had risen to approximately 7 million and almost all contemporary villages were already long established (with the few exceptions of industrial villages established in the late eighteenth and early nineteenth centuries). At the same time, almost all agricultural land had been brought into cultivation, including some areas which were ploughed at that time and were not to see the plough again until the Second World War. However, at this time the bubonic plague which had been crossing Europe in the previous decades, entered England through the channel ports of the south west, particularly Weymouth, in 1348. Estimates of the level of mortality in the initial plague years of 1348 to 1350 varied widely, but it is accepted that between a third and a half of the population died. The crowded ports and cities were hardest hit, as were the nucleated villages of the south east, but even in the heart of the plague-stricken districts some villages emerged relatively unscathed. There were approximately 300 local epidemics in the following decades. The plague continued in the years 1360—61, particularly in the north, and there were further outbreaks in 1390—91 and 1405—7. It disappeared in various regions during the next century but the West Country was affected again in 1592 to 1593. Finally, after the particularly disastrous outbreak in 1665, bubonic plague disappeared from England for reasons which are still not wholly certain. But it appears that the black or house rat was replaced by the brown or field rat, which lived in less intimate contact with man. At the same time, buildings were now of such a nature that they provided a less hospitable environment for vermin.

The effect of the Black Death on individual villages varied greatly. Some were totally destroyed, for example Ringstead Parva in Norfolk, but few were totally unaffected and many lost a large section of their labour force. What is certain is that the Black Death and the successive returns of the plague over the next twenty years created an economic situation which was in many respects the very opposite of that which had flourished during the period of village expansion, and in many areas a gradual process of settlement retreat began to take place. Poorer land was abandoned in areas hard hit by the plague, as were thirty villages in the Breckland area of Norfolk alone. One effect of the contraction in the population was to place the surviving village workers in a position of advantage. At the same time, surviving landlords were able to purchase their deceased neighbours' estates at disaster prices, though initially this was of little advantage to them unless they could find labourers to work the land. From the period of the plague onwards, the village labourers pressed their demands for higher wages, while Parliament, which represented the yeomen or substantial farmers, passed a series of Statutes of Labourers aimed at stabilizing the economic situation by holding down wages. A struggle developed between labourers and landlords which culminated in the revolt of Wat Tyler in 1381.

However significant the effect of the plague may have been on individual villages, it was probably not as great as the changes which resulted from new farming practices which were adopted in the late fourteenth and early fifteenth centuries. Even in Roman times, wool and wool products (particularly the *birrus britannicus,* a hooded woollen overcoat) were in great demand in Europe. At this time the demand for wool and cloth was steadily rising. In the early stages of the development of this semi-rural industry, demand had been met by taking up the long-fibred fleeces of English sheep, which had previously been exported via the wool staple in Calais (part of England until 1558), principally to northern Italy and the Low Countries. However, as the cloth trade developed in the eastern counties, the Cotswolds and the south west, the supply became insufficient and only an expansion of home wool production could satisfy the needs of the English clothmakers. By the beginning of the fifteenth century wool and meat prices had risen considerably, and with the diminished labour supply landlords began to enclose land for livestock and particularly extensive sheepfarming. Villagers found themselves evicted from settlements which were incorporated into the sheep runs, for they were no longer needed as a labour force. As a result, many villages weakened by the plague and migration to the towns were now abandoned either forcibly or voluntarily. In the period between

1450 and 1485, over 113 villages were abandoned in the Feldon area of south Warwickshire and this area of ancient settlement, close to the Cotswolds, became predominantly a sheepfarming region.

In the early decades of the sixteenth century concern was being expressed both in Parliament and elsewhere. The evidence of government inquiries, such as that of Wolsey's Commissioners in 1517 and 1518, reflected a similar situation to that recorded by many pamphleteers, Bishop Latimer's sermons, Sir Thomas More's *Utopia* and Shakespeare's *Pericles*, where the depopulating landlord is denounced as the great whale who has swallowed the whole parish 'church, steeple, bells and all'. However, these complaints were made mostly after the main flood of depopulation had already taken place and the evidence of the Commissioners showed that most of the enclosure of this period had taken place before Henry VII came to the throne in 1485. The first Act which sought to control the forced depopulation of villages (one protecting the Isle of Wight) was passed in 1488. Pamphlets such as 'The Decaye of England only by the Great Multitude of Shepe' (*c.* 1550) are an indicator of the changes which the sheep depopulations brought in their wake. Today many isolated farms stand on the site of what was once a village or a hamlet in the early medieval period, but which was reduced to a single farm at this time. In the country as a whole, there were estimated to be 16,000 villages in the early thirteenth century. In two centuries at least 3,000 sites were abandoned as a result of these changes.

If the changes to agriculture and village life were essentially local and gradual, it was decisions of a different order which led to the destruction of one of the principal features of the early medieval countryside. The smaller monastic houses were suppressed in 1536 and the larger ones in 1539. By the time the chantries were suppressed in 1547, the monastic movement had already disappeared as a principal feature of the English countryside. The effect of their suppression was to release large areas of land some of which fell into the hands of ancient landed families, but much went to an increasingly important group, the Tudor squires. The fifteenth century had witnessed the gradual decay of the feudal system, and as the authority of the sheriffs declined, law and order became a major problem in many rural areas. The Crown devised a system of appointing a number of country gentlemen of substance and standing as Justices of the Peace, with authority to try offences locally and to keep order. In many instances, quite literally, the Tudor squires built their mansions with the stones from the old monastic houses (as at Compton Wynyates). The increasing use of gunpowder in the fifteenth century weakened the defensive security of the castle, as was graphically demonstrated at Bamborough Castle in 1464, when the Earl of Warwick forced its capitulation within a week. The erection of new castles virtually ceased, and increasingly the newly wealthy landlords and merchants (particularly the sheep farmers and wool merchants) built houses and mansions in the square-headed perpendicular style so typical of this period and marked the beginning of a long tradition in English rural life, that of the country house.

During this period the population began to recover after the Black Death, and by 1541 it had risen to 3 million. It increased to 4 million by 1600 and to 5.5 million by 1651. As has been shown, enclosure continued in the sixteenth century to the point where, in many areas, there were few remaining open fields. In the upland areas, particularly the Cotswolds, after enclosure the open field was divided by dry stone walls and an arable rotation with sheep feeding on roots became the predominant farming pattern. In most areas mobile power in the fields was provided by oxen, which were preferred to horses because they were less prone to illness and, being fed on hay and straw, did not compete directly with humans for scarce grain supplies. Horses were used principally for transport and war, for which they were of particular importance (the export of horses was only permitted under licence after 1563). A principal reason why villagers may have preferred oxen was that in times of trouble horses were always requisitioned.

In 1523 Fitzherbert produced his *Boke of Husbandrye* and Thomas Tusser, himself a failed farmer, produced in 1557 *A Hundred Goode Pointes of Husbandrie*. This doggerel calendar of the farming year which gave a monthly checklist of things to be done around the farm became a Tudor bestseller, and it has been reprinted in almost every subsequent generation. In most areas during this period a wage-earning economy was well established, but enclosures continued to provoke deep resentment among the working population. The rising, first in Somerset in 1549, which quickly became of national significance under Robert Kett in Norfolk, had no lasting effect, but it drew the Tudor Parliament's attention to the problems of depopulation, the destruction of houses and the conversion of arable land to pasture. The cumulative effect of these changes was to increase the number of landless labourers: in the parish of Myddle, from 7 per cent in 1540/7 to 31 per cent in 1631/60. The Tudor Poor Laws were linked to an offence called 'vagrancy' and contemporary records show that alongside the growing wealth of the sheep farmers and wool merchants. as displayed in their country houses and large estates, there was a rapidly increasing class of landless vagrants, a fact of which Shakespeare was clearly aware.

During the sixteenth century, the price of wheat had risen from 5s a quarter at the beginning of the century to 14s a quarter by its end. The disruption of the Civil War in the mid seventeenth century caused a continuous rise in the value of agricultural goods until the 1660s, when farm prices began to fall. In 1673, a duty was imposed on imported grain, which led to a substantial increase in the extent of arable farming. Between 1732 and 1766 Britain once again became a food-exporting country (for the first time since the Roman period) and this was achieved not only through the expansion of the arable areas but also by the application of new techniques and understandings. The Agrarian Revolution has been frequently described (as in Lord Ernle's classic account of the development of British agriculture, published in 1912) as if it was a relatively sudden and complete transformation of the rural economy which resulted from the work of a handful of pioneers, in the way that the Industrial Revolution affected, over a relatively short period of time, urban and manufacturing areas. However, the so-called 'Agricultural Revolution' was in fact a long-drawn-out process of improvement, adaptation and development spread over several generations. On the one hand its roots lay in the advance made by the monasteries and the Tudor squires; while in the twentieth century, it was still possible to find, in the early decades, farmers engaging in practices which the Agrarian Revolution was supposed to have made obsolete (Ted Smith of Cirencester Park Estate retired as Britain's last oxman in 1963). By the same token, the decline of the small farmer was a long and protracted occurrence which resulted from a long-term process of reorganization and change in land use, accompanied by the expansion of the cultivated area and the adoption of new methods and practices. The advance in ley-farming and the adoption of rotations which included legumes and roots, long pre-dated the eighteenth century. Turnips, sainfoin, rye grass, clover, trefoil and lucerne were all introduced in the seventeenth century, encouraged by such books as Sir Richard Weston's *Discourse on the Husbandrie used in Brabant and Flanders* (1645). However, it was in the mid eighteenth century that this 'Norfolk system' was well publicized through the work of 'Turnip' Townshend and Coke of Holkham.

At the same time, improvements in cattle and sheep breeding also have a long history, and the pioneer breeders of the eighteenth century achieved successes with animals which had been subjected to experiment and improvement over many generations. Among cattle breeders Robert Bakewell was the most famous pioneer. Using Lincoln stock, he bred animals which fattened rapidly and had a higher proportion of flesh to bone. The Colling brothers, who farmed near Darlington, developed the famous Durham Shorthorn cattle and soon after came Tomkins' Herefords and Lord Leicester's Devons. Between 1710 and 1795 the average weight of beasts sold at Smithfield increased from 370lb to 800lb for beef cattle and from 28lb to 80lb for sheep. Coke's annual sheepshearing from 1784 to 1821, which had started as an annual meeting between landlord and tenants, gradually turned into one of the most important agricultural meetings in the country and was attended by many hundreds.

Jethro Tull, in the early years of the century at his father's farm at Hawberry near Wallingford, developed a machine for planting seeds in rows, an invention which was based on church organ pipes. But this invention did not receive publicity until the appearance of *Horsehoeing Husbandry* in 1731. At the same time the steady expansion of the cities created a domestic market for agricultural products, and large numbers of livestock made the long journey to the cities (for which cattle had to be shod and pigs had to be fitted with a special boot). From the 1750s, the newly established Society of Arts offered premiums and prizes for agricultural improvements: in 1771 Mr Makins of Clare, Suffolk, received the sum of fifty guineas for inventing a plough which would cut hollow drains. With rising demand at home and a market overseas, the village in general and farming in particular prospered in the mid eighteenth century, and this prosperity is reflected not only in the large country houses which characterized the period, many of them built by merchants, manufacturers and financiers, but in the more humble rectories and houses which can still be seen in almost any village.

Karl Marx, writing in the nineteenth century, saw the periods of enclosure, principally in the sixteenth century and between 1750 and 1850, as having a dramatic and transforming effect on the countryside, creating a landless rural proletariat who had been ousted from their smallholdings and whose place had been taken by recognizably modern capitalist farmers. It can be seen that the process of enclosure was an almost constant feature of the English countryside from the early medieval period, though it had periods of intensity, of which the second half of the eighteenth century was the most significant. Enclosure by Act of Parliament was a mechanism of the eighteenth and nineteenth centuries, and during this time some 5,286 enclosure bills were enacted, of which 3,105 effected the enclosure of open-field arable land. Although the rate of enclosure varied from time to time, the periods of greatest activity were 1760 to 1780 and 1790 to 1812. In those two periods 7 million acres, or 21 per cent of the total surface area, were enclosed. By the late seventeenth century and early eighteenth century all agricultural commentators were extolling the virtues of enclosure. The familiar Midlands countryside of rectangular fields marked by hawthorn hedges and fences dates from this period. In some cases enclosure meant that the farmer found it more convenient to move from the centre of the village to a new house surrounded by farm buildings in the middle of this holding. Farm names such as Botany Bay, New Zealand, Trafalgar and Waterloo allow the dates to be guessed with some accuracy.

The eighteenth century was the Golden Age of the small English provincial town. Improved roads and the need to service the residents of the large houses in the district, brought trade and wealth to many small country towns. However, despite the prosperity of farming in the post-enclosure period, many writers shared Oliver Goldsmith's (see Chapter 2) regret at the passing of the old pre-enclosure village and the emergence of a more stratified rural society in which the landowners and farmers were significantly wealthier but the number of landless, frequently unemployed, labouring people had clearly risen. This was partly a consequence of the expansion of factories in the urban areas, which removed from the countryside many of the old craft and cottage industries. The walls around the squire's park, the keepers who kept the villagers from his game, and the high box pews of the eighteenth-century church, all served to accentuate social divisions in the late eighteenth century. As the lesser gentry (sometimes called the parish gentry), who had filled the parish registers and the heraldic visitations for many generations, began to disappear, so the gulf between the few wealthy and the many poor began to widen. An Act of 1740 required paupers to have a scarlet letter P sewn to the back of their coats (though there is little evidence that this was enforced), but it is certain that from the middle of the eighteenth century church burial registers recorded an increasing number of people described as 'paupers'.

The last decade of the eighteenth century saw the Napoleonic blockade of England and, partly as a consequence, a period of rapid inflation. In the period 1765—94 the price of a quarter loaf fluctuated between 6d and 8d; in 1795 the price had risen to 1s 3½d, and in 1801 it had risen to 1s 5d. On 3 December 1800 the King issued a proclamation appealing to the wealthy to eat less, so that there would be more food for the poor whose sufferings were now very apparent. (There is no evidence that Parson Woodforde, famous for his meals, obeyed this injunction.) William Cobbett, a Tory radical, never ceased to ridicule the new agricultural practices and to lament their effects on the rural poor. Even realistic and reasonable men, such as Arthur Young, Secretary of the Board of Agriculture from 1793, who approved of the new farming methods, were horrified at the effect that these changes were now having on the poor and wished that more could be done to alleviate the attendant misery. The picture of the eighteenth-century countryside created by the picturesque movement, as exemplified by Blaise Hamlet and the cottages ornée in Windsor Great Park, bore no relation to the poverty and misery of most villages. Day labourers existed on a diet of bread, supplemented occasionally by a little bacon, cheese and such vegetables that they could grow in their gardens (the growing of potatoes only became widespread in the nineteenth century), and lived in crowded, damp and insanitary conditions. Nathaniel Kent, one-time bailiff to George III at Windsor, wrote in his *Hints to a Gentleman of Landed Property* (1775) that a cottage should have half an acre with fruit trees and a vegetable garden and a pigsty. 'Nothing', he wrote, 'can reflect greater disgrace upon a gentleman than miserable hovels at his gate, unfit for human creatures to inhabit.' The century ended with the widespread implementation of the Speenhamland system of outdoor relief which was a means of providing supplementary income, from parish funds, for those who were the principal victims of the changes in the countryside which had occurred in the previous decades.

Thus it can be seen that much that is recognizably modern in village life had its roots deep in the past. The countryside has not been shaped by sudden changes but by a steady process of transformation and adaptation. English history is cumulative and many of the attitudes and understandings which can be found in the contemporary village have their roots deep in changes which have taken place in the village centuries ago. For in the village the past is ever present and its influence can be felt at every turn.

4

The Village in the
Recent Past

The previous chapter has sought to show that the origins of the contemporary village lie much further back in history than is often imagined. The traditional village was not an ideal peasant community but contained many features that are recognizably modern. However, many people's idea of what a village is, or what it should be, has been shaped by evocations of the nineteenth-century village. It is true to say that in many ways the contemporary village is viewed through the prism of the nineteenth-century rural community, for the 'golden afternoon' of the late Victorian and Edwardian countryside has printed itself indelibly on the English imagination. Today, as has been suggested, it seems that at a time of profound change and turbulence in our society people need to identify with, and in a sense seek refuge in, this vision of the past. Thus, modern bookshops are full of reprints which describe in detail the countryside of that earlier time and the lives of those who lived in it. Such perceptions powerfully influence the way in which the modern countryside is perceived by many people, particularly those who move into rural areas, and they are a significant force in the shaping of some aspects of village life.

In large measure this picture of English rural history is owed to the artists and writers of the 1920s, who, having had their imaginations seared by Sanctuary Wood and Passchendaele Ridge, cherished such memories as comforting symbols of the world that had vanished as a consequence of the 1914—18 War. However, in reality there was little that was romantic, picturesque or even 'golden' about the nineteenth-century countryside. Most of its inhabitants knew the harsh realities of rural poverty and the claustrophobic atmosphere of village life at a time when villages were contained and isolated settlements in which there was limited mobility both of people and ideas. Many of the clergy who moved away from Oxford and Cambridge in the mid and late nineteenth century for family livings in country villages have left testimonies in their diaries to the deep sense of shock with which they encountered the squalor and misery of many of their parishioners and the brooding sense of violence and brutality, drunkenness and disease which dominated much village life. The rural simplicity and 'community spirit' which are described with such a wistful sense of loss in many of the books referred to, was in reality the brotherhood of hard work and poverty and the sisterhood of keeping house in circumstances where hunger, dirt and disease were almost ever-present. Blood, sweat and hunger are well known as strong social adhesives, and much that is now called 'the loss of community spirit' in fact refers to the passing of these primitive conditions in rural England.

At the beginning of the nineteenth century the French wars had a mixed effect on the English village. At one level landowners and large farmers saw commodity prices rise sharply and the capital value of land increase significantly, principally as a result of enclosure and the consolidation of farm holdings. However, the farm labourers were called upon to provide an army which, by 1815, had risen to half a million men, principally recruited into the county militia regiments. The consequent shortage of men in the villages resulted in the famous 'petticoat harvests' of the Napoleonic Wars. The wartime prosperity of agriculture accelerated the process of enclosure and there were approximately 2,000 Acts of Parliament at this time, which, in many areas, almost completed the process of enclosure. The end of the war saw the enactment of the new Corn Law of 1815 to protect farmers against a fall in prices by prohibiting the sale of foreign corn on the home market until the price had reached a certain threshold (80s per quarter for wheat; 40s for barley and oats). But in reality the period of prosperity was over, and wheat which had sold for 126s a quarter in 1812 made only 44s a quarter in 1822. Hardship was widely experienced in rural areas, particularly in the grain-growing south and among the returned soldiers and sailors for whom little provision had been made (as Thomas Hardy noted). As prices fell many country banks went bankrupt, taking with them into liquidation the savings of many small farmers and rural tradesmen. Landlords everywhere were inundated with requests to waive the rent, which in many cases they acceded to in order to keep tenants on the land. The number of owner-occupier farmers fell sharply after the war and in 1819 the Central Agricultural Association was set up, with local branches, to protect the interests of the farming community. The widespread rural distress precipitated extensive rioting in the eastern counties in 1816, principally in Littleport, Wisbech, Ely and Upwell. This was put down with great severity by the magistrates (many of whom were clergy).

The distress of the period was felt keenly in the village and farmers particularly resented the combination of high taxation (needed to repay war loans) and the sharply rising cost of providing for the poor under the terms of the Poor Law. Nationally, the cost of the Poor Law rose from £20 million in 1792 to £106 million in 1815. In Dorset there was a 40 per cent rise in population between 1792 and 1831, but during the same period the cost of the Poor Law rose by 214 per cent. All contemporary records point to a sudden and alarming rise in pauperism and violence in the countryside, which even the harsh regulations of the period and the efforts of the magistracy failed to stem. The judicial whipping of women ceased only in 1820, and burglary ceased to be a capital offence in 1837. But the villagers themselves probably regarded the laws (of 1671) relating to game and poaching as among the most harsh. Contemporary sources indicate that, by the late 1820s such was the desperation of many people in the village that there existed almost a state of armed warfare between gamekeepers and hungry villagers. At the time when a labourer's family struggled to survive on as little as 1s a day, the open-market price of a pheasant was approximately 5s and a hare 2s 6d. Many country houses still have a room referred to as the 'justice room' in which the local landowner-magistrate administered law and order in the neighbourhood. But the village reserved its hatred for the agent rather than the master. For the gamekeeper, though born in the village, was licensed to inform on his neighbours and to enforce, with mantraps and spring guns, the harsh Game Laws. It is estimated that between 1833 and 1844 no less than forty-two gamekeepers were killed in fights with poachers. The poacher, who became something of a folk hero in mid nineteenth-century village life, was singled out for particular attention by the magistrates, and in 1830 one-seventh of all convictions were for offences against the Game Laws.

Early snow in October 1829 marked the beginning of a particularly long and cold winter which reduced many village labourers, who were hired by the day and unemployed for long periods in the winter, to a state of desperation. Between 1801 and 1850 the population of England and Wales doubled (rising from 9 million to nearly 18 million). In short there was not enough work for all the able-bodied men and, despite the fact that women and children worked when they could find work, cottage incomes were very small. Many Victorian village families existed for years on end on home-baked bread, horse beans, home-made cheese, turnips and swedes, with meat and potatoes as a very occasional luxury. Most cottages had a piece of land attached on which vegetables were grown and it was the ambition of every family to keep a pig (though not all were able to do this). The pig, of the large fatty type rarely seen today, was the cornerstone of the cottage economy for it provided the only reliable source of protein. Its diet was very mixed and included household leftovers, windfall apples, acorns, roots and greens. So severe was the situation during that winter that by the spring of 1830 the 'Captain Swing' riots had begun, principally in the southern arable counties where lack of competition from industry meant that wages were at the lowest. The labourers' fury was focused on the new threshing machines which they regarded as robbing them of their winter work, for on an arable farm threshing by hand represented a quarter of the year's total work. Spasmodic outbreaks of machine breaking, sheep stealing, animal maiming and arson (the most feared of all rural crimes) continued for a number of years as an expression of the desperation of the rural poor.

The problem of rural poverty had occupied the minds of people, particularly the ratepayers, for many generations. Under the terms of the 1660 and 1691 Acts, a pauper could only obtain help from a parish in which he or she could claim a 'settlement'. In effect this was the parish in which the person had been born or had worked for a year (as a consequence all employment in villages at this time was for one week less than a full year). Until the second half of the nineteenth century, one of the most vexed questions involving poor relief was the issue of where the responsibility for a particular individual lay. Parishes went to great lengths to avoid having to accept responsibility for a potential pauper and this had a particularly deleterious effect on rural housing. The last quarter of the eighteenth century saw a great extension in outdoor relief and the Speenhamland system of 1795 was an attempt to preserve the situation by subsidizing low wages out of the rates on a scale calculated by the price of bread and the number of children in a family. An Act of 1782 allowed the building of workhouses for the aged, sick and disabled. However, the considerable increase in the rural population in the 1820s and 1830s resulted in a situation with which the Speenhamland system and its subsequent modifications was unable to deal. The Poor Law Amendment Act of 1834 (usually called the new Poor Law) sought to cope with this problem by prohibiting outdoor relief and restricting relief only to the workhouse. As a result the country parishes of England and Wales were formed into 600 unions under Boards of Guardians and workhouses were built in many country areas. Three quarters of the Guardians were farmers who, at a time of agricultural distress, were principally concerned with lowering the burden of paupers on the rates. The harsh regime of the workhouse in which families were strictly divided has become a byword in country areas, so much so that people were reputed to have committed crimes purposefully because prison was to be preferred to the workhouse. The threat of the workhouse (a number of which were very well built, and have subsequently been turned into old people's homes and are still referred to as 'the Union') was for a long period a potent force in rural society. But workhouses were not the answer to such an extensive problem and many unions found it impossible to discontinue outdoor relief as the 1834 Act had envisaged.

A year earlier, labourers in the southern counties were faced with yet another cut in their weekly wages, which, in Dorset, where it is acknowledged that the lowest wages were paid, had fallen from 9s in 1830 to 8s in 1831 and 7s in 1832. Faced with a further cut of 1s, a group of workers from the Dorset village of Tolpuddle, rejecting the traditional rural means of expressing discontent (rick burning, machine breaking and arson), and their leader George Loveless prevailed upon the vicar, Dr Warren, to visit local farmers and speak for a minimum wage of 10s. This Dr Warren did, but when after a while the promises were dishonoured he found himself unable to pursue the matter further. It was then that Loveless turned to the Grand National

Consolidated Trades Union led by Robert Owen, and formed a Friendly Society of Agricultural Labourers to negotiate directly with the farmers. It was this action that led to their arrest by local magistrates (after consultation with Whitehall) and their subsequent conviction and sentence in March 1834 to seven years transportation, under the Mutiny Act of 1797. The case of the Tolpuddle Martyrs aroused national feeling against the injustices of village life and exposed to national observation many of the tensions (not least, religious) which existed in the countryside at the time. The dominant picture which emerges from this episode is that of a countryside in which the magistracy were already profoundly anxious as a result of the agricultural disturbances; and in which the farmers, who, with high taxation and the tithe burden (although this was somewhat eased in 1837), were often forced, when they appeared before the squire at his rent table, to ask for the waiving of rents. At the same time the labourers were trying, in the words of George Loveless at his trial, ' . . . to preserve ourselves, our wives and children from utter degradation and starvation'. Loveless and four other labourers were Methodists; two of them were lay preachers. They all eventually received a full and free pardon from Lord John Russell on 14 March 1836.

Recently, historians have shown that the traditional view, which sought to establish that there was cause and effect between the Enclosure Acts and the subsequent distress in the rural community in the early nineteenth century, is in need of some modification, not least because the worst distress was experienced in the southern counties, where enclosure had largely taken place at a much earlier period. The rapid fall in agricultural commodity prices, the high taxation and tithe burden (income tax was reimposed in 1842, having been abolished in 1816), the end of the European wars and the disbanding of the county militia, together with a fall in the demand for agricultural labour, and a sharp increase in the rural population in the 1820s and 1830s, were all factors which combined to make the countryside at this time a place of hardship, hunger and poverty. For many, the village had become little short of an open prison, from which escape was sought whenever an opportunity presented itself; the road out of the village led to London, Queensland and Ontario, to the army depot and the troopship. The 1830s saw the beginning of a major movement out of the villages to the industrial areas and also the start of an officially encouraged programme of emigration as an attempt to solve the problems of rural society. As Pamela Horn records, between 1835 and 1837 6,403 people from twenty counties in southern England were helped by their parishes to emigrate, principally to Canada. Of these, two-thirds came from East Anglia. In 1850 the Bicester Board of Guardians were continuing their earlier work of encouraging emigration and helped a group of people from Lower Heyford to go to Canada and from Launton to go to Australia. By 1853 24,000 people had received assistance which had allowed them to emigrate. In the early period they chose Canada and in the later period Australia and New Zealand. Many Anglican clergy and Methodist ministers played a prominent role in encouraging emigration as a solution to the problems of the countryside. In 1857 the Methodist minister from Bodney in Norfolk assembled a large party, which left on the 'Southern Eagle' for Tasmania; it seems that the village never recovered from this exodus and it may be one of the few examples of depopulation by emigration. In the winter of 1873 a party of 500 labourers and their families from a number of south Midlands parishes left Plymouth on the steamship 'Mongol' and arrived on 13 February 1874 in New Zealand, eventually settling in the area around Dunedin.

However, the agricultural depression which followed the Napoleonic Wars came to an end in the late 1840s, and the early 1850s saw a gradual rise in agricultural prices as a result of increased demand from urban areas. The desperate years of the 1830s and early 1840s gave way to a gradual improvement in the middle years of the century as farming became more profitable and other changes began to transform village life. While the situation of the country church will be discussed in Chapter 11, no account of the mid nineteenth-century village is complete without acknowledgement of the contribution made by the clergy during this period. The residence legislation of 1817 and 1836 required the parochial clergy to live in their parishes, whereas previously, many churches were served by itinerant curates. The newly resident clergyman and his wife and family frequently took a lead in developing a whole range of locally based activities and initiatives aimed at improving the conditions of village life. In this he enrolled the assistance of the landowners and principal farmers, but in almost every case it was the clergyman who provided the driving force in this radical reshaping of village life in the mid nineteenth century. Though some villages had charity and parochial schools which dated from Tudor times, much village education was given in dame schools, which were probably little more than child-minding devices, with a limited amount of teaching done by retired soldiers, clerks or craftsmen as a secondary employment. George Crabbe recorded in his poem 'The Borough' (1810) a description of Reuben Dixon, a shoemaker who ran a small school in the parish; and Parson Woodforde agreed with the village schoolmaster to have his servants taught to read and write for 4s 6d per quarter. The enduring monument to the work of the mid nineteenth-century parochial clergy is neither the system of parochial institutions nor the elaborate restorations of the parish church, but the system of parochial primary education which they established, largely through their own efforts (and in many cases their own money). This system, in many of its essential features, has remained unchanged to this day. The primary school, with its separate entrances for boys and girls, its prominent foundation stone (in all probability bearing a date between 1840 and 1870) and schoolmaster's house attached, was considered an essential part of the parochial machine in the mid nineteenth century, and it was in the school that the clergyman did his most important and enduring work. By that time statesmen and property owners were united in the opinion that the education of village children was a question that could no longer be overlooked and that schooling could most effectively be carried out by the resident clergyman.

In this period parochial clergy gave, and raised from the prominent members of the parish, considerable sums for the building of schools. Apart from the day school, the school building would have housed a night school (for teaching adults to read and write), the Sunday school, village lectures, penny readings and the meetings of missionary and philanthropic societies. At the same time the schoolroom was the focal point of village life, in which the clothing club displayed its wares, the provident society received contributions, the labourers and cottagers' cattle insurance club conducted its business, and tickets were handed out for the shoe, coal, and blanket clubs. In the schoolroom, until the later village halls were built, the lantern shows, musical evenings, harvest suppers and other festivities which formed the annual cycle of local activity at this time were held in opposition to the rival attractions of the many village pubs. Behind all these activities were the local incumbent and his family, whose lives were marked by an activity and a busyness totally absent from the pastoral work of the clergy of previous generations. The visitation returns for Oxfordshire for 1855—60 record that 85 of the 178 villages had schools which had been either built, repaired or enlarged during that period. In 1851, the census revealed that Church of England schools were educating 76 per cent of the children in the country and it is reasonable to believe that this percentage was considerably higher in rural areas. In 1870 the Forster Education Bill established the axiom that secular instruction was secular, and that instruction given in any school was to be suitable for the children of parents of any denomination. The churches were given until the end of the year to complete their system of parochial education, after which the board schools filled the gaps that remained. However, despite the great emphasis placed on schooling as the means by which the life of mid-Victorian villages could be improved, the very poverty of many village families meant that if there was the prospect of a day's work — picking stones, weeding, beating or bird scaring — the children would be unlikely to attend school that day.

But schools were only one of the weapons with which the clergy sought to confront the violence, drunkenness, disease and brutality which prevailed in many rural areas. As magistrates they worked to impose stricter licensing controls on the large number of public houses and beer houses that existed in even the smallest village. The clergy were particularly active in trying to persuade farmers and other employers not to pay part of the weekly wage in beer. At the same time, the clergy sought to provide suitable recreational occasions, especially during the annual week's holiday at Martinmas, which would draw the villagers away from the village ale house and its dance tent erected at the rear for the holiday week. The coaching inns, established in the late eighteenth century, bore no relation to the seedy ale houses which many clergy identified as the breeding ground for vice and violence in the village. The activities which took place in the village school in the evenings, the establishment of village institutes and reading rooms, were all partly designed to lesson the attraction of the ale houses. The *fête de campagne*, 'rustic sports' and harvest festivals were likewise all part of the clergy's campaign to promote 'innocent amusements'. In many villages in the spring of 1856 the clergy organized such occasions to celebrate the signing of the Treaty of Paris which ended the Crimean War.

The clergy worked also to improve the lot of working men, as can be seen by their evidence given to the various royal commissions. The Agricultural Gang Act of 1868 was a notable victory for the clergy: it officially ended child labour in the fields (though in reality it lingered on in many areas). However, the clergy were painfully aware that the very poor state of rural housing at that time was another major contributory factor to 'rural vice' and to the high levels of disease. Villages varied considerably between the closed villages in which a squire owned most or all of the land; those villages where a few larger farmers effectively ran the community; and the open villages (made up of smallholders and craftsmen), many of which were notorious rural slums. The squalor of much rural housing became a mid-century scandal highlighted by the Government's Blue Books on living conditions and public health published in the 1850s and 1860s. Between 1851 and 1861, in 821 rural parishes covered by the investigation, the population had increased from 305,567 to 322,064, while the number of houses had fallen by approximately 3,000 to 66,109. In a sample of 5,375 'typical cottages', 8,805 bedrooms were occupied by 13,432 adults and 11,338 children. The clergy were acutely aware of the moral and sanitary implications of this situation and worked hard to persuade landowners, the principal farmers and the property owners to 'do their duty'. Earlier Lord Shaftesbury, the liberator of the slaves, had been publicly assailed as the owner of an estate on which there were particularly poor housing conditions. By the middle of the century many squires were practically rebuilding their villages, influenced by Loudon's *Encyclopaedia of Cottage, Farm and Villa Architecture* published in 1833. These model cottages, normally providing accommodation for a village family, comprised a living room, a scullery, a larder and three bedrooms upstairs. Between 1849 and 1851 Charles Higgins, squire of Turvey in Bedfordshire, built forty-eight cottages; in 1847 he had built a school, and earlier he had obtained medical qualifications in London so as to be able to treat the destitute sick in Turvey and the surrounding villages. There are many examples of mid and late nineteenth-century estate villages being virtually rebuilt on 'model village' lines: Preston-on-Stour is one such example. In this village in the 1860s the West family virtually rebuilt the centre of the village and added a school in the picturesque style of the period. At the same time concern for rural health and cottage economy led to a spate of 'improving' publications, such as *The Cottager's Monthly Visitor,* which the vicar and the squire sought to circulate within the village.

A change which profoundly influenced almost all villages in the mid nineteenth century was the improvement in communications which resulted from the building of the railways. It was this which finally broke the physical isolation of many country areas, and for about two generations all the important journeys in rural areas were undertaken by train. The first Turnpike Act was passed in 1663, but it was not until the mid eighteenth century that the turnpike system was established. By 1750 thirteen main roads out of London had been turnpiked for almost the whole length to such destinations as Bristol, Hereford, Chester, Manchester and Berwick. In 1784 John Palmer first conceived the idea of regular coach services in and out of London to all parts of the country. His special Royal Mail coaches were consistently improved and they increased in both speed and punctuality so that they had no rivals for smartness and efficiency in the early nineteenth century. Painted in maroon and black, with scarlet wheels, they travelled at an average of twelve miles an hour, with the mail locked in the mailbox under the seat of the armed guard. During the 1830s turnpike roads and the larger road coaches allowed relatively swift travel for the wealthy few (a coach took approximately eight passengers inside and twelve outside). The coach which left Stow-on-the-wold at 6 a.m. stopped in Oxford at 10 a.m. and arrived in Oxford Street in London by 4 p.m. Carriers' wagons and carts also had already developed a sizeable network of services, with local inns serving as collecting and despatching points. However, by the end of the century, relatively cheap rail transport was transforming the countryside. There were very few horse-tram roads in rural areas; one ran from the docks at Stratford-upon-Avon, sixteen miles southwards to Moreton-in-Marsh, and preceded by approximately fifteen years the great railway boom of 1845 and 1846. In those crucial years 650 Railway Acts authorizing 9,000 miles of track (today's total is only 11,000 miles) were passed. By 1860 almost every main-line station was finished, and within the next twenty years the total railway system was constructed by which many very small villages and hamlets were connected to a national network of communications.

The railways were the principal means by which the countryside experienced the breakdown of the economic and social containment which had characterized pre-industrial rural England. The railways integrated even the remotest areas into a regional and, increasingly, a national economic system. Daily newspapers, the telegraph system (which became a post office monopoly in 1870) and 'railway time' which superseded local time (which often depended upon the vagaries of the church clock) were all creations of the early phase of railway building. Whereas villagers had previously depended on the 45,000 packmen who still provided the service of bringing many goods to the remoter villages, in a relatively short time the railways brought foodstuffs from across the British Empire. The shelves of the village shop (virtually a creation of the railway age) were now well stocked. The locally made smock which had been worn for centuries by country people began to disappear in the mid-1860s as factory-made suits became more widely available. The coming of the railways resulted in an immediate fall in the price to the consumer of such goods as coal and building materials and such agricultural commodities as fertilizer, marl and lime, and allowed the speedy transport of livestock to market, thus preventing the loss of condition involved in lengthy journeys on drove roads.

Landowners and farmers were enthusiastic supporters of railway building, for the network provided a means of transporting perishable commodities to the centres of population. In 1852 the building of the Worcester—Evesham railway opened up about 1,000 acres in the Pershore—Evesham area for market gardening and soft-fruit growing. London received broccoli trains from Cornwall, butchers' trains from Perth and turkey trains from Norfolk. But it was the dairy industry which was the most radically affected, particularly after the London cattle plague of 1865 had destroyed the metropolitan dairy herd. In a short time farmers' lives were dominated by the need to get the milk supply to the railway station for transporting and to collect the empty churns from the first morning down train. Farm life in many areas became regulated by the railway timetable, for farmers quickly found that they could profit more from selling liquid milk to the urban centres than by processing it at home into cheese or butter. However, only investors in the main-line railways made profits and many people were slow to realize that branch lines with unnecessarily large stations on cross-country routes (many wealthy farmers owned sidings) were unlikely even to pay their way. Within the village the station almost immediately became an important focus of activity, of news and information. Next door to the station was the railway inn whose saloon bar provided a convenient waiting room for passengers and whose public bar was a mess room for the porters and gangers. The stationmaster joined the upper ranks of village society as an important person, a status emphasized by his uniform. But, like the Methodist minister, he was not of the village. He was an employee of the railway and expected, or hoped for, a move up the line to a more significant station. His very presence was a symbol of the decline of localism in the Victorian village. The railways created much-needed rural employment and many farm workers left to join the railway building gangs. The number of those directly employed by the railways rose from 250,000 in the 1870s to 600,000 in 1914; a large proportion were recruited in rural areas.

Finally, it was the railways which opened the countryside for the urban population and the urban middle classes were quick to extol the value of recreation amidst the beauty of the countryside. Even in its earliest period there were many, such as Wordsworth, Ruskin and, later, Hardy, who saw that this movement would profoundly change the countryside in many areas. In 1865 the Commons Preservation Society was formed to preserve from enclosure such open spaces as remained. In the following year on 7 March a trainload of 120 men disembarked at Berkhamsted and tore down the fences that had been put up to enclose the common. At the same time, while the earlier Great Western route to Cornwall was principally for goods traffic, its rival the London and South Western Railway ran a line into Cornwall via Okehampton largely for the developing tourist traffic. In 1871 bank holidays were introduced.

However, for most villagers the railway became an essential part of mid-Victorian country life and it played a most significant role in breaking down the economic and social narrowness of the pre-industrial countryside and the isolation and containment which had been such a feature of villages in the earlier period.

In 1846, faced with the massive Irish potato famine and despite the protests from farmers, Peel was forced to repeal the Corn Laws; but the worst fears of the farming community were not realized for another thirty years. In the intervening period farming enjoyed years of unparalleled prosperity as it strove to meet the increasing demands of the new urban population. The period from 1850 to 1873 is often referred to as the 'high farming' period, when English farming enjoyed a golden age: a time of high investment and high returns. A symbol of the growing professionalism of the farming community was the founding of the Royal Agricultural Society of England in 1838 (it was known as the English Agricultural Society until 1840). As early as 27 June 1838, within a month of its first meeting, the Society proposed prizes for essays on such topics as 'The best mode of keeping roots', 'Improved rural economy abroad', and 'Insects prejudicial to plants and others'. It had also begun to make plans for prizes to be offered at its first Show which was held in Oxford in 1839 on 'Mr Pinfold's pasture ground, Holywell' (now Mansfield College). It was indicative of the transport problems of the time, that Thomas Bates' four Shorthorn cattle, which won four of the five prizes for the breed, and £70 in prize money, had to travel from Kirklevington in County Durham to Hull, where they were transported to London by boat and trans-shipped to a barge which took them by canal to Aylesbury; from there they walked to Oxford — a distance of twenty-one miles. The Royal Show quickly became a focal point in the agricultural calendar and the Society played a major role in the application of scientific methods to farming. Encouraged by the Society, mid-Victorian farmers and landowners became passionately interested in new machinery, such as the Ransome YL plough, first manufactured in 1843 and still selling in considerable numbers one hundred years later. Improved livestock breeds and model farmsteads also attracted considerable attention in the Society's journals. Peel's Land Drainage Act of 1846 resulted in £12 million being borrowed for the drainage of approximately 3 million acres.

When the Crimean War began in March 1854, agricultural prices again rose steeply. The new scientific approach to farming which followed the founding of the Rothamstead Experimental Station and the scientific discoveries of Leibig who demonstrated a relationship between plant nutrients and the composition of the soil and inspired chemists to analyse manures, led the way to the manufacturing of fertilizers and to the importing of vast quantities of Peruvian guano. The importance of drainage for arable crops, the design of appropriate buildings both for dairying and fattening bullocks, the practice of confining animals in stockyards so that the manure could be collected, together with the adaptation of barns for steam-powered threshing, roots slicing and chaff cutting, soon became common on many farms in the villages.

Many farm workers were taken to see the Great Exhibition of 1851 at which the new reaping machines were displayed for the first time. They viewed them with a sense of amazement and the same foreboding with which the older men had viewed the threshing machine of the 1830s. However, when the reapers were introduced and steam power was installed on many of the larger farms, the farm workforce was already declining and in some areas a shortage of labour was caused by the Crimean War and by the higher wages paid by the railway builders. While the number of farmers remained roughly the same, the size of the workforce now began to decline significantly. In the towns the real wages of unskilled workers were only slightly better, and in some places housing conditions were worse, but the opportunities for economic advancement beckoned and, most important of all, the social and moral pressures associated with the traditional village were absent. The first absolute decline in the rural population started in Wiltshire and Montgomeryshire during the 1840s and spread to Cambridge, Rutland, Norfolk, Huntingdon, Somerset and Suffolk in the following decade. One of the lasting legacies of this period of agricultural prosperity was the decision of many farmers to move out of the village itself and live at the centre of their land. The pattern of farmhouse and associated buildings standing a little way out of the village, so typical of any parish in the Midland counties, dates in the main from this period.

By the mid nineteenth century, both in terms of labour and output, farming had ceased to be Britain's largest industry and this was reflected in the gradual shift of political power and influence to the urban industrial areas. The repeal of the Corn Laws had been a clear sign of the declining political and economic influence of the landed interest, and although, in the age of Palmerston, the countryside's loss of influence had been disguised, from the late 1860s it manifested itself with growing and unmistakable clarity. In the late 1850s agriculture accounted for 10 per cent of the gross national product; by the late 1890s it had declined to only 6 per cent. In 1851 the total population had grown to 18 million, but the census indicated that only 50 per cent now lived in rural areas and a peak had been reached in the number of people employed in agriculture (approximately 2 million). While in 1851 23.5 per cent of the population was employed in agriculture, by 1861 this figure had declined to 16.8 per cent and it declined further, in 1891, to 11.6 per cent. As has been noted, a considerable amount of the surplus labour now moved overseas, and in the 1860s and 1870s approximately 20,000 labourers emigrated from rural areas to Australia and Canada each year. Whereas the early stages of the Industrial Revolution had seen a great increase in industries based in the countryside, by the late nineteenth century many rural communities had reached or passed their peak and the widespread use of steampower had stimulated the growth of industries in towns, frequently near navigable water or a railway junction. By the end of the century many of the craft industries were beginning to disappear from rural areas, and after 1875 corn milling was revolutionized by rolling mills, which led to the widespread closure of many of the small water-powered rural mills.

The collapse of British farming in the years following 1873 was both sudden and complete. In the years 1870 to 1874, wheat sold for an average of 55s a quarter; during the years 1895 to 1899, the average price had dropped to 28s a quarter. The development of steam-powered metal ships, the extension of the American railway system, and the opening of the Suez Canal placed British markets within the range of America, Canada, Argentina, Australia and New Zealand. For these countries, food was the currency by which they were able to pay for English manufactured goods. The cost of transporting a quarter of wheat from Chicago to Liverpool fell from 11s 11d in 1860 to 3s 11d in 1900. The natural monopoly which British farmers had enjoyed was destroyed in a relatively short time, and between 1870 and 1880 the percentage of home-produced wheat consumed in this country dropped from 61 to 27. In 1882 the first cargo of frozen mutton left New Zealand, and, within seven years, one million carcasses a year were being imported. The value of wool on the domestic market was halved between 1870 and 1900. In 1879 the first shipments of American and Canadian cheese began to arrive. As food from the colonies began to flood into this country, so the average price of food to the urban consumer began to fall; the price of a 4lb loaf in London fell from 10d in 1867 to 5d in 1901. At the same time the price paid to the farmer for his crops began to fall; wheat, which had reached 74s 8d a quarter during the Crimean War, fell to 42s 10d in 1879, 31s in 1886, 26s 2d in 1893, and reached its bottom price of 22s 10d in 1894. To add to the disastrous prices Britain appeared to enter a period of relatively unstable weather conditions, with exceptionally wet summers in 1875, 1877 and 1878 and the disastrous year of 1879. This was followed by a number of exceptionally dry summers in 1892, 1893, 1895 and 1896. At that time also, foot and mouth disease and pleuro-pneumonia decimated cattle and liver rot attacked sheep. Land prices began to fall steeply after 1878, and, by 1890, numerous farmers, especially those who had purchased with heavy mortgages in the boom period, had either gone bankrupt or were forced to cease farming. Many farms were simply abandoned, and houses and estates were let at minimal rents to shooting and hunting tenants who made little or no attempt to cultivate the land. P. J. Perry records that in the period 1875 to 1902, farm sales in Dorset increased by 10 per cent and in Huntingdon by 30 per cent. The Royal Commission of 1893 reported that the value of agricultural production had been halved in recent years, and in the following year the price of wheat was the lowest for 150 years.

The hardship for many farm families during this desperate period is part of the folk memory of the farming community. Those farmers who survived, and the hardy upland farmers, particularly from Scotland, who moved into vacant southern farms, did so by diminishing their cereal acreage and concentrating almost exclusively on livestock farming and particularly milk production, where the impact of foreign competition played a less significant role. They also reduced labour as well as their own personal expenses. The farmer who, twenty years before, could send his children to private schools and hunt twice a week, found that he was now struggling to survive. In 1891 Pemrose McConnell wrote in the Royal Agricultural Society's Journal of the Scottish colony around Ongar, Brentwood and Chelmsford. These farmers were known more for their low standard of living than for their technical innovation, but they managed to survive and prosper largely by selling milk to London. In the last quarter of the nineteenth century it is estimated that 30 million acres went from arable to grass and it is noticeable that many of the sheep-breed societies were formed during this period (Oxford Down 1888; Hampshire 1890; Dorset Down 1891; Lincoln 1892; and Romney Marsh 1895).

Within the village the effect of the agricultural depression was particularly harsh on the labourers, as farmers looked for every available opportunity of economizing on labour costs. Almost every innovation during this period had the effect of reducing the amount of labour needed on the farm. Even the introduction of the Dutch barn reduced labour costs, as thatching was no longer required. The last years of the boom period in the early 1870s had seen a more determined effort on the part of the agricultural workers to win for themselves some share of the new prosperity. In February 1872 Joseph Arch had addressed a meeting of labourers under the chestnut tree on the green at Wellesbourne, protesting against a wage of 12s per week. This action led to the formation of the National Agricultural Labourers Union in December 1872. Considering the nature of his cause, Arch gained support in remarkable places including that of the Hon the Revd J. W. Leigh of Stoneleigh, who persuaded his brother to increase wages to 15s per week. Although Arch succeeded in drawing attention to the problems of agricultural labourers, and was later elected as a Liberal Member of Parliament, the cause of higher wages was lost, with much else, in the years of the farming depression which came after 1873.

The effect of this depression can be seen from the rent which Christ Church, Oxford, received from its estate at Westwell near Burford which declined from 39s per acre in 1813, to 26s per acre in 1873, and eventually reached 11s per acre in 1894. In every area marginal land was abandoned and economies in farm staff were reflected in the general deterioration in traditional standards. The countryside of the last two decades of the nineteenth century was characterized by overgrown hedges, weedy, waterlogged fields, and dilapidated buildings. Many landowners were forced to take land in hand and others had no option but to sell at disaster prices. Considering the desperate state into which the countryside fell in the last quarter of the nineteenth century, it is even more remarkable that this period should be remembered as 'the golden afternoon of the English countryside'. Many farmers were reduced to 'dog and stick' farming in order to survive, and life in the village was correspondingly harsh. Late nineteenth-century rural society was increasingly polarized between the few wealthy and the many relatively poor, with only the clergyman and the doctor occupying the middle ground. The effect of the enclosures early in the century, and the farming boom in the middle decades, had been to concentrate land ownership in fewer hands. To counter increasing political criticism of this fact, a survey was conducted in 1873. Although it showed that there were approximately one million owners of land, its detailed findings only served to reinforce the view that land was concentrated in the hands of very few people. Of the 966,275 owners of land, 73 per cent owned less than one acre; 1 per cent of the landowners owned 56.6 per cent of the land and 7 per cent of the landowners owned 80 per cent. In Northumberland and Rutland over half the land was occupied by estates of over 10,000 acres.

The last quarter of the nineteenth century marked the zenith of the English country house, which was one of the principal casualties of the First World War. Recent research has shown the durability of the English aristocratic families, but during the nineteenth century the ranks of the traditional landowners were joined by many manufacturers and merchants whose fortunes had been made either in the industrial areas or overseas. The occupants of the country houses lived lives of great luxury on a scale unlike that of the early nineteenth century or the generations which preceded it. Hunting and shooting played a dominant role and it is hard to exaggerate the importance of the hunt in Victorian rural society as a focus of county life. However, by the early twentieth century, Lloyd George's 1908 budget with Increment Value Duty and Undeveloped Land Duty, precipitated a trickle of land sales between 1910 and 1914, which became a deluge after the war, when the top rate of death duties on estates of over £2 million rose by 40 per cent. If *The Times* leader writer, who wrote that rural England changed hands between 1918 and 1922, was exaggerating, it is certainly the case that a quarter of 'the rural estate' was sold during this period. The carnage of Flanders had robbed many landed families of their heir. At the same time, changed lifestyles, higher income tax, death duties, the shortage of domestic staff, the increased wage of farm labourers (which rose from 13s a week before the war to 30s a week in the post-war period), rationing, and the depressed state of farming all took their toll. Some estates were sold in their entirety, but almost all landowners were forced to sell a sizeable proportion of their land, frequently to the tenant farmers. In the post-war period the leadership in country life was already beginning to pass from the occupants of the large houses to the farming community.

The war also accelerated the centralization of industry in urban areas. In the traditional village, farming had existed alongside a host of processing and manufacturing trades. Locally available raw materials were extracted and worked; clay was dug for pots, bricks and tiles; stone was quarried and dressed for buildings; wool was woven and spun into raw material for cloth, hosiery, knitted garments; hides were tanned to produce leather; corn and industrial crops were milled, baked, malted and brewed; straw was manufactured into hats and bonnets; hemp was made into rope and every sizeable village had a number of carpenters, wheelwrights, harness makers and blacksmiths. But in the post-war period the village craftsman slowly abandoned the unequal struggle with factory products, which were preferred to the locally made boots, clothes and kitchen equipment. By the early years of this century the rural community was regarded as the ailing sector of the economy.

Thus it can be seen that in the majority of villages the last quarter of the nineteenth century was a time of stagnation, poverty and hardship, when the rural community increasingly became aware of itself as a community of 'the left-behinds' (as Bishop Sheppard has used this term of modern city centres). The most energetic and ambitious had already left the village for the urban areas or the colonies, and the village was seen as a backwater, where nothing but low wages and a harsh and demanding life could be expected. Amelioration of these conditions depended almost entirely on outside intervention, which, in practice, meant the interest of a benevolent squire or clergyman with sufficient income to support his good intentions. Housing conditions were particularly bad in many villages despite the fact that there was often an oversupply of houses, albeit in a near ruinous condition; and a part of the reason why model villages were so popular on estates was because much rural housing was too poor to be adequately improved. Even the Addison Act of 1919, which sought to provide 'homes fit for heroes' had relatively little impact on rural areas, where few council houses were built.

However, the building of the parish hall, either to commemorate Queen Victoria's Golden Jubilee in 1887 or her Diamond Jubilee (1897); the 1893 Mundella Education Act which required children to stay at school until they were eleven, and until thirteen or fourteen in many areas in accordance with local by-laws; the 1873 legislation on the secret vote (though many land workers did not qualify until 1884); the establishment of county councils in 1888, and district and parish councils in 1894; all represented gradual changes which were to have an accelerating impact on the village in the years after the First World War. But perhaps it was the more widespread availability of the bicycle, with developments such as chain drive and pneumatic tyres in the 1890s and the addition of three-speed gears and gas lamps in the 1900s, which did more to change the life and outlook of many villagers. For the bicycle represented another major onslaught on the localism and containment of traditional village life and was swiftly reflected in the marriage registers, as marriages between couples who were from the same parish began to decline. But it was the old age pension which came into operation on New Year's Day 1909 which perhaps had the most lasting effect. It was introduced at a maximum rate of 5s a week, but this was enough to relieve many old people of the fear of the workhouse.

When war was declared the village labourers, farmers and gentlemen's sons flocked to join the County Yeomanry or a more prestigious regiment. Such was the poverty of the rural diet at this period that the army could hang no more potent symbol than a side of beef outside its market-town recruiting depots. Some English villages furnished the army with almost all their menfolk who were fit to serve, and probably several who were not. It is recorded that Buckland in Berkshire provided 79 recruits from a total population of 302. The parish of Barley in Hertfordshire, with a population of 500, furnished 141 servicemen, and a further 39 men who were Barley-born also served. Of these the names of 77 (almost half) are recorded on the role of honour, including nine members of one family, seven of another family and four of two others. The comradeship which was such a prominent feature of the army at this period was partly based on the fact that recruitment was local. The war struck the villages hard; at the Battle of Loos in September 1915, the Second Battalion of the Royal Warwickshires went into battle with 667 men; at the end of the day there were no officers and only 140 men still alive. The village of Bookham in Surrey lost 60 men who joined the forces in August and September 1914, and as a consequence found that they had to withdraw from the Dorking and District Football League. The first four weeks of the Battle of the Somme, in 1916, provided *The Times* with sixty-eight closely printed columns listing the names of dead private soldiers. In 1917 another 30,000 farm workers were recruited for the army. The names of many of those who left the village are recorded on the war memorials in the church and on the village green; the lists of names often seem disproportionately large by comparison with the size of the village. Those who remained were required to help with the farming and with the great increase in food production which was achieved during the war. But in many villages few men were left and, in 1916, Lord Montague of Beaulieu engaged a woman, Miss Hilary Dent, as his gamekeeper.

When the war was over and the land sales began, the old order, of which the country house had become so inextricably a part, was coming to its end. Tractors were now seen on some farms and the occasional car in the village street; both were signs of the coming displacement of the horse. The horse was the centre of traditional rural society and its needs, abilities, and timetable set the pace and tempo of village life, which was radically altered by the introduction of tractors and cars. Thus the countryside began to enter the period of post-war depression, a period during which it became even more aware of itself as a backwater.

The Contemporary Village

There are two ways of describing any village. At one level it is the sum of its component parts and may be studied under such headings as housing, facilities and services, education, employment and transport, but such a description will not account for what a village feels like to live in and what has given it its distinctive nature. This chapter and the next seek to describe the contemporary village in these two ways; this chapter is concerned with its formal aspects, under the headings mentioned above; Chapter 6 is concerned with the village as a community, or, rather, as a community of communities.

Certainly, until the First World War, and in many places for considerably longer, the village remained essentially a community, centred around the farming year, with which almost all its residents were either directly or indirectly involved. In recent decades, accelerating and far-reaching changes have transformed the village, so that today it bears little relationship to the occupational community of previous generations. Villages have ceased to be physically isolated, small-scale settlements, providing the labour force for the surrounding farms, and, so radical have been the changes, that some commentators have suggested that it is now inappropriate to use the word 'village' to describe them. From being occupational communities, modern rural settlements have become communities of choice where, with very few exceptions, people have moved both into and away from the village according to their preferences and desires. Whereas in the nineteenth century the village was largely shaped by local factors and internal considerations, the modern village is increasingly aware of the significance of external factors mediated through the planning system and the operations of local and central government. If, in the nineteenth century, villages grew slowly and organically, today the scale of change has dramatically altered and new housing developments, the re-routing of a road, or the establishment of a military base, can quickly transform the character and nature of a village. If spatial distribution and low population density are what principally distinguish rural areas from urban areas, the effects of the development of relatively cheap personal transport have dramatically affected the countryside and rural settlements. While in the nineteenth century villages on the main roads had the best facilities and had the most lively community life, today it tends to be those off main roads which are considered more desirable. Villages astride a main road tend to be divided by the constant heavy traffic, and the main road symbolizes the fact that almost all the village's needs are met from outside. By contrast, it is the smaller, less accessible villages and hamlets which have retained a greater sense of their own identity and a more tangible feeling of community.

It may be suggested that the recognizable modern village dates from the early 1950s, when it was first noted that the process of rural emigration which had dominated the previous hundred years was being counterbalanced by the process of urban decentralization. While there had always been a small out-movement of people from urban areas, particularly into the accessible dormitory villages, the chronic post-war housing shortage, together with the extensive programme of rural electrification and the near completion of the rural sewerage and water supply system, suddenly made the countryside a more attractive place in which to live. Between 1951 and 1961, the rural population increased by 0.6 million, but between 1961 and 1971 the increase was 1.6 million. Clearly, the impact on individual villages varied considerably, but certainly those in the more accessible countryside experienced a period of revival, when public transport by road and rail raised the prosperity of the village and, for a period, relieved its isolation without greatly weakening its identity. However, in the less accessible areas depopulation continued. In the last thirty years the area within the Yorkshire Dales National Park has lost 22 per cent of its population, and as a result services and facilities have tended to contract at an accelerating rate.

However, other factors have contributed to the post-war change in the nature of village life, including the widespread availability of the private car; the sharp decline in public transport; and the implementation, as a result of the county structure plans in the early 1970s, of a planned approach to the countryside (initially in terms of land use). At the same time, changes in personal preferences, particularly those of the middle classes, meant that a house in a village became increasingly desirable for commuters, the retired and the occasional residents (second home owners, tourists and visitors). The extent and impact of these new elements in the rural population are examined in Chapter 8. At this stage it may be noted that almost all villages since the 1950s have lost any last vestige of being a homogeneous occupational community and have become a community of communities, comprised of different, and at times competing groups, with different understandings about the nature of contemporary rural settlements.

In an increasingly mobile society, retirement migration has become the most significant contemporary demographic phenomenon and certain selected areas have been radically affected by the demands of occasional residents. The local impact both of in-migration and local attempts to control it can be seen in Warwickshire, which is a county that has received significant in-migration in recent decades. In the period 1951 to 1961, of every three people who moved into the county, two moved into towns and cities and one into the villages. By the period 1961 to 1967, the number moving into the villages had risen to equal the number moving into the towns. The early 1960s saw a rapid growth in the rural population, a trend which was reflected in national demographic changes. The effect of the implementation of the county structure plan in the period 1976—81, was that the balance that had existed in the early period was restored, and the number of people moving into the villages was only half the number moving into the towns and cities.

In the period up to the 1960s, when people spoke of the problems of the countryside they were referring to depopulation and the gradual tightening of the spiral of decline in rural facilities and services; since the 1960s, the problems have been of a different nature and have been caused by repopulation in all but the most remote areas. In such a context, individual villages no longer change principally as a result of local factors, but in a manner determined by planning decisions.

The Planned Village

In the eighteenth and nineteenth centuries some estate villages were planned, in the sense that they were built (or rebuilt) in a uniform style to an overall design pattern. However, the majority of English villages were unplanned, and houses and other buildings were sited and designed as a result of local preferences, styles and the availability of building materials. The unity of house styles, the similarity of scale but the great variety of design and detail and the randomness of siting are what make many English villages so attractive, particularly in the areas where stone has been extensively used, such as in the Cotswolds and in the ironstone villages of Northamptonshire and Rutland. Indeed, in some areas the buildings are grouped in such an effective and pleasing manner that it is hard to believe that there was not some overall plan. However, it was not until the Town and Country Planning Act (1932) that the opportunity was given for the preparation of planning schemes for rural areas. At this stage a developer was not obliged to apply for permission, but if the subsequent development failed to conform to the provisions of the scheme then demolition without compensation could be ordered.

In the mid 1930s, public opinion was alerted by campaigners such as Professor Joad and the Council for the Preservation of Rural England (which in 1969 changed its name to The Council for the Protection of Rural England) and became increasingly concerned about uncontrolled, sporadic ribbon development in the urban shadow countryside, which led to the Ribbon Development Act (1935) and the Green Belt Act (1938). At the same time, there was widespread concern in the late 1930s about the changes which were taking place in the countryside in general and, in particular, the loss of agricultural land to urban development. This found expression, in the early 1940s, in three important government reports: the Barlow Report on the Distribution of the Industrial Population (1940), the Uthwatt Committee Report on Compensation and Betterment (1942) and, perhaps of greatest significance to rural areas, the Scott Committee Report on Land Utilization in Rural Areas (1942). Taken together, these reports laid the foundations for an all-embracing and effective planning system for rural areas. The Scott Report may be regarded as one of the most comprehensive pieces of work undertaken on the English countryside, the recommendations of which in the areas of agriculture; the revival of villages and country life; rural housing and public utilities; village institutions and playing fields and the whole area of access to the countryside by the non-rural population; country parks and common land, formed the basis for much subsequent legislation. These recommendations led directly to the Town and Country Planning Interim Development Act (1943) and the Town and Country Planning Act (1947). At the same time, the report by John Dower, which was presented to the newly formed Ministry of Town and Country Planning in 1945 (followed by the Hobhouse Committee Report of 1947), resulted in the establishment of the National Parks Commission (1949). Also, reports on wildlife conservation, footpaths and access to the countryside were published in 1947.

The Town and Country Planning Act (1947) established a planning system based on the preparation of county development plans and provided the framework for planning for the next twenty years. Needless to say, much of the emphasis was on urban planning and few of the original CDPs contained policies or proposals for rural areas, apart from defining areas of exceptional natural beauty (either as National Parks, or, later, as Areas of Outstanding Natural Beauty, national or local nature reserves and Sites of Special Scientific Interest). However, there were policies of directing development away from first-class agricultural land and policies aimed at improving facilities in market towns and large villages, both of which were recommendations of the Scott Committee. The overall effect was to control urban sprawl and to avoid, where possible, sporadic and ribbon development in the countryside, together with the protection of the best agricultural land and of areas of special historic, scenic or scientific interest. In the 1960s, the 'Countryside in 1970' series of conferences (chaired by the Duke of Edinburgh) had focused attention on the rapidly changing rural scene which had resulted from greater mobility and increasing use of the countryside for leisure and recreational purposes. The Countryside Act (1968), which may be seen as part of the government's response to the leisure explosion of the 1960s and the influx of car-borne visitors, brought into being the Countryside Commission which replaced the National Parks Commission and had considerably enlarged responsibilities and powers.

The effect of the Town and Country Planning Act (1968) which later was consolidated with unrepealed sections of previous acts as the Town and Country Planning Act (1971), was to establish a new procedure, which required local authorities to prepare structure plans which were to contain statements of the authority's intentions and general proposals for development and land use, and were to provide a framework for the more detailed local plans. As a result of the Skeffington Committee's recommendations (1969), which pointed to the inadequacy of previous consultative procedures, a much greater degree of public participation was built into the new procedures. Thus, the early 1970s saw the production of the County Structure Plans for the rural counties, which were often subjected to a lengthy public inquiry (in the case of Warwickshire the Structure Plan was approved by the Secretary of State in 1975). The plans provided some of the most detailed information on the countryside and were prepared on the basis of extensive surveys of such issues as the location and scale of employment; housing; the transport system; the extent of conservation; recreation and tourism and facilities and services. The plans were originally designed for a fifteen-year period and are subject to review every five years.

At the same time, the Local Government Act of 1972 had considerable consequences for planning. Under the 1968 Act planning had been a county responsibility, but after 1972, planning became a shared responsibility between the County Council and the Rural District Council (after 1974, the District Council). The counties were made responsible for preparing and for keeping the structure plan under review; the new District Councils were given responsibilities for the preparation of local plans and control of development taking place in their district (with certain exceptions, the most significant of which related to mineral extraction; strategic development; gypsies; and waste disposal). The Parish Councils have the right to be consulted over developments in their area and some Parish Councils have initiated parish plans. Thus, for the village, planning, in the sense of permission to build or alter buildings, is a District Council responsibility; the Parish Councils, so often referred to as the grassroots of democracy, have found it difficult, both individually and collectively, to articulate a clear voice. In part this related to the different understandings of the village referred to above, found in the contemporary countryside, and represented on any individual Parish Council.

It is not possible to do more than summarize the general approach which is enshrined in the county structure plans of the early 1970s. While villages were to a large degree self-sufficient in earlier centuries, they never have been entirely isolated economic units but have depended upon local markets. The cattle market was the hub of the old rural society and markets were found in the country towns and larger villages spread across the countryside at roughly eight-mile intervals (which allowed those who lived farthest away to walk into the market and return between the morning and evening milkings). At the same time, as has been noted in Chapter 3, villages were located roughly 1.5 to 3 miles apart (or more in upland and marginal areas); this allowed villagers to walk out to their fields and return having done a day's work. Thus, the pattern of English rural settlements was dictated by the farming and transport constraints of a pre-industrial society. The first significant change to this pattern (apart from changes resulting from demographic fluctuation), occurred in the nineteenth century, when the railways integrated even the most remote country areas into a regional and national economic system. Locally, the railways had the effect of making certain market towns of more significance than their neighbours and this led to the decline of some market towns and large villages which were not on the railway system.

In the 1950s, when those who wrote about the problems of the countryside were principally concerned with depopulation and its likely long-term effects, it was suggested that many villages would continue to decline in population and that some would eventually disappear, as they had become 'functionally redundant'. It was not possible to foresee the significance of the out-movement of urban dwellers into the countryside, which gathered pace in the 1960s and became a major demographic phenomenon in the 1970s. However, despite the radical nature of these changes, the settlement pattern remained almost entirely unchanged. In County Durham a policy of selected settlements was formulated in the mid-1950s, in which 121 category-D villages, regarded by the County Council as obsolete, were designated for no further development, which meant they would be allowed to slowly die.

The policy, originally contained in the 1951 County Development Plan, was fiercely resisted locally and became the subject of innumerable public inquiries. By 1970, only eight of these former mining settlements had been cleared. (Cumberland also designated category-D villages but no sites were cleared.) At the same time a few villages were abandoned as a result of areas being designated for military use (as in west Norfolk) or as a result of flooding for reservoirs.

However, although the settlement pattern has changed little, it has been widely acknowledged, since the early decades of this century, that the level at which services and facilities can economically be offered in the village has been steadily rising, and that the cost of acceptable minimal facilities has also been increasing, particularly in medicine and education. The combination of these factors led to the development of new approaches to rural planning which have their origins, in this country, in the work of Harold Peake, who came to the forefront of rural planning affairs at the end of the First World War, and Henry Morris, who was Chief Education Officer for Cambridgeshire between 1922 and 1954. Both saw that it was not possible to maintain a highly dispersed system of provision and that it was necessary to concentrate facilities and services in particular selected rural centres which would serve an extensive hinterland. In the United States and in Germany, W. Christaller and A. Lösch had developed theories and models of rural development which suggested that facilities and services could be provided where there was a critical 'threshold population' which would create the necessary demand. Thus, it was possible to create models of rural development based on hierarchies of settlements and needs, which took account of the fact that more specialized services required larger catchment areas.

The county structure plans reflected these insights (known as central place theory), for they uniformly proposed the selection and development of 'service centres' (variously called capital, key or category-A villages). Public investment, in the form of schools and council houses, was directed to these selected settlements which were also designated for residential and industrial development. By concentrating the provision of all but the most basic services in such centres, it was suggested that a rural area was able to retain a degree of integrity and autonomy and not become completely subordinate, in economic and social terms, to the neighbouring large town. Thus, today, the key village tends to have more shops and services than would be expected for a settlement of that size, for it provides for the population of the surrounding smaller settlements, and is the hub of the local transport network.

The key or selected settlement policy can be regarded as the principal agent of planned change in post-war rural Britain, (though it must be remembered that approximately a third of the countryside is subject to further planning constraints as a result of its designation as one of a number of specially protected areas, including national parks). However, its implementation has not been without continued controversy. Initially, Christaller's work was criticized for according little significance to topography, and, more recently, commentators have suggested that the rigid implementation of this policy has been detrimental both to the larger key villages, which have been greatly increased in size over too short a time span, and to the smaller settlements which have experienced very strict control on their development, and, in many cases, have experienced population decline in recent years, accompanied by the loss of all local facilities and services. It is noticeable that there has been a tendency for those in the lower income groups, who are particularly dependent on the public provision of services, to move out of the smaller settlements into the key villages. Parents, particularly those without private transport, whose children are at secondary school, are likely to find living in a remote hamlet with almost no public transport links, very difficult, and a significant number have moved to the larger settlements. At the same time, the smaller settlements are a particularly popular choice for the retired and second home owners. Thus, in certain areas, a pattern of social zoning has emerged in the countryside, whereby the smaller hamlets and villages tend to be populated by the relatively affluent, who are less dependent on the public provision of services and facilities, while the key villages attract those who need ready and frequent access to such services.

Housing in the Village

The Scott Report (1942) which noted the particular nature of the rural housing problems, drew attention to the existence of a significant number of derelict houses in many villages. The level of out-migration, particularly in the remoter upland areas, had led to a situation in which a sizeable proportion of the housing stock in many villages had been left empty and was in varying stages of decay. It was part of the paradox of rural housing, in the early decades of this century, that while those houses that were occupied were often severely overcrowded, such houses stood alongside others which were empty. In the period after the Second World War, when there was an acute shortage of urban housing, it was the existence of empty country cottages and land on which to build new homes, that attracted people from urban areas into the village; a movement which gathered momentum in the subsequent decades. Approximately 4 million houses were built in the inter-war period, and, although the majority were located in the suburbs, a significant number were built in the accessible villages, many of which took on the nature of discontinuous suburbs.

Throughout the countryside it is impossible to ignore the way in which villages were affected by the arrival of so many commuters, retired people and occasional residents in the post-war years. Those cottages and houses which the Scott Committee observed to be decaying and dilapidated, have been extensively renovated and restored by the new village residents. Many villages, which once had an air of poverty and neglect, became, in a few years, cherished and well cared for. However, this work of restoration and repair, which changed so many of the older houses in the village, is often contrasted with the uninspiring and repetitive nature of some new building in rural areas during this period, which, in its style and layout, was often unrelated to the old village.

Inevitably, the desire of so many people to live in the countryside now that the old disadvantages of physical isolation and poor facilities could be more easily overcome, resulted in a rapid rise in the price of rural housing. At the end of the 1920s a semi-detached suburban house cost approximately £600 (a detached house £1,000); in the village, houses could be purchased for even lower prices and almost all villages will testify to the fact that certain cottages were sold in the inter-war period for as little as £80 or £100. While all the incidences of cottages being sold under £100 in the years after the Second World War and being resold thirty years later for £30,000 to £40,000 need not be individually true, nevertheless they underline the fact that in the early period rural housing was relatively cheap, so much so that the working men could and did purchase their own cottages — today, it has become both scarce and extremely expensive. Cottages in attractive parts of the countryside such as the Cotswolds, which are near main-line stations or motorways, are particularly sought after, as has been mentioned above, and two- or three-bedroomed cottages in many Cotswold villages now (1985) sell for prices ranging from £50,000 to £75,000. It is villages of this nature which are spoken of by planners as having been affected by the processes they term 'gentrification' and 'geriatrification'. In many villages the old village community can afford to live only in council houses or in rented estate cottages (though there are relatively few of these in the countryside as a whole), or in agricultural tied cottages. The old village community which used to live in the centre of the village, in many cases has moved either to its margins or away from the village altogether.

The first council houses were built in the period after the First World War, principally for ex-servicemen. But council housing plays a statistically less significant role in the rural areas than it does in urban areas. (On average it comprises 20 per cent of the housing stock in rural areas as compared with 30 per cent in the nation as a whole.) It is sometimes suggested that farmers, who were often in the majority on the rural district councils, were cautious about introducing council houses into the villages which they represented, partly because such a move would disturb a situation in which the tied cottage system played a predominant role, and partly through fear of introducing undesirable families. Although such generalizations are hard to maintain, some rural areas do possess little local authority housing and in other villages it has been located in an insensitive manner, either on the edge of the village or, in a few cases, as a block of housing standing on its own as much as a mile outside the village. Council housing has become particularly important in rural areas to the old village community at a time when it is impossible for them to compete for the private housing stock. As a consequence, the 1980 Housing Act, which allowed tenants to purchase their council houses, has been viewed with particular alarm in rural areas. It has been suggested that should a council house be resold, in the present market conditions of unequal competition between affluent outsiders and less well-off local residents, there is an increasing likelihood that the former council house will be purchased for retirement or for occasional residence. In individual villages as much as 50 per cent of the local authority housing stock has already been sold (though this is well above the average for rural areas). The percentage of rural council housing that has been sold under the 1980 'right to buy' provision, is 45 per cent above the national average. Inevitably sales tend to be the highest in the smaller villages with the least council housing, in areas of high scenic value. However, under the terms of the 1980 legislation, in certain designated areas (particularly National Parks) the District Council can exercise an option to buy back ex-council property if it is resold within five years. In 1984 the Government proposed a further extension of the right to buy to old people's accommodation (either local authority or housing association tenancies). But the prospect of losing such accommodation was regarded as such a significant threat to the future of rural communities that a rural lobby succeeded in resisting these proposals.

For generations the agricultural tied cottage has been a subject of contention and difficulty in the village. Though the number of evictions was never large, even in circumstances where the farmer and his staff enjoyed good relations, the constant threat of eviction was deeply resented. In 1966 there were twenty court cases in Suffolk (although not all these ended in eviction). Eventually, the legal position of the agricultural tied cottage was changed by the Rent (Agriculture) Act 1976, following a long campaign for the termination of this form of tenancy by the National Union of Agricultural and Allied Workers. Under the new system, if a farm worker is required for whatever reason to leave tied accommodation, there is an obligation on the District Council to provide accommodation. A farmer can only invoke this procedure in cases where it can be proved that repossession of the cottage is essential for the running of the farm. This compromise has meant that the insecurity from which farm workers once suffered has been removed, but, at the same time, in certain cases farmers can repossess a cottage where it is essential for the running of the farm. However, this arrangement is dependent on the availability of local authority housing in rural areas.

The problems of rural housing result principally from the scarcity of supply and consequent high cost. Rural Voice has noted that in the mid-1970s private house building accounted for 82 per cent of all new homes in rural areas, as compared with 54 per cent nationally. At this time, the number of local authority houses being built in the countryside was considerably less per capita than in urban areas. Even private building has been severely curtailed in many areas, partly as a result of the planning policies contained in county structure plans, which sought to centralize new building in the key villages and service centres, and partly because those who bought houses in the village were often not disposed to encourage further new buildings in that village. This phenomenon, sometimes referred to as the 'drawbridge mentality', whereby newcomers to a village are among the most vociferous in resisting any further development, is a significant feature of the rural housing situation. Commentators on rural housing have noted that villages are particularly deficient in housing for special needs such as the elderly, the disabled, young couples and single people. At the same time, in certain areas, a significant proportion of low-income families live in mobile homes, caravan parks or use out-of-season holiday accommodation.

Following a period of low activity in the early 1980s, the house-building industry has begun to expand. Clearly, most of this increase has been provided by private developers seeking to meet the demands of commuters and retired people. However, a notable feature of recent years has been the development of the housing association movement in rural areas, sometimes called 'the third arm' of housing policy, particularly since the report of the National Federation of Housing Associations working party on Rural Housing (chaired by the Duke of Edinburgh) in 1981. In the main, housing associations have been connected with urban areas and particularly with the special needs of inner cities, and have looked on small schemes in rural areas with disfavour. Also, the need for such housing in rural areas has not been demonstrated in terms of the local authority housing lists; principally because people do not apply for what does not exist (this is often referred to as a 'hidden need'). While some counties such as Northumberland and Cumbria are well served, many rural areas have had little or no housing association development. Recently the Development Commission and the Housing Corporation (which was established in 1964 and regulates the affairs of housing associations) have assisted in the development of starter homes and new shared ownership schemes (where the occupant pays rent on a proportion of the value of the house and has a mortgage for the other part) which have been expanded in many areas including North Yorkshire and Cumbria. Some self-build schemes have been developed, but increasingly it appears that housing associations may play a more significant role in meeting the demand for low-cost housing in rural areas. The National Agricultural Centre Rural Trust has worked to encourage the formation of county housing associations in the areas where there is no housing association willing to meet rural needs; to date, associations have been formed in Shropshire, Wiltshire, Suffolk and Gloucestershire. The Trust has the benefit of a revolving fund that can purchase sites and hold them for housing associations while planning permission and Housing Corporation approval are obtained. This is of particular value in rural areas where many sites have complex associated problems and where other purchasers are readily available.

Thus it can be seen that a combination of unequal competition between affluent outsiders and less well-off local inhabitants; a decline in the number of council houses and the disappearance of the private rented sector, together with the concentration of private builders on the 'executive end' of the market, has created a situation in which many have found it impossible to find adequate housing in the village. This may be regarded as the 'hidden need' in the village and has led to the large-scale out-movement of people who might otherwise have stayed in the village. Their place has been taken by others, and it can be said that the constraints of the housing situation in rural areas have contributed significantly to the changing social profile of the village.

Facilities and Services in the Village

The degree to which rural households were self-sufficient in the period before the mid nineteenth century must have varied enormously, but, from that period, the local cash economy developed considerably as households purchased those goods and services which previously they had either gone without or obtained locally. Village shops, as has been noted, were essentially a nineteenth-century creation and their widespread development led to the demise of the packman and the decline of the smaller markets. By the late nineteenth century, most villages had a number of small shops, including a general stores, a butcher and a baker, which took their place alongside the established craftsmen such as the cobbler, tailor, wheelwright and smith. The many small pubs and beer houses, mentioned in the previous chapter, were also a prominent feature of village facilities in the nineteenth century. A large number of these shops and beer houses were essentially part-time occupations and were either run by women or combined with a farm or with some activity such as a carrier's round. Before licensing rules restricted the number of inns and ale houses, a sizeable village had perhaps more than a dozen, and until 1872 beer could be sold at any hour of the day or night. By the late nineteenth century and the early decades of the twentieth century, there was already a tendency for the range of small part-time businesses to contract and for a single general stores to become the principal retail business in the smaller villages. At the same time, as farming became a more specialized and technical activity so its ancillary services tended to become both more centralized and specialized. As the tractor took over from horses, so this led eventually to the closure of many village wheelwright's shops and smithies.

In 1943 the Agricultural Economics Research Institute of Oxford University undertook a survey of a rural area in north Oxfordshire. In the twenty-two villages contained in the survey, only two had piped water and mains sewerage; six had only piped water and the remaining fourteen had neither. Under the terms of the Rural Water Supplies and Sewerage Act (1944) generous grants were made available for installing piped water, sewerage and sewage disposal, but although considerable progress was made with the former, mains sewerage facilities were still lacking in many rural areas because of the high unit cost. Since 1974 these matters have been the responsibility of the regional water authorities, and by that time all villages in the north Oxfordshire survey area had both piped water and sewerage. Following the nationalization of the electricity supply industry in 1947, a large number of rural electrification schemes were carried out, with the result that within a period of seven to ten years electricity was available in almost all rural areas, with only limited exceptions. A survey of 1963 revealed the extent to which electricity was being used in agriculture: 85 per cent of all farms were connected to the public supply. Gas has never been a rural service and is not available in most country areas, as the cost of reducing the mains pressure for a small group of houses is uneconomic. Despite the considerable advances that had been made in the post-war period, it is important to note that the provision of public utilities in rural areas is a relatively recent phenomenon and that there are still a few isolated pockets in which certain supplies are not available.

In the post-war period, three mutually related and interdependent factors have significantly altered the provision of services and facilities in rural areas. First, the level at which services can be provided economically has risen sharply in recent years, partly because they have become intrinsically more costly and sophisticated, as with health and education, and partly because they now serve a wider catchment area. This has inevitably meant that, with the exception of a small combined post-office and general stores, almost all facilities such as schools, banks, medical centres, specialist shops (including chemists) and professional services now can be found only in the key villages and market towns. Clearly, as mentioned above, below a certain threshold it has become impossible to provide services economically. Putting exact figures to these thresholds has always been problematic, not least because local factors play such a significant role. However, in 1967, R. J. Green and J. B. Ayton suggested the following threshold figures needed to support certain services:

Service	Population
Grocery shop	300
Butcher	2,000
Single doctor	2,000 – 2,500
Draper	2,500
Household goods	2,500

Baker	3,000
Chemist	4,000
Home nurse	5,000
Primary school	5,000
Three-doctor practice	6,000
Health visitor	8,000
Secondary school	10,000

Second, as has been mentioned above, a variety of factors encouraged the centralized provision of services particularly by these providers. Thus, all organizations which maintain a network of outlets have followed a policy of centralization and concentration on the key or service villages. This has led to the closure of a number of banks, tax offices, registries and DHSS offices, with consequent effects on the employment pattern. Single-doctor country practices, which were once relatively common, have been superseded by group practices, frequently operated from a medical centre in the key village, with its own dispensing facilities. Some doctors hold surgeries in village halls, schools or other buildings, though the complexity of modern medical procedures and the need for adequate support and records place severe limitations on this practice. Since 1944 great stress has been laid on the development of group practice, and while this has undoubtedly improved the level of medical care available in the village, and rural practice allowances are paid to country doctors, the difficulty of access and the distance that people now have to travel both to the doctor and to outpatients' facilities, chiropodists, clinics and hospitals, have become major problems. A large number of village pubs have been closed and many of those that remain rely on 'passing trade', a restaurant or holiday accommodation, or have become part-time employment for the landlord and his family.

Third, the change in the social profile of the rural community has of itself precipitated significant changes in the provision of services and facilities. Not unnaturally the process of population substitution, whereby many locally born families have left the village and their places have been taken by the retired and commuters, has changed the nature of the demands which are made on local facilities and services. Many of the retired and the commuters retain close links with neighbouring urban areas to which they go for shopping and other facilities and services. It is part of the paradox of the contemporary countryside that the influx of more affluent people has not necessarily arrested the decline in services and facilities, but, in many cases, has accelerated this process. In some less attractive areas which are not favoured by new villagers, the local demand generated by the old villagers has meant that services which might otherwise have been lost, have been maintained. This is the case in the industrial-mining countryside of some areas of the east Midlands. In other areas, the increasing significance of tourism and the leisure use of the countryside has changed the nature of many local shops, which in some areas have become almost exclusively aimed at this market.

While larger villages have retained a modest range of services and facilities, the smaller settlement may only have a single village shop with a sub-post office, together with a telephone kiosk and a postbox. The modern village shop survives, as it has always done, by supplying a range of goods and services including daily and Sunday papers, foodstuffs and household requirements, sweets and confectionery, cigarettes, and possibly also an off-licence as well as agencies for such things as dry cleaning and shoe repairs. The abolition of retail price maintenance greatly affected village shops, which are now principally used for perishable, supplementary or forgotten items, rather than for the main weekly groceries. However, a number of less mobile and elderly people do rely upon the village shop for all their purchases, and its convenience and the lack of transport costs compensate for the higher prices. The sub-post office is frequently an important part of the village shop and the salary which it generates (current minimum salary £2,000 in 1985) makes an important contribution to the viability of the whole enterprise. However, recent changes introduced by the Department of Health and Social Security in the methods of payment of benefits has depressed the turnover of the local sub-post office. In Cambridgeshire, which has slightly over 300 villages, between 1982 and 1984 ten villages lost their last remaining village shop, eight their sub-post office. No village shop can hope to compete in price with the out-of-town, twenty-four-aisle super store, but many people still place a high value on personal service and convenience. The success of many village shops in tourist areas depends upon lengthy opening hours and the development of a strong Sunday trade.

It is widely acknowledged that village shops make an important contribution to the general wellbeing of the village community and the village shop with a post office is a focal point for information and the co-ordination of many services needed particularly by the elderly and the less mobile. Some Scandinavian countries, notably Norway, support small village shops from central government funds in recognition of this aspect of their overall contribution to the village; and in Sweden, common carriers who deliver groceries, post, newspapers and prescriptions in remote areas are linked to the social services. The specialist officers of the Council for Small Industries in Rural Areas (CoSIRA) provide business advice and training courses for those who run village shops, and the Rural Community Councils also provide support for local shopkeepers by means of campaigns, competitions, meetings and advice; all of which are designed to draw attention to the problems and demonstrate the methods of overcoming them. One example of this is the development of a link-up between one of the three major rural shop groups and a garage chain to provide joint services in rural areas. In some areas mobile shops, banks and advice centres have been used to replace closed services but a large area is needed for these to be operated economically and with certain services security is a major problem.

It is often argued that social services need not be so extensive in rural areas because of the absence of the stresses of the urban environment and the existence of supportive neighbours. At the same time certain elements of the population are significantly under-represented in the rural community, notably one-parent families. However, physical isolation and the attendant loneliness and lack of social contact can create other problems, and the number of elderly people in the rural community (as has been mentioned above) creates particular problems in certain areas. While many villages are able to support their elderly residents in a way that might not be possible elsewhere, nevertheless the increasing number of elderly people in rural areas places a considerable strain on the personal and domiciliary social services. In a highly mobile society many elderly people have become isolated from their families and the home help scheme provides much valued assistance. 'Meals on wheels' is an important part of domiciliary services, and in many rural areas the meals are supplied from school kitchens and village halls. It is suggested that in most rural areas 'meals on wheels' cost approximately 15 per cent more than in urban areas, while social service work as a whole can cost approximately 30 per cent more per client.

In part, as a consequence of the effectiveness of domiciliary services, and as a result of their own self-reliance, country people appear to go into 'part 3' accommodation (old people's homes) at a significantly older age. The average age of entry in Warwickshire to the 26 old people's homes with 1,000 places is 81 years. In order to overcome some of these problems volunteers are of particular importance in the rural areas, and members of the Women's Royal Voluntary Service play an important role in distributing meals on wheels throughout the villages. At the same time, lunch clubs have been established in many villages. These provide not just a meal but a place of meeting and contact for elderly people.

Village Schools

In recent years nothing has focused attention more closely on the problems of the village than the situation of rural schools. Many villages owe their school to the efforts of the mid nineteenth-century country clergy, who shared with others a belief in education as the panacea for most social and economic ills. The village school, with its foundation stone dating from between the 1840s and the 1860s, with its separate entrances for boys and girls and with school master's or mistress's house attached, is the enduring monument to the pastoral work of many mid-Victorian clergy. It was in the school that they spent much of their time and energy and it was the centrepiece of their work in the village. Not only was the school used for teaching but it also accommodated the meetings of an educational, charitable, social and recreational nature which were organized by the clergy. In short, the school was the hub and centre of village life, and in the days when it provided education for all ages, many schools, even in smaller villages, had between 100 and 150 children on the roll.

In recent years the changes in the social profile of the village, together with the decline in the birthrate since 1964, and the restructuring of education, have resulted in a very different situation. Dr Horn recorded that, in 1938 Oxfordshire still had forty-three all-age schools. The 1944 Education Act which set up the system of primary and secondary schools (later divided between grammar and secondary modern, with a few technical schools) led to the closure of many of the old village all-age schools or their conversion to primary schools and the appearance of the school bus. The Plowden Report (1967) is usually regarded as having sounded the death knell of many remaining village schools for it led to the establishment of policies designed to ensure that the minimum size of schools was fifty pupils and three teachers. Today, it is widely believed that the significance of the interaction between the community and the school was significantly underestimated in this report. However, by the 1970s and early 1980s, it was clear that the declining birthrate in the earlier period had led to a decline in the number of primary school children. Nationally the numbers of primary school children declined from 5.2 million in 1972 to 4.7 million in 1977. In Warwickshire, between 1978 and 1983 there was an 18.4 per cent fall in the numbers of primary school pupils and a 4.2 per cent fall in those of secondary school pupils. The effects of the declining birthrate are now being felt in the secondary school sector and it is suggested that, in Warwickshire, before 1991, there will have been a 24 per cent fall in the numbers of secondary school pupils.

Total pupils in Warwickshire

| | AUTUMN TERM | AUTUMN TERM | CURRENT PROJECTIONS |
	1978	1983	1991
Primary	53,909	44,017	44,000
Secondary	34,266	32,837	24,000

Clearly, such large changes in the numbers of pupils have radically affected the structuring of education in all counties, as has the advent of comprehensive patterns in many areas, following the legislation of 1965.

While rural people have accepted the necessity of travel to

reach certain facilities, most expect primary education to be available in the village, but recognize that children will have to travel to secondary and post-sixteen level education. Inevitably, as a result of falling school rolls, many primary schools have been closed and it is suggested that in the last two decades approximately 25 per cent have been shut. In almost all cases this has only been achieved in the face of strong opposition by the villagers, who see the school as an important centre of village life and a symbol of the village's community life and future. At the same time, in some small villages the school is a significant provider of part-time employment. The strength of public opposition to such closures has caused some reconsideration of this policy in recent years, and the commissioning of research projects from Aston and Cambridge Universities. However, it is clear that the cost per pupil is inevitably higher in smaller schools and that the optimum economic size for a school is over 200. Certainly, costs per pupil rise sharply in schools below 100 pupils. In Suffolk in 1978, the average cost of a pupil in the county per year was £398; the cost of a pupil per year in a 30-pupil primary school was £473; in a 25-pupil primary school £600; in a 20-pupil primary school £775. But many voices (not least the National Association for the Support of Small Schools) have sought to convince the Department of Education and Science and county councils that there are high costs to be met in other sectors as a result of the policy of centralization. Advocates of village schools point to the importance of a stable environment where the parents can be involved in the life of the school, and where teachers tend to stay for considerable periods and to know and be known by the community. In some cases such teachers contribute considerably to the life of the village outside school hours. However, it has to be recognized that children in village schools can be educationally and socially stranded, with few facilities to compensate and little competition to spur them on. The fact that a group of children may be taught by the same teacher for five or six years may not necessarily be of benefit to all the children. In the smallest schools a child may be the sole member of an age group, with the next nearest in age being one or two years older or younger. This and other factors account for the lack of academic stimulation, the restricted social development and the lack of competition which critics of small rural schools believe to be significant factors.

In many counties any primary school of under forty or fifty pupils must be considered as under constant reappraisal. Local authorities under continuing pressure to reduce educational spending, by the Department of Education and Science, which accounts for 60—70 per cent of expenditure in the non-metropolitan counties, have attempted to rationalize the provision of primary schools and are now concerned with the secondary level. However, as a consequence, long journeys have to be undertaken by many children. School transport is provided for children under eight who live over two miles from the school and for children over eight if they live over three miles from the school. (Currently, in areas of heavy traffic on narrow roads, there is some discussion as to whether the most direct or the safest route should form the basis of calculation.) It is suggested by some that the problems of travelling outweigh the benefits of social contact and a better educational environment for younger children. Recently, a government circular has tried to encourage county councils to safeguard some rural schools, particularly in upland areas such as Cumbria, the Pennines and the North Staffordshire border, where wintry weather can seriously disrupt journeys over a considerable period.

In rural areas secondary schools are usually found in the large villages and key settlements and need a catchment area of between 10,000 and 12,500, which may mean as many as sixteen to twenty-five villages. The sharp fall in school rolls which primary schools have recently experienced is now moving into the secondary age group and many secondary schools will find it increasingly difficult to maintain a wide choice of academic subjects. Except in a few instances, distance virtually rules out co-operative ventures at the secondary level and the only way improvements can be made is by increasing staff/pupil ratios, often by use of peripatetic staff for such courses as music, remedial education, separate sciences and modern languages. The adoption of a three-tier school system has by its nature increased the population thresholds needed to maintain viability at each level.

However, despite the fact that education is the least flexible of public services, it was in this area that the earliest experiments were carried out in the provision of centralized facilities for a cluster of small villages. The development of the village colleges, principally by Henry Morris (Chief Education Officer of Cambridgeshire 1922—54) was a concept which owed much to the Danish Folk High School movement. The village college sought to provide an integrated educational resource for a cluster of villages, providing both secondary education for the children and the base for adult education and youth work, both statutory and voluntary. More recent experiments have been undertaken in clustering primary schools, for example in Norfolk, so that a group of three small schools become one educational unit with a single headteacher but a staff member for each school. These schools are all within a few miles of each other, and, in one example, two schools provide education for the 4—8 age group, while all the 8—11 age group go to the third school. In one Oxfordshire village the local people 'bought' a third teacher for the school (with a roll of fifty-eight) after the county had reduced the staff to two. In one Cambridgeshire village the school was purchased and reopened in 1978, when the authorities closed it; this example has been recently followed in Devon.

In a village where the school has been a significant and important feature of village life for many decades, the prospect of its closure will unite the village community against what they regard as an external bureaucratic threat. Former pupils, parents of former and current pupils and those who have moved into the village only recently, will unite to resist this outside threat. As in church matters, the school is seen by the villagers not as part of the overall educational provision for the county, but as *their* school. No matter what standard of education is provided by the school it will be defended by anxious villagers, who rightly detect that its closure is a significant threshold in the downward spiral of decline in village life. Research has shown that the closure or the possibility of the closure of a village school almost inevitably leads to some families with young children moving away to larger settlements where their children can walk to school. The rural lobby has been particularly active in drawing attention to the problems of rural schools and in part it has achieved some reconsideration of earlier policies.

Employment in the Village

The rural policies of different countries reflect varying approaches to the problems of rural revival. In some Scandinavian countries it is believed that the provision of the facilities and services is of the greatest importance. In this country public policy has always reflected the belief that it is necessary to provide jobs in rural areas in order to halt depopulation; for instance, the Countryside Review Committee Report (1977) recognized the crucial role of the local economy and of jobs as the foundation of rural community life. Since the beginning of this century there has been a steady decline in rural jobs, principally as the result of specialization and centralization. The mills, dairies and outworkers which were such a prominent feature of village life in the last century, found that their work had been centralized into urban factories. One medium-sized Cotswold village recorded that twenty-four businesses had disappeared during this century. The replacement of the horse by the tractor in the mid-1930s meant a sharp decline in those jobs related to the horses, its harness and implements. In the mid-1970s there were not enough shoeing smiths to meet the rising demand for their services as a result of the increased popularity of riding as a recreational activity.

At the same time, the numbers employed in farming have fallen steadily throughout the decades of this century. In the last twenty years there has been approximately a one-third decline in the number of jobs in agriculture and while this rate of decline has slackened, commentators suggest that agriculture will continue to be served by a contracting labour force. While nationally slightly under 2.5 per cent of those employed work in agriculture, in most rural districts the figure is between 5 and 8 per cent and even in the more remote rural areas it rises only to 20 per cent. The 1984 Ministry of Agriculture figures indicate that there were 159,300 full-time farmers; 67,000 part-time farmers; 7,850 salaried managers; 160,700 regular full-time workers; 60,000 regular part-time workers; and 96,000 seasonal/casual workers.

To help arrest the depopulation of the remoter countryside and declining employment opportunities in all rural areas the Development Commission was established in 1909 by Lloyd George when he was Chancellor of the Exchequer, to advise the

Government on the use of the Development Fund, which represented money set aside to help deal with the economic and social dimensions of rural deprivation. Many of the original tasks of the Commission, in connection with rural roads, agriculture and fisheries research, forestry, harbours and inland waterways have been transferred to other departments and recently the Commission has concentrated on rural employment, primarily by assisting small businesses. In 1969 the three separate bodies which had been funded by the Commission to pursue this aim — the Rural Industries Bureau; the Rural Industries Loan Fund, and the Rural Industries Organizers — were merged into a new organization, The Council for Small Industries in Rural Areas (it was transferred from the Treasury to the Department of the Environment in 1971; and, in 1976, separate agencies were established for Wales and Scotland). The Council for Small Industries in Rural Areas (CoSIRA) aims to assist small firms employing no more than twenty people and in country towns with under 10,000 population. The other main agency carrying out the Commission's economic work is English Industrial Estates, which undertakes the construction of new factories and is now the largest industrial and commercial landlord in England, developing and managing property, in assisted areas, for the Department of Trade and Industry, and supporting the Commission's work in rural areas, principally in the Rural Development Areas, which are priority areas designated on criteria established by the Government. In such areas English Industrial Estates carry out a programme for building workshops and small factories of between 1,500 and 5,000 sq ft. They are also concerned with the conversion and building of premises in partnership with local authorities, and with making grants to help convert existing redundant buildings, principally agricultural buildings, into craft workshops or for light industrial use. CoSIRA also provides an advisory service and supports small rural industries with technical and financial services.

Employment in rural areas has a number of particular characteristics; for instance, the number of jobs in the service sector is much higher in rural than in urban areas. In most rural areas the ratio of services to manufacturing jobs is 2:1, in the remote countryside it is 4:1. Many jobs in rural areas are relatively low paid and the five lowest paid industrial sectors (agriculture, clothing and footwear, timber, distributive trades and miscellaneous services) form a high proportion of the jobs available in rural areas. There is also an above-average representation of those industrial sectors where the number of people employed is declining, the most obvious example being agriculture. At the same time, there is an under representation of those sectors which are expanding, such as professional and scientific services, insurance and banking. Furthermore, the small-scale nature of rural enterprises and the centralization of all major services means that career prospects can be severely truncated. This is particularly the case in clerical, managerial and professional work sought by many of those who obtain higher qualifications. In many country towns the industrial structure is dominated by one or two firms. Some of these are related to agriculture or branches of large national companies, attracted to rural areas by the availability of a labour market where there is little competition. The disadvantages to the local population of this kind of industrial structure are threefold: the lack of variety in job types; low wages; and dependence on the fortunes of a single company, for inevitably branch factories are particularly vulnerable in times of recession.

It is clear that lack of employment opportunities is one of the main factors behind the continuing out-movement of people from many of the remoter rural areas, and provides the main justification for the Development Commission's approach to halting rural depopulation. Many young people are forced either to commute long distances to work or to consider moving from the village. This may be a solution to their individual problem but the real problems of rural depopulation are left to be faced by those who remain. In some areas it is suggested that tourism and recreation may provide an increasing number of jobs. But frequently the employment created by tourism is seasonal and supplementary. Many rural areas have considerable reservations about the benefits of tourism and an increasing dependency on what is termed 'the ice-cream economy'.

It is well known that registered unemployed in rural areas do not reflect the total situation, particularly with regard to married women, for whom, in many of the traditional rural industries, there have been few jobs. The number of women working in rural areas is substantially less than the national average; in some places about half. However, as a whole, the extent of unemployment in rural areas is frequently underestimated, not least because figures are often given for a whole district council area. In October 1981, there were 407 people under eighteen years of age unemployed in the Stratford District Council area. Of those 102 lived in Stratford, but 305 were spread in small numbers across the many small villages of south Warwickshire which comprised the Stratford District Council area. The situation of young people, often isolated, without transport, is particularly disheartening. Rural youngsters, who may visit Job Centres infrequently, find it particularly difficult to get employment and are often poorly informed about the extent of government training programmes. The Manpower Services Commission Youth Training Scheme has provided a number of one-year schemes in rural areas (shortly to be increased to two), though some of these have proved difficult to operate because of the financial constraints and the high costs incurred in travelling. The small number of large employers in rural areas has meant that there has been difficulty in obtaining Mode A places, and travel to Further Education colleges may involve a long journey. Despite the success of the Approved Agricultural and Horticultural Scheme, operated in the main by the county agricultural colleges, there remains a significant number of youngsters in rural areas who are neither employed nor on government training schemes.

A further constraint to employment in rural areas is the attitude of some members of the new village community, who regard the countryside principally as a place of residence, retirement and recreation and do not see it as a place of work. It is well known that the new rural population frequently seek to defend the countryside and the village against what they regard as intrusive and incompatible industrial and commercial developments. As a consequence, planning permission in rural areas (despite government encouragement, as in Department of the Environment circulars 22/80 and 16/84) has been difficult to obtain for any form of commercial enterprise, with the exception of certain craft industries. As the majority of new villagers see the village principally as a residential area, delivery lorries, and industrial processes which create noise or smell, are resisted fiercely. Nevertheless, some progress has been made and the Department of the Environment has sought to encourage district councils to take a more favourable attitude, particularly towards the conversion of redundant farm buildings for light industrial use. This has led in some rural areas to the development of a number of small industries. Such developments can be found among the firms belonging to local enterprises trusts, groups of agencies in craft homes (built by the Development Commission) and in workshop conversions on the estates of private landowners, of which there are now many examples. However, despite these encouraging developments, rural unemployment remains a significant though largely hidden phenomenon.

Transport in the Village

Throughout this consideration of the problems of the contemporary village, the consequences of physical isolation and low population density have been highlighted. For the rural resident the cost of mobility, whether it is by public or private vehicle, will inevitably be higher than in urban areas and access will have a direct bearing on almost all aspects of life. As has been shown, rural planning philosophy has been dominated by the concept of the key village, surrounded by a rural hinterland, which was originally designed to be served by readily available public transport. The maintenance of an adequate public transport system was regarded as a critical component of the key village concept in its original form.

While, in the period before the First World War, almost all local transport was provided either by horse-drawn vehicles or by rail, in the 1920s and 1930s an extensive rural bus service was developed. In 1930 the regulatory license system which controlled local operators for fifty years was set up with the enactment of the Road Traffic Act (1930), and country bus services entered a period of steady growth which continued until the 1950s, when they reached their zenith. In 1951, the number of passenger miles travelled nationally by bus was 50 million and exceeded by 10 million the number of miles travelled by car. Most rural people in this period had relatively easy access to bus services which, together with the yet unpruned rural rail network, provided a widespread and relatively low-cost service.

The local railway station, in many large villages, was one of the centres of village life and the railways played an important role in intergrating remoter areas into a regional and national economy. Before the widespread use of lorries, the railway, supplemented in some areas by the canal, was the most appropriate and economic means of moving most agricultural commodities, as well as fuel and building materials. However, between 1961 and 1965, Dr Richard Beeching initiated a programme to reduce the extent of rail network, for his report had shown that much of the rail network was under-used; for instance, it had become clear that 90 per cent of the country's freight was carried on only 50 per cent of the rail system. In four years 2,000 route miles, 900 freight depots and 700 stations were closed. The majority of these closures were in rural areas, and Norfolk lost 70 per cent of its rail network in the 1960s. This brought to an end the period of branch rail travel and resulted in the closure of the station in many villages. The publication of the Serpell Report in January 1983 raised fears about the closure of some parts of the remaining rail network, particularly such rural routes as the Settle—Carlisle line. In recent years there have been experiments with rail buses which have proved successful, particularly in the eastern counties, and certain lines favoured by commuters have been saved from possible closure as the distance which commuters (particularly 'three-day' commuters) are prepared to travel has increased. It seemed inevitable that, as a result of operative deficits and the deterioration of the track, the Hereford—Oxford line would have to be closed. However, since the formation of a Promotion Group of regular users in 1978, the line has marketed its services for both business and tourist use much more effectively and has seen a 20 per cent increase in passengers.

In the post-war period the increasing availability and use of private cars dramatically altered the local transport situation. In 1951 there were only 3 million private cars, but in 1971 this figure had risen to 12 million (between 1961 and 1972 the number of private cars doubled). The growth of mass car ownership has been a major factor in reducing the need for rural buses, and between 1951 and 1977 the number of passenger miles travelled by car increased from 40 million to 240 million. From 1965 to 1975, the number of passengers carried by country buses fell by approximately 30 per cent. In 1971 the Lincolnshire Road Car

Company (a fully owned subsidiary of the state-run National Bus Company) carried 56 million passengers over 18 million miles of route; in 1979 it carried only 29 million passengers over 13 million route miles. But it was not simply the rise of the private car that led to the decline in the use of buses. Television substantially reduced off-peak evening travel requirements; the five-day week and longer holidays resulted in fewer journeys to work; and changes in the rural population also had a significant effect. At the same time, increasing labour, vehicle purchase and running costs have together resulted in the gradual reduction of the rural bus service to the point where some rural areas were almost without a bus service. While, in major urban areas, 25 per cent of all travel is currently by public transport and 66 per cent by car, in rural areas only 14 per cent is by public transport and 81 per cent by car.

The level of car ownership and usage in rural areas reflects both the relatively poor provision of public transport and the need of country people to travel to centralized facilities and services. In many villages it is noticeable that families with relatively low incomes find it essential to maintain an elderly vehicle or face the possibility of being dependent upon few and infrequent buses. The Family Expenditure Survey of 1977 demonstrated that average weekly household expenditure on transport and vehicles is significantly higher in non-metropolitan districts (14.5 per cent of total household expenditure) than in metropolitan districts (12 per cent). As might be expected, the average expenditure on transport increases as population decreases. However, transport involves other costs than these of financial expenditure, principally those of time and effort. The priority which rural people give to transport is reflected in their concern for such changes as the contraction of the petrol station network, government proposals to increase fuel tax and phase out the Road Fund Licence, and concern about the poor state of secondary roads. Finally, although the level of car ownership in rural areas is significantly higher than in urban areas, there are still a large number of rural households without any means of transport. A recent survey of Oxfordshire Women's Institute members showed that 40 per cent of women in the survey area could not drive, and 50 per cent did not have a car available to them during the day (because the husband takes the car to work). It was indicated by the General Household Survey of 1980 that, nationally, 58 per cent of households had at least one car. However, research in rural areas indicates that approximately 70 per cent of households own a car and that 80 per cent have regular access to a car. But this leaves a significant proportion of households, who have been termed 'the transport poor', who neither have a car or have regular access to a car and have to rely on the public provision of transport services. A survey of one village in south Warwickshire in 1981 revealed that 25 per cent of the households had no car. Of these, 83 per cent were pensioners.

There has been much detailed analysis of the rural transport situation in recent years, and it has demonstrated that there has been a steady and significant decline in the provision of services since the 1960s, despite the fact that direct subsidies became available as a result of the Transport Act (1968). This enabled local authorities, with central government help, to make limited grants available towards socially necessary but loss-making services. In addition, fuel tax refunds were increased and grants towards the price of new buses were introduced. The 1968 Act established the National Bus Company, but rural counties were not given general responsibility to develop and co-ordinate public transport until the Local Government Acts of 1972 and 1973. Since the mid 1970s, government funding has been available to support rural transport, but perhaps more significant has been the relaxation of licensing which started with the 1978 Act and was further extended in the Transport Act (1980) and the Public Passenger Vehicle Act (1981). This significantly eased many of the remaining restrictions on conventional transport and attempted to encourage competition between operators of local services. Following experiments in areas of Hereford, Devon, and Norfolk, the Government is currently proposing the abolition of the Road Service Licence and the encouragement of competition in the provision of services. Between 1972 and 1982, transport subsidies have increased thirteenfold and a pattern of rising subsidies for declining services has become established. The effect of current proposals would be to bring to an end the period in which cross-subsidizing (by which profitable city and inter-urban corridor routes subsidize loss-making rural routes) was possible and the end of the role of the county councils as co-ordinators of rural transport services. Opinions are sharply divided as to whether this 'free for all' will lead to a significant contraction of rural bus services or whether deregulation and competition will be the spur to the provision of a better service.

A village in the North Walsham area of Norfolk, which was the subject of a recent survey, may be regarded as typical of the remoter countryside: 30 per cent of the households have no car. In 1975 the village had 115 bus services per week; in 1981 this had fallen to 72 and in 1983, 42. The service was withdrawn in 1985. A private operator was persuaded by the local Women's Institute to introduce limited twice-weekly services, though these bypassed the centre of the village. Transport illustrates better than most other aspects of village life the ability of country people, in certain circumstances, to explore alternative methods of meeting needs. The relaxation of the licensing regulations has allowed the development of car-sharing arrangements and community bus schemes (such as 'Bee Line' in north Warwickshire and 'The Villager' in the north Cotswolds area) as an important supplement to existing transport provision. In areas where there are no services the community bus links the remoter villages to existing bus and train services. The legislation of 1978 and 1980 made it possible to freely advertise sharing schemes and social car schemes are now operated by the WRVS and the WI in many areas, for shopping trips, journeys to hospitals and doctors' practices, and to collect prescriptions. Community mini-buses need careful planning and much voluntary commitment if they are to avoid being a loss-making proposition. However, they now operate in many areas. At the same time, the 1980 Act made it legal for school buses to take fare-paying adults and, in some areas, postbuses have been developed, as in the Wadebridge area of north Cornwall. However, despite these and many other enterprising initiatives transport remains a considerable problem in many rural areas, particularly for low-income families and the elderly.

In recent years there has been an increasing tendency to see the countryside as a prosperous and relatively affluent area and to associate deprivation with urban and inner-city areas. While the extent of the problem is of much greater proportions in urban areas, nevertheless there has been a tendency either to underestimate rural deprivation or to deny its existence. At one level it is difficult to assess the extent of deprivation in rural areas, because when faced with declining services many country people, particularly the elderly, stoically accept the situation and somehow seem to make alternative arrangements. However, multiple deprivation and social disadvantage is a significant phenomenon in all rural areas and particularly affects the non-mobile, low-income and elderly groups. Emigration is the ultimate protest against disadvantage and deprivation and there is still in many rural areas a significant out-migration of low-income families. Some observers have pointed to the 'culture of poverty', and to the vicious circle of poor housing; poor education; poor health; limited employment opportunities and low incomes. Like most rural problems this can be seen in its most exaggerated form in remote upland areas.

In many rural areas the problem is not the existence of facilities and services but their delivery to those who need them, particularly in remote villages in which almost all elements of the rural infrastructure have been removed. Inadequate services penalize those who do not have a car; village shop prices can be as much as 20 per cent higher than those of the supermarket in the local town. In recent years there has been a growing awareness of the extent of deprivation in rural areas and a more concerted attempt, particularly by voluntary bodies, to draw attention to this situation and devise possible solutions. While many such organizations, particularly the Rural Department of the National Council for Voluntary Organizations, the Rural Community Councils and the Women's Institutes have a long history of campaigning on such issues, in October 1980 Rural Voice was formed as an alliance of the nine principal rural organizations, with the purpose of ensuring that the Government, the media and the general public understood the problems of those who live in the country. Among other things Rural Voice has sought to demonstrate that rural deprivation and poverty can exist side by side with a prosperous agriculture and can be obscured by the arrival of more affluent commuters, the retired and occasional residents. This lobby (not least through its magazine *Rural Viewpoint*) has sought to contend with the urban image of the countryside as a contented, affluent, integrated and neighbourly community, well provided with adequate services and facilities. By contrast, the rural organizations have pointed to a situation in which children are taken by bus many miles to schools in neighbouring towns; youngsters have nothing to do in the village and have little prospect of local employment; newly-weds have no prospect of purchasing a house in the village, as house prices have risen beyond their reach; and elderly people lead increasingly isolated lives in villages which are deprived of all services and facilities.

In all counties (except Norfolk) the Rural Community Councils have played a major role in stimulating voluntary services which supplement, and in places replace, withdrawn statutory or lost local services. At the same time, they have campaigned on such issues as rural health, the lack of low-cost housing, various aspects of rural transport and the closure of schools, the possible closure of rural telephone boxes, post offices and letter boxes, the lack of recreational facilities and other issues relevant to rural areas. Increasingly, villagers have come to realize that central and local authority funding will not be available to replace or extend services and that they must call upon their own resources. Thus, in many villages, community transport schemes have been organized, shops run by volunteers are established in the village hall; mobile facilities are encouraged to visit the village; and room has been set aside in the village hall for a doctor's practice and other medical clinics. The message of all this activity is that much can be done to ameliorate the condition of country villages by the efforts of those who live there.

Finally, those who comment on these aspects of village life frequently point to the lack of co-ordination which exists between the various central and local government departments, whereby decisions regarding transport, schools, the location of public services and other aspects of village life are taken by different bodies frequently concerned about the maintenance of a county (or nationally) wide network. There have been a number of calls for a more integrated approach to the social and economic problems of rural areas, as can be seen in France. From the perspective of an individual village, decisions which can greatly affect the future of life in that community seem unrelated to one another. The parish council can provide the principal means of relating to these decision-making processes; since local government reorganization, their powers have been significantly increased. It is the parish council which has the local knowledge and is able, through district councillors, county councillors and direct communication with decision-making bodies, to exert influence in these matters. Parish councillors, in common with other village residents, know at first hand the problems of deprivation in the modern village and can campaign vigorously for the alleviation of the social and economic problems which affect many rural communities.

The Village as a Community

> 'A little world of our own . . . where we know everyone and are known to everyone and authorised to hope that everyone feels an interest in us.'

This description of her village by Mary Russell Mitford in the 1820s evokes an image to which the term 'community' would be readily ascribed. Contemporary accounts of village life and the changes that are currently taking place in the countryside are dominated by a concern for such issues as transport, schools, employment, housing and the provision of facilities and services. However, these are the quantitative aspects of village life, alongside which needs to be placed an assessment of the qualitative aspects: what a village actually feels like to live in. In this context the word 'community', with its varying connotations, is frequently used; indeed, in modern English, the words 'village' and 'community' have become almost interchangeable. People who wish to describe a sense of community in urban areas often speak of a certain part of a city as being 'like a village'. Community has become one of the 'comfortable words' of modern society and is used in a wide variety of contexts, namely community care, community policing, community development, Rural Community Councils, etc. But, despite its widespread use, the term 'community' has such a variety of meanings and connotations that it eludes precise definition. Social analysts who wish to use it in their work customarily preface their study with a detailed definition of what they mean by the term 'community'. After reviewing ninety-four such definitions, one writer was forced to concede that 'beyond the recognition that people are involved in community, there is little agreement on the use of the term'. A number of writers specifically reject the term because of its vague and imprecise meaning.

The term 'community' came into specific usage when social anthropologists employed it to describe the small-scale, preliterate societies about which they wrote. These communities were customarily described in such terms as ' a body of men inhabiting the same locality and having identity of character; some joint ownership of property; some degree of political organization; a sense of fellowship and a uniform set of religious beliefs'. Traditionally, definitions of community have had two elements: 'confined locality' and 'people having something in common'. A well-known definition is that of MacIver, who described a community as 'an area of living marked by some degree of social coherence'.

However, the term only came into general use when it was recognized that the social conditions of advanced industrial society appeared to lead to the gradual attrition of those social patterns which had characterized traditional village life and to which the word community had been widely ascribed. In contemporary urban society, with high levels of mobility and a culture which was becoming increasingly privatized, observers noted that there was a widespread weakening of the bonds of kinship, a general decline in the social significance of the family, the disappearance of community foci and a general undermining of the traditional basis of social solidarity. Much of the thinking concerning the concept of community can be traced back to the work of Tönnies in the 1880s. He constructed two ideal types of social relationship. The ideal type of the homogeneous, small-scale, cohesive, kinship-based group, to which he gave the name *gemeinschaft* or community, accords in many of its essential features with the traditional pre-industrial English village. The other ideal type, *gesellschaft* or association, is the characteristic form of modern industrial society. It was suggested by such sociologists as Redfield that there was a continuum between these two ideal types, and that societies, as they developed from their traditional to their modern form, increasingly approximated the *gesellschaft* ideal type, in which people are involved in a variety of different roles and activities, among different people, in different locations, in contrast to the confined and integrated social patterns of traditional society. Redfield, whose work is particularly suggestive for the study of English villages, charted the interaction between the 'lesser culture' — the traditional folk culture of a rural community, and the 'greater culture' — the metropolitan urban culture of modern society. Against this background it is possible to see that in the eighteenth and nineteenth centuries the 'lesser culture' was gradually supplanted by the 'greater culture'; it was this process which Hardy and other commentators observed at close quarters. The traditional community life of the village broke down under the impact of such manifestations of the 'greater culture' as the railways, factory-made clothes, imported foodstuffs, newspapers and, eventually, the wireless and television. The effect of these and other changes was to break down the local containment of traditional village culture, first in economic and physical terms; later in social and cultural terms. Community, in the sense of *gemeinschaftlich* society, was the product of these constraints; once they were removed, that almost indefinable sense of community tended to evaporate in a more mobile and privatized society. The Middle Ages (in the sense of traditional understandings of community) ended in many country villages, it has been suggested, with the invention of the bicycle.

Community studies have been undertaken by social anthropologists in this country predominantly in small, declining, isolated, upland villages, where local people have been particularly aware of the erosion of the traditional culture as a result of depopulation. Such accounts have often sought to record the apparently static and unchanging nature of village life before it disappeared, as a result of the impact of urban values and understandings. However, this chapter seeks to demonstrate that what is meant by community life has not disappeared in the contemporary village but has been significantly transformed as a result of changes which have taken place in rural communities in recent years. It may be demonstrated that there has been a significant change in the understanding of the term 'belonging to the village', and that today two predominant understandings of this term coexist in contemporary rural communities and account for an important part of the differentiation between the old villagers and the new.

In the social context that Mary Russell Mitford was describing, community as an expression of the social solidarity of isolated rural settlements was above all else the product of constraints. The physical, social, kinship and economic constraints of traditional, agrarian society produced a form of social life which is readily recognizable. Belonging was thought of principally in terms of *identification.* A villager belonged to the village in the sense of being totally identified in both his family and his work life with a particular settlement, and, as a consequence, many English surnames are in fact place names. For the traditional villager, the village was akin to a total institution (in the sense in which Erving Goffman used the term) in that it was an institution with which the villager was totally identified, and, at least in the eyes of an outsider, one which defined and accounted for the villager. In the days of limited mobility, people belonged to a village in which they lived, worked, brought up their family and died, in a way which is not true of modern mobile society. This sense of belonging had much to do with the knowledge that one's past and one's future were bound up with a particular settlement (a fact which was codified in the Elizabethan Poor Laws) and with a sense of place in both the geographical and the social sense. The nature of agriculture at that time demanded that much manual work should be performed by groups of people (it needed seven people to form a threshing gang); while, in domestic life, a man and a woman would need the help of their neighbours and kinsmen at certain times, and these exchanges reinforced ties of obligation within the village. Traditional farming conferred on villagers a high degree of economic interdependence and social discipline which gave the village an inner coherence and unity. Many folklorists have pointed out that in traditional society money is seen as corroding these ties and that the finder of 'the crock of gold' is likely to meet misfortune, for money freed people from the reciprocal dependencies which were the basis of traditional society.

Poor communications necessarily restricted the range and number of suitable marriage partners and the majority of marriages at this time were local. In the period 1857 to 1866, in the parish of Ringmer in Sussex, it is recorded that in seventy-five marriages half the brides and bridegrooms came from the parish, and of the remainder almost all had been born within twenty miles of it. Such a situation meant that almost everyone in the village was related to a single kinship plan and kinship relations were of considerable importance. Inevitably, the self-contained nature of traditional village life produced a pattern of close-knit, overlapping, social and kinship relations in which one person stood in a variety of relationships to another, as workmate, as drinking partner, fellow committee member, and first cousin. However, the contained, small-scale nature of village life meant that people had to maintain a degree of social formality and distance between one another. There are many accounts of the claustrophobic nature of small-village life, in which every action is watched and discussed and where a person cannot escape from his background or the reputation of his family. The containment of village life led to a degree of intimacy which became, for many, close to insufferable and thus 'he keeps himself to himself' became a village virtue. A village was no place to live a very private life, and it has been suggested that a mild form of paranoia was relatively common. The intimacy of daily life demanded certain symbolic boundaries and the maintenance of a degree of social distance. Customarily, country people did not go into each other's houses, and the house became a refuge from what could otherwise be the overpowering intimacy of a small community. Women referred to each other and were referred to by men in a formal way, in marked contrast to the instant intimacies of modern urban society.

Belonging to such a traditional rural community was principally a matter of *identification*. Perhaps this can be most clearly seen when the constraints which held traditional society have been largely removed. Nothing mystifies new arrivals more than the lack of involvement of many of the old villagers in the life of the village. Among the old village families, there are in any village a significant number who play little part in the organized aspects of village life.

By contrast, the new villagers tend to understand the phrase 'belonging the the village' in terms of *participation*. For them it is important to be involved in and committed to organizations and activities which take place within the village; that is the only way, in their terms, of demonstrating both to the village and to themselves that they belong to this particular settlement. They tend to be critical both of those old villagers who seem, in their eyes, 'not to care about what goes on in the village', and of those new villagers who take no part in village activities. Such criticism, in both instances, is based on the assumption that the only way in which people can demonstrate that they belong to the village is through participation. Nowhere is this dichotomy between *identification* and *participation* more clearly demonstrated than in the life of the church (as will be shown in Chapter 12). It can be seen in almost any village that there is a marked distinction between the attitude of the old village community, who identify with the church and are concerned by any threat to it, but who in the main attend it rarely; and that of the new villagers who see themselves either as belonging to the church if they participate in its life and worship, or as not belonging to the church if they take no part in its activities. It is fundamental to any understanding of the nature of village life today to appreciate that these two concepts of community, seen in terms of *identification* and *participation*, coexist in almost every village; the first is the dominant view of the old villagers, the second is that of the new villagers.

However, it would be wrong to think of the village as a single community. Traditional rural society has been portrayed by social anthropologists as if it were a single entity which, although it may have a relatively simple economy, has an extremely complex society structure. It is easy to underestimate the degree to which traditional rural society was comprised of identifiably separate communities. Recent analysis has sought to show that there was a marked difference between the landowners, the clergy, the professional people and large farmers and those who made up the majority of the villagers — the farm workers and smaller farmers. This latter group Hobsbawm and Rudé called 'the dark village', in contrast to 'the official village'. The history of the countryside in the nineteenth century can be portrayed as a steady widening of the gap between these two groups. Many social historians, including Marx and Engels, have sought to portray nineteenth-century rural history as a tearing apart of the reciprocal ties of obligation which once held together the rural community as a common whole. Recently, Newby has described the agricultural workers as a sub-culture based on a neighbourhood association with workmates which was virtually impenetrable to outsiders and was sustained by isolation, kinship links and the need to co-operate in times of family crisis and common work.

If it is not possible to see the late nineteenth-century village as a single community, the contemporary village can be seen as a social entity comprised of a series of indentifiable, and increasingly separate, interest groups. In short, the modern village is a community of communities comprised of groups of people who have different understandings about the nature of the village and the future of the countryside. Village life today is the product of the interaction between these groups, with their different understandings of the nature and function of the modern village. (The three dominant communities are the subject of the next three chapters.) The changed nature of social encounter has done much to break down the old integrated view of the village as a single community, for the majority of people do not now meet in the course of daily events in the village street, but travel almost everywhere by car. The decline of social encounter has meant that gossip (ranging from a friendly interest in one's neighbours to malicious criticism), which was a powerful integrating factor, has ceased to be of such importance. The oft-heard cry 'nobody tells me anything' bears witness to declining social encounter in many rural communities. At the same time, changes in the village have significantly reduced the importance of those community foci which were once such powerful integrating factors. Before piped water, when everyone had to draw water from the village pump, this became a powerful symbol of village integration. Similarly, the closure of the school means that the mothers who used to gather outside the school gate at 3.30 p.m. no longer meet to exchange news and information. The closure of the shop and other community facilities has a similar effect of reducing the number of community foci which play such an important role in maintaining that sense of the village as a coherent social unit.

Today in many small villages and hamlets the only remaining such focus of village self-awareness, apart from the church, is the village hall. In the medieval period the nave of the church fulfilled many of the functions for which the village hall is now used, and church sales, meetings and business transactions all took place there. The sharper divide between the sacred and the secular, which was one of the consequences of the Reformation, led to these activities being banished from church premises. The modern village hall dates from the mid nineteenth century when many squires and clergy established 'village institutes' or reading rooms, with newspapers, table games and non-alcoholic beverages as an alternative to the lure of the public house. Village halls as they are known today mostly date from the period after the First World War. Both wars did much to encourage the building of village halls, but state financial assistance was made available only after the Second World War (although Carnegie Trust grants were obtainable in the 1930s). The halls range from elaborate brick or stone structures designed and built by the squire with a full range of kitchens, committee rooms and other facilities, to the army huts from both World Wars to be found in many villages. Aid for village halls came at a time when many of the village huts (as they were often called), which dated from the early 1920s, were falling into disrepair. Today many wartime buildings, often wooden structures, are falling into disrepair and are being replaced, with parish, district and county council grants, by more appropriate buildings.

Within the village hall the Women's Institute holds its meetings, the Scouts and Guides parade, the trainer of dogs holds classes, the mothers and toddlers club meets, election candidates appeal for support and voters cast their votes. The parish council meets in the hall, as does the Over Sixties club, the youth club and the flower show and charity committees; members of the amateur dramatics group give their annual performance in the hall, and at Christmas it is decorated for the village children's party. A few villages have more than one available building, (there are some social clubs, WI halls and a number of church and British Legion halls in rural areas), but the vast majority of villages have only one building.

The distinction between those who see the community in terms of identification and those who see it in terms of participation is highlighted by different attitudes towards the village hall. In those villages where the hall has been renovated or replaced, it may be thought of as a community centre rather than a village hall. The concept of a community centre, with its implications of high levels of participation and involvement, is significantly different from that of a village hall, which is often a modest building unused during a part of each week but nevertheless a powerful symbol of the self-identification of the village. By definition a community centre has a membership but a village hall is there for all the village to use. Many villages find it difficult to sustain anything like the programme of events which some enthusiasts would wish for. Inevitably, the television, that potent symbol of privatization in modern society, is blamed for the decline in interest, particularly among the old village community. When homes were less comfortable, the warmth and conviviality of the village hall was something that few could resist; today, when all homes are considerably more comfortable and television entertainment is constantly available, it is often difficult, even in the larger villages, to attract a sufficient audience for some village activities. In an age of privatized lifestyles, the organizers of village activities often complain that 'it is difficult to get people to come to meetings' and that 'people do not go out at night any more'.

Certainly, newcomers have revitalized some aspects of village life, but inevitably their tastes tend to be somewhat different, and few villages now have the dances and whist drives which were once the staple of village hall programmes only a few years ago. Not infrequently the hall is significantly busier during the day with the old people's lunch club, the children's playgroup, the after-school group, the weekly doctor's surgery, the post office and the community shop and, in the car park, the mobile library and the wet-fish van. New villagers have introduced badminton, keep-fit classes and the judo club, and in many villages these have taken the place of the drama groups, uniform organizations and whist drives that were once the main functions in the hall. In the evenings the hall is more frequently used for private functions, eighteenth-birthday parties, wedding anniversary and family celebrations, punctuated by the occasional Young Farmers Club dance. The village hall is also the base for the annual flower show, which is one of the events in which old and new villagers join together in a common cause. Many villages have a horticultural society: some of these societies date from the last century, when much was done to try to improve cottage gardens and the domestic production of food. The cultivation of fruit and vegetables is still fiercely competitive, but in a friendly way. However, flower shows, once a feature of almost every village's annual calendar, are now relatively rare in the smaller settlements.

Many village halls and their management committees find increasing difficulty in maintaining the fabric of the building. Such committees often rely on hire charges and fund-raising events to keep the hall open, but find that they are beset with problems. Among these is that of having to meet new minimum standards for environmental health and fire equipment in order to be granted a public entertainments licence by the District Council under the provisions of the Local Government (Miscellaneous Provision)

Act of 1982. Since the local authority rather than the magistrates has become the licensing authority, much higher standards have been applied and the withholding (or the threat of withholding) licences has been invoked where these standards are not met. The pattern of usage of the building on which these standards are based is not always that found in the majority of small villages, and the cost of upgrading such halls has proved to be heavy. However, the Licensing (Occasional Permission) Act of 1983 now allows such organizations not run for private gain to obtain permission to sell alcohol at their social events. This may prove particularly helpful to villages which do not have a pub, if the village hall committee is prepared to run a bar at local functions.

Any village hall management committee can obtain help and advice from the county Rural Community Council (and from the Village Halls Forum). The Rural Community Council is an independent, voluntary organization which receives substantial funding from the Development Commission towards its activities to stimulate community development in rural areas and to improve the social fabric of the countryside. The first Rural Community Council was started in Oxfordshire in 1921 and was principally concerned with educational and social work in the villages. It realized that the establishment of village clubs and institutes was of particular help in achieving this goal and a revolving fund was started in 1924 to support the building and improvement of village halls. Music and drama festivals (supported by the Carnegie Trust) followed shortly afterwards. By 1926 there were seventeen Rural Community Councils and they now exist in all counties except Norfolk. The Councils form a means of liaison between local voluntary organizations (particularly village halls) and statutory authorities; they advise and assist the village hall committees, and often act as agents for the County Association of Parish Councils, the Playing Fields Association and other voluntary groups such as the local history, music, drama societies and conservation organizations. Most Councils organize and run Village Ventures competitions (a scheme which gives awards for imaginative local projects), the Best Kept Village competition and other such activities and they act as a bridge between the local authority and the local community in encouraging and supporting voluntary initiatives and local activities. Most Rural Community Councils have a Field Officer, who is actively involved in supporting local initiatives such as housing associations, community transport schemes, community shops and other local facilities. The Field Officer is able to act as a focal point for transmitting concern about rural facilities and services to the appropriate authorities. The Best Kept Village competition, for which Rural Community Councils are probably best known, originated in New Zealand and was brought to the United Kingdom by Lord Bledisloe when he retired to Gloucestershire, where the first competition was run by the county branch of the CPRE. In many areas the role of the councils has been to initiate work some of which, as in drama, music, old people's welfare and rural crafts, has now been taken over by the other bodies.

Two of the most regular users of the village hall are the Parish Council and the Women's Institute. The formal aspects of the Parish Council's work as the third tier of local government have been discussed in the previous chapter. But the Parish Council also has an important role in many villages as the co-ordinator of a range of village activities. Not infrequently the Council includes representatives from the various communities, each of which has different concerns about the village, based on different understandings of what the village is as a social unit. While the traditional view of the village as a single integrated community may predominate in the thinking of the Parish Council, detailed items on the agenda reveal that, in effect, different councillors are representatives for different groups within the village. The manner in which these groups interrelate can, and frequently does, result in a degree of conflict over particular issues. On the whole, villagers do not like conflicts to be brought into the open, for this itself is a contradiction of the traditional view of the village. Not infrequently, new villagers inadvertently articulate points of controversy and bring hidden conflicts into the public arena. This allows older village residents to affirm their unity as a group and to blame conflicts upon newcomers, who frequently can be made the scapegoats for internal difficulties and conflicts which long pre-date their arrival.

It is suggested by some that men's clubs have never really succeeded in the village (though there are many British Legion huts and other men's groups, both sporting and non-sporting), because men essentially regard their homes as a refuge from their work, while women, so it is said, are happy to leave the scene of their work for the monthly meeting of the Women's Institute. Certainly, the Women's Institute numbers among its members more rural people than any other such organization, and in many village households the calendar is firmly marked at the date of the Women's Institute monthly meeting. The Institute, which was started among farmers' wives in Ontario in 1897, was established in this country in 1915 when the first Institute was opened at Llanfairpewll in Anglesey. It owed its existence to the efforts of a Canadian widow, Mrs Aldred Watt, who had settled in this country. By Christmas 1915, four Institutes had been formed in Wales and three in England. At this stage great emphasis was placed on the need to conserve and increase food supplies at the time of wartime shortage. Lady Denman, the first Chairman of the movement's National Federation, not only stressed this aspect of its work but also was associated with the recruitment drives for the Women's Land Army and with the need to set up village industries to stem the exodus of young people from the countryside. In the Second World War the number of Institutes grew to 6,000 and once more their services in the production of fruit and vegetables came to the fore (the 'jam and Jerusalem' image dates from this period). The movement also has social and educational aspects and has done much to bring a fuller life to women in the countryside through its programme. Its non-political, non-sectarian approach helped to widen its appeal, for in the countryside at this stage many of the social activities were run by the church, the chapel or the Conservative party. As the Institutes developed many formed dramatic groups, choirs and folk-dance teams and became engaged in such activities as fund-raising for local charities and organizing demonstrations on domestic subjects. More recently, with a membership of 355,000, in a very large number of the villages and hamlets of under 4,000 people, the WIs have become increasingly concerned with campaigning on those issues which directly affect the lives of country women. In this context the Women's Institutes were a founder member and have played a significant role in the development of Rural Voice.

As the nature of community has changed in country villages, so has understanding about leadership which plays such a significant role in the shaping of community life. Certainly, in the period before the First World War, most villages had a formal leadership structure in which the squire, the clergyman, the schoolmaster, and their wives, all played different but acknowledged roles. The social structure of the village had a commonly understood hierarchical aspect which permeated all activities. For instance, Ambrose noted that the batting order of a village cricket team in the inter-war years almost exactly paralleled the rateable value of each team member's house. Some commentators have noted the way in which, from the mid nineteenth century onwards, the village attempted to develop institutions which were insulated from the formal authority structure. The chapel and the pub (so different in many ways) were both outside the formal authority structure of the village and represented alternative communities within the village. However, even in this period, as Newby has noted, while many who held subordinate positions in the village hierarchy adopted attitudes of deference on public occasions, this did not prevent them from having their own views about the worth of the traditional leaders of the local community. Within the informal village community a 'head man' often emerged; he occupied a position of considerable authority and his status was often recognized by the formal leadership structure. He is seen as an unofficial mayor of the village. However, the strength of the traditional structure, and the power that it exercised in a small community, was so great that the characteristics of respect for authority became part of the village tradition. As a consequence village people became adept at avoiding possible confrontations with their leaders and were reluctant to accept positions in the village which were conspicuous or which might place them in a position of authority over their neighbours. It was noted during the First World War that regiments recruiting largely in rural areas often found it difficult to persuade people to become NCOs because there was a reluctance among country people to accept such a role.

The break-up of the old authority pattern in the village has been slow, and, certainly in the formal aspects of village life, the authority of the squire still remains of considerable significance, even though his (or in some instances, her), actual power is much diminished in contrast to the days when he was the major employer and the patron of all village activities. It is sometimes said that the disbandment of the Home Guard at the end of the Second World War represented the last phase of the formal authoritative structure in the village. But perhaps what is surprising about contemporary villages is the degree to which attitudes persist. Certainly, in the remoter countryside, the leadership of the squire and the clergyman is still in many places welcomed and valued, though today such a role has to be earned by the worth of the person rather than assumed as a function of office.

The breakdown of the old isolation of the village and the arrival of the new villagers quickly dissolved some aspects of the old authority structure, as members of the new village community were elected to the parish council and became prominent in other aspects of village life. Slowly the pattern of leadership and authority in the village became more complex, as different people assumed leadership roles in different areas of village life. Today the diversity of leadership in the village represents the diversity of the social profile of a modern rural settlement. In any village there is a tendency for various organizations to become the prerogative of a particular group, and an ability to identify territories and boundaries is an important part of understanding the dynamics of the contemporary village. Thus it can be seen that the village as a social unit is a complex phenomenon. There is a significant divide between the concept of community, commonly found among the old villagers, which is based on the traditional understanding of identification and that commonly found among the new villagers, which is based on participation. The village, for so long a symbol of unity and social integration, has become a complex, polycentric and fragmented social unit, which can best be described as a community of communities. The three dominant communities — the old villagers, the new villagers, and the farmers — are the subject of the next three chapters.

✤ 7 ✤

The Farmers

The view from any hill in England is one of a patchwork of fields, woods, hedges and farm buildings, for England, unlike some other countries, has a predominantly farmed landscape. Although the undulating ridge and furrow of medieval cultivations still can be seen in some areas, the contemporary English landscape was shaped by the parliamentary enclosures of the eighteenth and nineteenth centuries. The abandonment of the open-field system and the consolidation of farm holdings in that period created the modern pattern of rectangular hedged fields and scattered farmsteads. There are very few areas of England which have never been farmed and farming has advanced and retreated in marginal areas over the centuries; abandoned farm buildings can be found in even the most remote places. Such buildings serve to remind us that farming is in the last analysis an entrepreneurial activity. In a sense there is nothing new in farming, just new ways of balancing the three basic factors of land, capital and labour so that the cost of production is less than the market price.

The total area of agricultural holdings in England and Wales is 18.7m hectares* of which approximately 7m hectares is arable land, 5.1m hectares is pasture and grassland, 5m hectares is sole-right rough grazing (mostly in upland areas above 1,000ft); and 1.6m hectares is common rough grazing or woodland. Despite the fact that the area of land available for farming has been constantly contracting (it is said that an area equivalent to the Isle of Wight is lost to agriculture every year), in broad terms in the United Kingdom 75 per cent of the land area is farmed, with a further 5 per cent being used for forestry. Thus, there is a real sense in which farming is the defining characteristic of the landscape in a country which has been particularly favoured in terms of climate and soil type, and whose early prosperity was founded on farming.

* MAFF *Agricultural Statistics*, June 1985.

The village, as has been shown in Chapter 3, evolved as the home of the farming community and no account of the contemporary village can be attempted without an understanding of its past significance and its present impact.

In the popular imagination farmers form a large proportion of the village population; however, in reality, villages have always been mixed communities and the number of farmers in the contemporary village is surprisingly small. While in the mid nineteenth century, farming was still the predominant economic activity in the countryside, by the early decades of this century the proportion involved in farming in the national workforce had dropped below 10 per cent. This decline was essentially a decline in the farm workforce, for the number of farmers recorded in the 1851 census is roughly similar to that recorded in 1951. However, since then there has been a steady decline which has accelerated in recent years. In the period 1971—8 there was a 12 per cent decline in the number of farmers. In 1973 there were 454,000 farm holdings; in 1981 the number of farm holdings had contracted to 242,300. The National Farmers Union estimates that their membership contracted by 20 per cent in the ten years prior to 1975. Currently there are 159,300 farmers and 160,700 full-time farm staff.* The total farm labour force represents 2.5 per cent of the national workforce, but it is clear that the farm population is still contracting and some estimates indicate that there is an annual loss of approximately 2,000 farm holdings and 2 per cent of the farm population. Like other industries, agriculture is increasingly dominated by a small number of relatively large units and it is estimated that the 5,000 largest farms (only 2 per cent of the number of holdings) produce approximately 30 per cent of the national agricultural output and 50 per cent of the cereals output. 30,000 of the largest farms together account for 60 per cent of the national agricultural output and 20 per cent of farmers produce 90 per cent of the national agricultural output. Thus, farming in recent years has seen a steady expansion of the average size of holding and a corresponding contraction in total numbers. Today half the agricultural land in East Anglia is farmed in holdings of 500 acres or more.

* MAFF *Agricultural Statistics,* June 1985.

In an individual village it is unusual to find more than 20 per cent of the population connected with farming, and in many villages the figure is likely to be below 10 per cent. In the majority of villages today there are only three or four farmers who together farm the whole area of the parish. Indeed, there are now many parishes in which there are no resident farmers and it has been calculated that one-fifth of the land in East Anglia is farmed by 'absentee' farmers. It is possible to suggest that many parishes in lowland England have lost approximately one farm family per decade during this century, though in reality the rate of contraction has been rather less than such a figure would indicate.

In the village itself the impact of changes to the structure of farming in recent years can be clearly seen. Thirty years ago a farmer was able to make a reasonable living for himself and his family (and hunt two days a week in winter) on a farm of eighty acres. At that time, a farm of 250 acres would have employed between five and ten men and would have been considered a sizeable holding. In recent decades the number of farms in the 250—300-acre group has remained relatively static, but there has been a sharp fall in the number of farms under 150 acres, just as there has been a steady (though often exaggerated) increase in the number of large farms. Today when the average farm size has doubled since 1967 (and the average British farm is four times larger than the average EEC farm) the number of farms in any single parish is inevitably less.

While some countries, notably France, have developed rural policies specifically designed to support and maintain the number of small farmers, this has not happened in Britain. Many small farmers have been victims of the economics of scale, at a time when anything less than fairly large-scale operations have become uneconomic. With the high cost of machinery this is self-evident in the arable sector, but it is also true for livestock farming. When a single man can manage 120 cows (the average herd size in France is thirteen) or look after 150 or more sows, or shepherd 1,000 ewes, or tend 50,000 hens, small-scale operators have been at a severe disadvantage. Many elderly farmers on small acreages have found it difficult to keep up with modern practices and a significant number of small dairy farmers gave up when the Milk Marketing Board stopped collecting churns in 1979 and insisted on bulk tanker collections. Others are currently leaving, following the imposition of milk quotas in April 1984. The contemporary practice of lotting, whereby a farm when it is sold is divided into a number of parts, frequently purchased by neighbouring farmers, is symbolic of the way in which the number of farm units has contracted.

This chapter is principally about farmers rather than farming, but before discussing the contemporary situation of farmers in the village, it is necessary to say something about the development of farming in the decades of this century. Britain's naval power prevented food from being a significant strategic consideration in the early period of the First World War and it was not until 1916, following a particularly poor harvest, that the Food Production Campaign was launched. Throughout that war only a quarter of the food consumed in Britain and by its armies overseas was produced in this country. In the years after the war a period of depression again settled on the agricultural industry, following the repeal of the Corn Production Acts in 1921 (often called 'the great betrayal'). In 1923 the price of wheat, which had at one stage stood at 80s 10d, fell to 42s 2d. Throughout the 1920s and 1930s farming was in the grip of a deep depression which lasted right up until the eve of the Second World War. No account of contemporary farming is complete without an assessment of the lasting effect which those years have had on the attitudes and the folk memory of the farming community. By the 1930s, sour, soggy and degenerating land, full of speargrass, bracken and brambles, together with dilapidated and out-of-date buildings, were common in many areas. On the lighter, less fertile soil, particularly in areas such as north Norfolk, farmhouse windows gazed emptily over derelict fields which were rapidly disappearing under a cover of gorse, thistles, docks and ragwort. In many areas ditches and drains slowly filled, hedges began to thicken into copses and copses become woods. Landowners were forced to set aside the rent in order to ensure that tenants remained on the farms. In south Warwickshire the farming community can remember that a number of the most productive farms today were untenanted and covered with dense thorn bushes during the worst of the farming depression. Game, rabbits and wild flowers all flourished in this neglected landscape, giving a pleasant aspect to what was in reality a deep agricultural depression and the ruin of many farmers. At its worst almost any land could be purchased for £10 an acre, and less good land such as the flinty chalkland of the Sussex Downs or Salisbury Plains could be purchased for £2 an acre unfenced, or £5 fenced.

However, even at this time there were some farmers who were able to make a living, particularly those who followed A. J. Hosier and his 'open-air dairying' by use of a bail. In 1922 he initiated a low-cost dairying system on the Wiltshire Downs which allowed land previously uncultivated to return a profit. Death duties and bankruptcy had the effect of bringing new blood into the lowland farming community, particularly from the north west and from Scotland, from where a significant migration of farmers moved into Essex and the eastern counties. In 1932 it was estimated that a fifth of the Essex farmers and a fifth of the graziers in the Rugby district had come from these areas.

The early 1930s saw even lower prices, and in 1931, following the American stock market collapse, the world price of wheat stood at half the 1929 level. The Milk Marketing Board was established in 1933 to act as the sole buyer and seller of milk and to prevent the price of milk sold for butter and cheese from undercutting the price of milk sold liquid. Also, a method of equalization between producers was introduced, and this, along with the certainty of a market and a regular monthly cheque, encouraged a considerable increase in dairying, particularly at a time when the electric fence allowed more systematic grazing methods. Between 1933 and 1938 the volume of milk sold increased by 30 per cent, as the MMB promoted milk as a health food.

The onset of the Second World War saw the end of the long period of social and economic neglect in the countryside, during which farm buildings had been left virtually untouched since the 'high farming' period of the 1860s and 1870s. It is possible to argue that the German U-boat campaign during the Second World War was the most significant event in the twentieth-century history of British farming. For a period, the increase in domestic food production was literally a matter of national life or death and the Government established County War Agricultural Executive Committees with the widest powers to invigorate agriculture and, in particular, to plough up land which was not being used to the limits of its potential. The Ministry of Agriculture undertook a survey of farmland; planned and supervised local programmes of production; provided grants, advice and services; collected and distributed machinery, fertilizer and feedstuff. From being the most neglected and economically marginal aspect of the country's economy, agriculture was suddenly propelled to the front as vital in the fight for national survival. In 1939 Britain produced 30 per cent of its own food, but by 1945 the figure had risen to 80 per cent. During this period the percentage of farmland under cultivation almost doubled and again approached the levels of the 1860s and 1870s.

If, during the war years, schemes were hastily implemented to increase food production, such as the Dolfor scheme of 1941, which in a few weeks converted 750 acres of rough upland grazing in Montgomeryshire into a vast potato field, after the war years there was a period of more considered rationalization and consolidation. The Second World War contributed to the radical restructuring of British farming and the establishment of a permanent partnership between the State and the farming community, formalized in the Agricultural Act of 1947. As wheat imports started in the immediate post-war period so the farmers were determined that the depression which had followed the First World War should not occur again. In 1946 the National Agricultural Advisory Service (the predecessor of the Agricultural Development and Advisory Service) was set up and the Act of the following year established, among other things, a system of securing guaranteed prices (subject to the annual February price review) and a system of subsidies and grants for capital projects. At the same time it increased the security of tenant farmers. But above all it was the guaranteed prices which gave the individual farmer the confidence and assurance to develop his farm and to expand his farm business in the decades that followed. The Agricultural Act of 1947 created the economic conditions in which agriculture could expand in the knowledge that it had a guaranteed price for its products; between 1947 and 1951 net agricultural output grew by 20 per cent. Today, the great changes which are occurring in agriculture have principally arisen as a result of the realization that there are limits to both the amount of food that can be economically produced and to governments' willingness to subsidize this production.

It was in this period of post-war confidence that farming finally emerged from its craft period as a thoroughly modern technological industry. At the beginning of the Second World War there were still three-quarters of a million working horses on farms and they constituted a third of the mobile power. When Askham Bryan Agricultural College (in South Yorkshire) was built in 1952 there was extensive accommodation for working horses. Although milking machines had been introduced in the early 1900s, in 1939 only 15 per cent of the national herd was machine milked. The first effective tractor, the Ival, was marketed in 1902, and within a quarter of a century the descendants of this early tractor were rendering steampower obsolete for field work. The term 'mechanical agriculture' was first used in 1931, when the first farms were being run entirely without horses. Combine harvesters appeared in this country in 1928 and the introduction of the three-point linkage system, in the early 1930s, revolutionized the design of tractors. The Ferguson system allowed the tractor and implement to operate as a single unit and the depth of working could now be controlled hydraulically. The Dolfor project, mentioned above, was another significant landmark in the history of mechanization, for this was the first concentrated power farming project with twenty-two tractors, including lease-lend crawlers, whose drivers were the first men ever to plough an acre of British soil in an hour. In 1946 the first little grey 'Fergie' was produced from the Banner Lane Standard Motor Company's works in Coventry: a tractor which came to be regarded with particular affection by the farming community. In 1939 the combine harvester was still a rarity in the English countryside, but fifteen years later half the arable crops were harvested by this method.

In the pre-First World War period all grass conserved for winter feed was made into hay, but by the mid-1950s the making of silage in towers, clamps and pits was becoming an established practice on a minority of farms. The 1950s and the 1960s saw farming benefit from the relatively cheap imports of machinery and fertilizers and particularly feeding stuff, and at the same time there was heavy investment in improvements to farm buildings encouraged by government grants from 1957 onwards. While, in the early period, the buildings were often adapted from previous use and made of local materials, in this period new farm buildings were constructed in steel, corrugated iron and asbestos to specific design requirements.

Between 1948 and 1978 the average yield of wheat in England and Wales approximately doubled and this was achieved by improved varieties (noticeably short-straw varieties); the development of precision drilling and direct drilling; and the development of new pesticides, better drainage and, in some places, irrigation. At the same time, new crops such as forage maize and oil-seed rape began to make their appearance and the growing of sugar beet (initially introduced in the 1920s as a labour-intensive crop at a time of unemployment) was revolutionized by the development of monogerm seeds and precision drilling. Comparable increases in productivity were achieved in the livestock section (despite the setback of the 1958 foot-and-mouth epidemic), as a result of the introduction of new breeds, hybridization, crossbreeding and new development in the nutritional and genetical aspects of veterinary sciences. The first Charolais cattle were introduced in 1962, and they, with other Continental breeds, now account for 35 per cent of the beef breed artificial insemination carried out by the Milk Marketing Board. The post-war period was one of unparalleled growth in British agriculture. When the price of land fell for the first time since the war, in 1956, it was said of the previous ten years that a man who had lost money farming would lose money anywhere.

These and other developments transformed farming in the post-war period, and their impact can be seen in every village. Farming at this time joined the ranks of the capital-intensive industries as farmers sought to expand their business and to make the best use of new technical and scientific developments. In 1939 a farmer took a farm valued at £250 with sixteen men working the farm with horses; in 1969 the farm was handed over to his son with equipment valued at £50,000 and only three men. In south Warwickshire in the early 1960s there were 220 dairy herds, the majority with less than fifty cows; today there are only fifty herds (though these would certainly be producing more milk). But perhaps nothing exemplifies the changes which have overtaken farming in recent years more accurately than the change in the farm office. Thirty years ago, in many cases, a farmer would do the majority of his paperwork on a Sunday afternoon; indeed, it was only the income tax regulations of the Second World War which persuaded some farmers finally to keep formal accounts. By contrast, today, many farm offices possess a computer on which operational and financial information concerning the farm is stored, and which will provide an analysis of the breeding, past health records and present performance of an individual animal. While some farms have always been large businesses by any standards, in a relatively short period of time the average family farm has become a sophisticated operation requiring skills which previous generations of farmers neither possessed nor needed.

Farming is customarily spoken of as if it were a single industry, but, in fact, it is made up of a number of distinct elements which, although they are interrelated and to some degree interdependent, are in many ways separate and distinct economic activities. There is little in common between an upland hill farm deriving the majority of its income from sheep, where a key statistic is whether one breeding ewe per acre can be achieved, and a smallholding concentrating on mushroom-growing in a disused railway tunnel, or a 'concrete farm' such as a modern intensive pig unit. Historically, farming has been seen as 'two nations' of 'horn' and 'corn'. In the past the differences have caused no more than friendly rivalry and mild envy, but in recent years feelings of deeper antagonism and resentment between these two elements of the agricultural industry have been discernible. In a sense the division runs down the centre of Britain, separating the arable east from the stock-rearing west. However, all these enterprises are concerned with the process of breeding animals and growing plants for food, but not all have the same relationship with the land. A modern livestock unit will not be immediately recognizable for what it is and someone passing in a car may mistake it for a small industrial complex rather than a farm. In order to develop a typology of farming, it is necessary to consider a number of variables, including the nature of the farm (here the soil type will be of particular importance), the type of farm business and the size of the unit. While these are different criteria for developing a farming typology, they are closely interrelated.

If the continuum of English farms stretches from extensive upland livestock units to intensive horticultural units, the medium-sized, mixed family farm which combines arable cropping with

123

some livestock enterprises may be taken as the mid point. Mixed farming is not simply a matter of maintaining a diversity of enterprises so that poor returns in one sector can be balanced by better returns in another, it is principally a matter of developing interrelated enterprises so that the products, or byproducts, from one section can be used to improve the performance of other sections of the farm. Thus, the barley and straw from the arable side of the farm are used for feed for the livestock enterprises, while manure and slurry from the livestock are used to increase the arable yields. In recent years the average mixed farm has become noticeably less mixed. While a farm in the early decades of this century may have had beef cattle, a dairy herd, some sheep and a few pigs and poultry, as well as a range of arable crops, it is much more likely today that a mixed farm will specialize in only three or four enterprises. In recent years beef production has been intensified and has become much more scientific (a high proportion of cattle now have hormone implants in their ears). All cattle tend to be 'finished' at a younger age, and stocking rates have been increased particularly as a result of the greater use of nitrogen and more intensive systems of grassland management, as well as the development of cereal-fed beef systems. Sheep have always been valued on a mixed farm, partly for added fertility and partly to tidy up the autumn grass after the cattle have been brought in. Recently their numbers have increased significantly as a result of better marketing opportunities, particularly in Europe.

The second type of farm is the specialist arable farm on which there are no livestock, or else livestock play a relatively small role. Such farms have become common in the eastern counties, stimulated by favourable grain prices under the Common Agricultural Policy. In a relatively short period of time, Britain has become a country which exports a significant part of its cereal harvest: this has risen from 12 million tonnes in the early 1960s to 26 million tonnes in 1984. Agricultural technology has built in much greater reliability to cereal farming, so that the variation in yield between a good and a poor year is now only in the region of 10−15 per cent. The farming strategy of a mixed farm is often designed so that an even flow of work can be maintained throughout the year. On specialist arable farms this is not the case; the year is characterized by periods of great activity, principally between the onset of harvest and the end of the autumn cultivations and planting. This whole period is one of intense activity and a great deal of work has to be compressed into a relatively short period of time, as the speed with which the next crop can be sown is a critical factor. It is estimated that every week's delay in the autumn can cost one cwt of wheat per acre. By contrast, such farms have little work going on in the winter months and this unevenness in the monthly work has done much to stimulate the development of contractors in the grain-growing areas. However, farms which do not rely upon contractors are characterized by heavy investment in machinery (farmers like to have enough combine capacity for a quick harvest in a wet year). One large 3,000-acre arable farm with fifteen tractors and five combine harvesters (capable of harvesting 200 acres per day) has over £1 million tied up in capital equipment. A large farm with a major pea contract recently purchased over £250,000 worth of harvesting machinery. The price of machinery has also stimulated the development of contracting; today a combine harvester can cost more than the farm purchased twenty years ago.

Specialist livestock farms include all upland farms which depend on sheep and cattle; dairy farms, particularly in the grass-growing counties; and specialist poultry and pig units. In recent years dairying has been characterized by an increase in herd size; the introduction of self-feed silage and cubicles; sophisticated modern parlours which have taken the place of the old cowshed; rising yields; bulk tanks and the problems associated with slurry; and the popularity of Friesians and, latterly, Holsteins. However, within the European context, milk and dairy products have been in substantial surplus for a number of years, and late on the night of 30 March 1984 a decision was taken to impose quotas on milk production in all European countries. This single decision effectively brought to an end the period of open-ended guarantees which had existed for farmers since the end of the Second World War when governments were prepared to underwrite all agricultural production and to fund surpluses as a strategic reserve. The milk quota was pegged at the 1981 production level plus 1 per cent (which meant a fall of 9 per cent) and in this country it has been allocated to individual farms. The details of the debate which surrounds quotas lie outside the scope of this chapter, but the impact of milk quotas on the farming community has been considerable, partly because it has brought home to a generation of farmers who have come to believe that greater production is always a desirable goal that there are limits to production both in economic and political terms. Many believe that a system of quotas eventually might be extended to other commodities.

Specialist sheep farms are largely restricted to the upland areas, though the number of sheep in lowland areas has increased considerably in the last decade, so much so that some of the historic annual sheep fairs, such as that at Marlborough, have been revived. Grassland management in both upland and lowland areas has become much more scientific, as have the methods of forage conservation. The percentage of grass conserved as silage has increased from 19 per cent in the late 1960s to 35 per cent today. In recent years pig and poultry production has become increasingly intensified with more stock being kept in larger units, with increasingly sophisticated machinery and less labour and greatly increased productivity (a sow can produce twenty-five piglets per annum, a chicken 280 eggs). New types of buildings, including environmentally controlled houses, have allowed production to become almost entirely divorced from the land itself. It is common to say that pigs are either 'gold or brass' and that there is a four-year pig cycle which sees prices climb to a high level and drop back again as pig numbers and production rises and again exceeds consumption. The broiler industry may be regarded as the zenith of intensification, with chickens now being ready for the supermarket in eight weeks from hatching. Such methods demand high levels of stockmanship and the managers of these units are some of the most highly skilled members of the farm staff. In both these areas new 'welfare-sympathetic' systems have recently been introduced.

Finally there are a number of small, specialist farm holdings, principally concerned with the production of horticultural crops for the urban market. Alongside these are a number of farms specializing in fruit and soft fruits, and many of these have now developed 'pick your own' enterprises. A few of these farms are managed on an organic system and the products can command an even higher price in specialist outlets. Other specialist farms include fish farms and those which grow hops, bulbs and flowers, not to mention one farmer in Norfolk who specializes in lavender and another in Yorkshire who specializes in teasels for the cloth industry.

Tourism and leisure are not usually thought of as an agricultural crop, but they are of growing significance to the farming community in certain areas, as farmers attempt to diversify the enterprises on their farms when some more traditional aspects of farming become less profitable. The idea of having caravans in the meadow may offend the sensibilities of some farmers, but farmers are businessmen before anything else and tourism is only one of a number of new enterprises which are currently being considered. An increasing number of farms derive some part of their income from non-agricultural sources, principally by offering bed and breakfast accommodation. Many of the farmers (or their wives) are members of local groups which are co-ordinated by the Farm Holiday Bureau at the National Agricultural Centre. In Devon and Cornwall, 25 per cent of all farms derive a significant part of their income from this sector.

Alongside the classification of farms according to their enterprise mix must be placed a classification according to farm business. The farm business reflects the preferences, skills and choices of the farmer and it is often said that there are not a number of different types of farm but rather a number of different types of farmer. There is an almost infinite variety in the way in which farms are operated. Some are sophisticated and complex enterprises using all the modern aids to business and financial management (which may include selling part of the harvest on the futures market), while others are farmed in a less intensive and less demanding manner and in some cases in a style not unlike that of the 'dog and stick' farming of the 1930s. Like other self-employed businessmen, farmers have to weigh carefully the advantages and disadvantages of developing their business in particular directions and these have to be considered against family concerns, particularly the need for recreation and leisure. By tradition, farmers find this equation hard to balance and some of the more old-fashioned farmers pride themselves on never having taken a holiday or a day away from the farm. At the same time, farmers have different income requirements and the financial arrangements of neighbouring farms may differ enormously. Some farms, having been bought on large mortgages, with heavy investment in machinery and buildings, need to generate a large income to service bank and other loans. This situation will be reflected in the decisions the farmer takes about his enterprise mix and the way he farms the land. By contrast, the farmer with a farm which has been in the family for generations will be freer to choose from a wider variety of options and to plan not for short-term cash needs but for long-term growth (such as forestry). It used to be said that young men milk cows, middle-aged men keep beef cattle and old men keep sheep. If this was ever true, it is certainly not an accurate picture of modern farming, but it does testify to the fact that farmers make choices about their farm business on a variety of criteria which include their own preferences, lifestyle requirements and overall financial situation, and whether they have a son who will continue to farm the land.

Standard typologies of English farming customarily take the size of the farm as the principal indicator. Clearly, this is an accessible distinction, but it has to be seen within the context of other criteria noted above. On the basis of size, farms can be divided as follows:

Above 500 acres	Large or estate farms
350–500 acres	Medium–large farms
250–350 acres	Medium-sized farms
Below 250 acres	Small or very small farms

In the 1930s and 1940s the countryside was still largely farmed in units which did not exceed 300 acres. Although large landed estates comprised many thousands of acres, the land was customarily let as farms of a medium size, and, if the estate owner himself farmed, the home farm was not conspicuously larger than the tenanted units. Since the Second World War there has been a tendency both for the estate owners to take more land in hand and to farm an extensive acreage themselves. This gradual process of consolidation has accelerated considerably in recent years, following the introduction in 1975 of capital transfer tax in the place of estate duty (lower rates applied to farmed land) and the legislation of 1976, which gave certain family members rights of succession to farm tenancies for three generations. This legislation was modified in 1984. Also in recent years, many farmers have acquired more land, not least because the incentive to buy more land is very powerful when the cost is tax deductable and adjacent land rarely comes on the market. It is often said that this is the principal reason why the price of land has increased sevenfold since 1970.

However, the largest land holdings are not in the hands of private landowners but institutions such as the Crown, local authorities and government agencies, nationalized industries, conservation bodies, the Church Commissioners, the Forestry Commission, universities and colleges, and a variety of other organizations. There is a sense in which institutional farming has a very long history dating back to the extensive monastic farms of the early Middle Ages. In the 1970s and early 1980s the relatively poor performance of other sectors, coupled with the sharp rise in land prices, encouraged city financiers to expand their holdings of agricultural land. One insurance company has owned farms since 1887, but in recent years the acquisition of agricultural land has become increasingly attractive to the managers of investment and pension funds. The early 1970s saw a considerable increase in institutional land holdings, and in 1973, 75 per cent of all agricultural land sold was purchased by non-agricultural purchasers. Today it is estimated that over 750,000 acres of land are owned by city institutions; and a proportion of this land has been acquired by the sale and leaseback arrangements which permit the farmer to continue farming as a tenant. In some cases, farming companies undertake the actual work of farming on behalf of city institutions. While, nationally, institutional land ownership may account for only approximately 2.6 per cent of the total land areas, because city institutions prefer the best high yielding land, particularly in the eastern counties, this form of land ownership and farming has had a particular impact in certain areas. However, in recent months the imposition of milk quotas and the declared determination of the EEC to reduce surpluses by price restraint has led to a significant contraction by the institutional landowners of their agricultural land assets at a time of declining land values.

To the large city landowners may be added the company farms and large family farms, a number of which exceed 3,000 acres. However, discussions of farm size often appear to exaggerate the number of very large holdings most of which are in upland areas.

Of the 156,036 holdings in England in 1983, only 4,356 or 2.8 per cent are over 750 acres and of these only 639 are over 1,750 acres. In the five years 1979—83, there was an increase of only 40 farms in the acreage bracket 751—1,250 acres; and an increase of 68 in the bracket 1,251—1,750 acres. Though their numbers are small, such farms are very large businesses by any standards, with an annual turnover of several million pounds. One such company farm of 3,000 acres in southern England comprises 1,000 acres of cereals, a dairy herd of 260, and 3,500 sows producing 84,000 cutters and baconers annually. A number of farming companies are now quoted on the Stock Exchange.

The medium—large and medium-sized farms comprise the broad band of English family farming whose interests have been traditionally represented by the National Farmers Union. In the first decade of this century 90 per cent of farmland was tenanted, but by 1910 a flood of land sales had already started which continued up to the outbreak of the First World War. After the war, the pace of land sales continued to increase, and in 1921 the *Estates Gazette* concluded that a quarter of England had changed hands in the previous four years. Not since the dissolution of the monasteries had there been such a dramatic change in the pattern of land ownership. By 1946 the percentage of tenanted land had been reduced by 67 per cent, and this process was accelerated in recent years to the point where today only 27 per cent of farmland is currently tenanted. There is much concern in the farming community about the decline in the number of farm tenancies (currently, approximately 3,000 per year) and that recent changes in tax law have significantly altered the ancient landlord/tenant system. At the same time rents have significantly increased in recent years: by 76 per cent between 1979 and 1983.

The medium—large and medium-sized farms cover the whole range of agricultural production, but increasingly these farms have tended to become more specialized and to concentrate on a narrower range of enterprises. Perhaps the most significant factor in recent years has been the contraction in their labour force. Twenty years ago such farms were significant employers of labour, but today, many farms in this category, with two or three principal enterprises, are entirely run by the farm family. Indeed, the disinclination of many farmers to employ labour may be one of the principal determining factors in a farming policy. Inevitably, such a situation can place great pressure on a farmer and his family, for a medium-sized Midlands farm of 250 acres with 130 acres of cereals, a flock of 150 ewes and covered yards fattening 100 cattle per year, represents a considerable farm business.

Although farms of under 150 acres are classified as small or very small farms, here the other criteria mentioned above are particularly important. A five-acre horticultural enterprise might be regarded as very small in terms of acreage, but such an enterprise which produces 24,000 boxes of bedding plants annually, and at the peak of the season employs twenty people, with 1,000 paying customers visiting the garden centre on a good weekend, must be regarded as a substantial business. Small farms vary widely from the specialist livestock and horticultural unit to small-scale mixed farming enterprises and marginal farms in less favoured areas. Traditionally, such farms have been divided between elderly farmers farming small acreages and young men just al to get a foothold in the industry. The Smallholding Act was passed in 1892 to provide holdings for agricultural workers who had lost jobs in the farming depression or as a consequence of the widespread conversion from arable to grassland at that time. The provision of smallholdings was for a long period a part of Liberal party policy, and 'three acres and a cow' was a slogan coined by Jesse Collins, a Birmingham MP. When the Liberals came to power the Smallholdings and Allotments Act was passed in 1908, which charged county councils with the task of providing small farms for letting. In the early 1930s the Land Settlement Association was formed to provide small agricultural holdings for unemployed people from the depressed areas, particularly those of north and south Wales.

Behind all these schemes was the belief that the smallholding would be a stepping stone to a larger unit, but in fact this happened in only a very few instances. The existence or absence of the farming ladder is frequently debated in the agricultural press. Certainly, some extremely hard-working and enterprising people have been able to move from small acreages to a medium-sized farm, but their number is very small. In the early 1970s it was recorded that of the 15,000 smallholders who had had tenancies, only fifty-five had progressed to larger farms since the inception of the scheme. Traditionally, small farmers regard themselves as more independent than their larger neighbours, particularly with respect to the bank manager. But independence has to be traded off against income and many such units, particularly on poorer land, do not provide an income equivalent to an industrial or factory job. At the same time small farmers have become increasingly convinced that the financial context of farming in this country discriminates against them. In 1984 the Small Farmers Association sought to give voice to these concerns, particularly in the aftermath of the imposition of quotas on milk production.

In the nineteenth century many village residents such as the clergyman, publican, and some of the village craftsmen, were all part-time farmers. However, in the twentieth century, farming became predominantly a specialist occupational role in which all the members of the family were involved in full-time work on the farm. Recent statistical work has shown the degree to which this pattern has now broken down and the large number of farmers for whom farming is a part-time, spare-time or hobby activity. The 1980 statistics indicated that 46 per cent of farms provided work for less than 250 standard man days and could be regarded as part-time, and that 24 per cent of the farmers could be regarded as part-time. However, many such farmers would not regard themselves as part-time but would see themselves as supplementing a modest farm income by contracting, driving the school bus or doing some other paid job. Traditionally those involved in part-time farming have either been farmers on small farms who need an additional source of income, or those who have come into farming from another job and still need income from another source while they establish themselves as farmers. However, the overall impression is that part-time farming is much more significant within the farming community than is often realized.

Obviously it is impossible to generalize about the life of a farmer and his family because of the variety of English farms, yet this chapter aims to give some sense of what it means to be a farmer in the contemporary village. Clearly, the lives of farmers who operate an intensive poultry unit, or a 500-acre arable farm, or an upland sheep farm, are almost completely different. However, most farmers would agree that a mixed family farm represents the typical farming experience and in a sense is the parent root of

English farming from which all other forms of farming are a departure and a specialization. In describing the life of such a farmer and his family it must be remembered that this is not the common experience of all farmers, but that which will be readily acknowledged as within the mainstream of farming experience. A farmer on a medium-sized farm is likely to have inherited his farm from his father and he may well be the third or fourth generation of farmers to live in the house and farm the land. In his grandfather's time the farm would have had a wider enterprise mix including arable, a dairy herd, beef cattle, sheep, pigs and poultry; the farm would have been a more integrated unit, growing among other things oats and hay to feed the horses. Today the farm is likely to concentrate on arable, beef and sheep and in terms of farm income the arable sector is by far the most important. If the farmer has a son, making it possible for his son to succeed him is a concern which will overshadow much of his thinking and planning; 'keeping the name on the land' is powerful force in all farming communities, but recent tax laws have made this increasingly difficult. The farm is likely to be a company, with all adult members of the family as directors and (with the exception of adult unmarried daughters) involved in work on the farm.

In his father's day, the farm would have employed approximately five men, all of whom lived in cottages on the farm or in the village. Over the years, as men have retired, so the labour force has been reduced to the point where only one man, a highly skilled tractor driver, is currently employed. The relationship between father and sons on the farm is a particularly sensitive matter in the farming community; but today many farmers try to give their sons the responsibility of running some part of the farm at the earliest possible opportunity, though some farmers find it difficult to hand over the reins to the next generation.

Today's farmer is likely to envy his father's life as being comparatively leisured compared with the hectic pace of contemporary farming at some periods of the year. Despite the years of depression in the 1920s and 1930s, none the less there remains something attractive about the pace of farming in those days. Farmers are fond of saying that horses had one great advantage: that they needed to stop occasionally and to have one day off a week. By contrast, at certain critical times of the modern farming year, work is so organized that as one man comes off a machine another is ready to take his place. Just as the farmer may remember his father as a man with sufficient leisure to linger at markets and shows, so he remembers him doing almost all the office work on a Sunday afternoon. While his father was pleased if he was dry at the end of the day, the modern farmer is likely to suffer from eyestrain rather than chilblains. Many farms today have a small outbuilding converted into a farm office and the farmer or members of his family find it necessary to spend much time on the farm's paperwork.

It is hard to generalize about either the daily or the seasonal pattern of work on any one farm. In a sense the farming year (ploughing, sowing, haymaking, harvesting; ramming, lambing, fattening and fairs) begins, as does the church's year, after the harvest. Favourable weather is important at any time of year, but it is particularly important in late September and early October, especially on the heavier land, for the autumn cultivations and the drilling of winter crops has to be completed before the wet and cold weather sets in. A typical farmer is likely to be extremely busy during this period at the beginning of the farming year, for not only does he have to prepare and plant his winter crops but also to sell the last of the spring-born lambs and bring in the cattle before they begin to damage the grass. At the end of this period, by late October or early November, when the amount of rain has made further work in the fields impossible, the farming year enters a quieter period, assuming that the farmer does not have forage maize or sugar beet. The evening and morning feeding and the checking of cattle and sheep become the dominant feature of the daily routine throughout the winter months, and as the days get shorter this routine can take up most of the daylight hours. For the rest of the day, this is the time of year when hedges, ditches and drains receive attention; when the farm machinery is overhauled and checked; when supplies are ordered for the farm stores; and when the backlog of work in the farm office is tackled.

This period of the year is a particularly active one in the social calendar of the farming community, for when the fields are too wet to carry a tractor and the cattle are not yet on full winter rations, the 'function room' of the hotel in the square of the neighbouring market town is filled with meetings, discussion groups and annual dinners of farming organizations. Some farming clubs date back to the eighteenth century (such as the Canterbury Farming Club, established in 1793), but many of the local societies were founded after the Second World War, when the Ministry of Agriculture advisers encouraged their formation as the means of spreading new techniques and methods. Aston Cantlow, near Stratford-upon-Avon, claims to be the home of the first of these established in 1943.

This programme of activity culminates in the fatstock shows in the few weeks before Christmas. Some farmers are particularly busy just before Christmas when the first lambs are being born, and with Christmas poultry (though now produced on few farms). Throughout the winter months beef cattle will be leaving the farm in small groups as they reach slaughter weight. After Christmas lambing begins on lowland farms with the aim of getting the earliest crop of lambs for the Easter market. Broadly speaking, March is the main month for lambing in the lowland areas, late April/early May in the upland areas. Lambing is very hard work for the farmer, who may not go to bed for a fortnight but simply doze in front of the fire between regular checks of the lambing pens.

Early spring sees the beginning of the spring cultivation and the planting of spring cereal crops, to be followed by potatoes. The late spring sees further field work as arable crops are sprayed and every farmer is relieved when he is eventually able to turn the cattle out, though the 'early bite' comes from the application of nitrogen fertilizer rather than flooding water meadows, as in former generations. By the early summer, lambs are being sent to market and there is a slightly quieter period on the farm during May (when some farmers take a holiday), which precedes the mowing of the grass for hay or silage. However, this is notoriously difficult to time; if early, it can finish well before the Royal Show (the first week in July); if late, it can be at its height during that week, and can effectively run into the harvesting of oilseed rape and winter barley. With the onset of the grain harvest, another very busy period on the farm begins. Some harvests, in good weather, are now relatively short and can be over by mid-August; but if the weather is bad, harvesting can carry on well into September. Although harvesting with modern machinery and drying equipment bears little relationship to the tense, lengthy and difficult season it once was (stooks of oats had to stay in the field for three Sundays), nevertheless the harvest remains a period of very hard work, to be followed immediately by the autumn cultivation. And so the farming year comes full cycle.

A consideration of the farming year serves to underline the difference between farmers and other occupational groups. Despite the fact that farmers refer to agriculture as an industry and that industrial methods and means such as uniformity of layout, mechanization of routine, and reduction of labour in order to produce a higher return are widely employed, farming is essentially different from other industries and farmers form a distinct group in society. What holds farming together as a single occupational group is its concern with growing crops and stock. But the separateness and distinctiveness of farming as a way of life is maintained and reinforced in every generation by a number of factors.

First, farming has a long history of which the modern farmer is both the product and the inheritor. Like all occupational groups farming has a corporate memory and language, and a rich store of folklore and myth, which shapes a farmer's perception of himself and the farming community as a whole. Inevitably, this tends to be dominated by recollections of periods of great hardship; and the experience of the farming community in the late nineteenth century and in the 1920s and 1930s has cast a long shadow and, in an inarticulate way, it continues to influence the thinking of modern farmers.

Second, unlike other industries, kinship still plays a significant role and 75 per cent of today's farmers are the sons of the last generation. Clearly, reasons of inheritance will mean that this high figure will continue to be maintained in future generations (it may be compared with doctors and clergy, where such continuity is between 18 per cent and 22 per cent). In any area it is common to find clusters of farming families who are closely related and who form an identifiable and tightly knit social group. It is not uncommon for brothers to marry the daughters of the neighbouring farming families and so to reinforce this occupational kinship network which, in some areas, includes the majority of farmers in the area. In former generations, the co-operation between farmers was important at certain times of the year, when numbers of men and teams of horses were needed for a single job. While inter-farm co-operation is still important, it is now largely at the level of borrowing equipment. Merely to purchase a farm does not turn a person into a farmer in the eyes of the farming descendants of generations of farmers and landowners in a district, and those who purchase a farm often feel that it will take a generation or two for their family to be accepted in the local farming network.

Third, one of the principal effects of the Industrial Revolution in the nineteenth century was the separation of the functions of ownership and management. The village craftsman who owned his workshop was replaced by the modern factory system of invested capital, and employed managers and labourers. The traditional landlord and tenant system represented this division in a significantly modified way in the late nineteenth century, when very few farmers owned their farms. However, in this century, as has been mentioned above, farming has moved in the opposite direction to that of other industries, and ownership and management are increasingly invested in the same person — the owner-occupier farmer. Unlike most of the population, farmers are not employed persons but, in the majority of cases, they both own and manage the means of production. This means that a farmer will be equally concerned about the capital value of his holding and its operational profit.

Fourth, as has been indicated above, agricultural economics are unlike the economics of other industries and this has had the effect of further differentiating farming from other economic activities. Unlike other areas of the economy, since 1947, farmers and the state have entered into a partnership in which the state has played an active and important role. Following the 1947 Act, a system of subsidies was introduced which, in effect, guaranteed a floor price for agricultural commodities and this created conditions in which the great resurgence of agriculture during the 1950s and 1960s took place. Since 1973 this system, though significantly modified, has been continued, not as a subsidy from the national government, but by the fixing of intervention prices under the Common Agricultural Policy. In effect, farmers received an open-ended guarantee which dated from a time of food shortage, that all production would be underwritten by the government. However, food is a different type of commodity from consumer durables or industrial products. It has a relatively short shelf life and supply has to be carefully matched to demand. In such circumstances both shortages and surpluses can easily occur and it is said that only a 2 per cent fluctuation will produce major surpluses or shortages in agricultural commodities. While those who market services or consumer goods are able to stimulate a demand-led expansion, this is not possible in foodstuffs where consumption has recognized limits. It is only recently that the significance of those limits has become apparent to farmers, particularly through the imposition of milk quotas. However, it is likely that from now on production controls will play an increasingly important role in agriculture, which again makes farming a significantly different activity to that of other production industries. This is not to say that the market cannot be stimulated by advertising (and by the recent concern about diet) so that marked changes occur within the pattern of food purchases. In recent years the percentage of the family budget that has been spent on food has been declining; in 1930, 25 per cent of the average wage was spent on food, while today this figure is below 10 per cent. In 1984 there was a 10 per cent decrease in the amount of butter eaten; 12.5 per cent increase in the sale of skimmed milk; 5 per cent decrease in the consumption of fresh vegetables and potatoes; and a 25 per cent increase in the sales of frozen vegetables. In the last eight years there has been a 30 per cent decrease in the consumption of beef and lamb and 250 per cent increase in poultrymeat consumption. Such factors will inevitably affect the way in which a farmer plans for the future.

Finally, to the economic and commercial distinctiveness of farming must be added the less quantifiable, but none the less real, social distinctiveness of the farming community. Farmers form a distinct, and, to a certain degree, a separate and encapsulated group in modern society. The difficulties in farming in any period and the harsh realities of the times of agricultural depression have given rise to a sense of solidarity and community. Foremost among all occupational groups, farmers have a strong sense of group identity based on history, kinship relations and the widespread belief that they are operating in an increasingly hostile social environment. In short, farming is a world characterized by a degree of distinctiveness and encapsulation, and membership of this well-defined group is for many farmers and their wives a considerable part of their job satisfaction. The significance of kinship links in farming has already been noted, but the fact that the majority of farmers come from farming families, as do their wives and friends, of itself makes farming a close-knit and self-contained world. This is reinforced by the fact that more farmers attend agricultural colleges than follow mainstream tertiary education. (However, this is a relatively recent phenomenon and, in 1972, 76 per cent of farmers had no formal agricultural training.) Furthermore, farming is not thought of as a job, but as a way of life which is absorbed from childhood and is largely based on practical experience and local knowledge. The nature of farming, as a way of life, means that family and farm life are very closely interwoven and until relatively recently it was not uncommon to find that decisions concerning the purchase of new stock or equipment for the farm had to be made, not simply on farming criteria, but within the context of the needs of the family for new clothes or some improvement to the home. Some farmers' wives, particularly those who do not come from a farming background, can find the all-pervasive nature of the farming environment difficult to cope with, at least in the early days of marriage. Although farming marriages are noted for their stability, since the Matrimonial Causes Act (1973) and the Matrimonial Proceedings and Property Act (1984), divorce in a farming family has become a particularly serious matter and can, in exceptional circumstances, lead to the sale of the farm.

Tristram Beresford has noted that some farming areas which are remote or marginal may be regarded as 'unwomanworthy'. Certainly the incidence of unmarried men in the farming community is noticeably high and tends to increase in the remoter areas. Recent statistics have indicated that while 17 per cent of English farmers are unmarried; 28 per cent of Welsh farmers are unmarried. Even the social life of the farmer tends to be dominated by farming and it is likely to comprise a round of contacts and engagements with other farmers at NFU meetings, at farmers' discussion groups and clubs, at agricultural and fatstock shows, and at a variety of recreational occasions which vary from bowling and darts to shooting and hunting. This has the effect of further reinforcing the farming community as an enclosed and self-contained world with its own rules of behaviour, customs and traditions, standards of dress and modes of speech. While, in the nineteenth century, farming was the activity of the majority of country people, today these factors taken together have produced a situation in which the farming community, even in rural areas, has become a small, distinct and separate world.

But perhaps the most dramatic change in farming, and the one which farmers find least easy to understand, is the way in which farming appears to have lost the social support it once enjoyed: today it operates in an increasingly critical, and at times vehemently hostile, environment. The two World Wars served to indicate that farmers were the producers of urgently needed food, the most vital and foremost human need. Such a role needed no justification and almost anything could be legitimated (particularly during the war) if its end was to produce more food. Even as the national food situation became less critical in the 1960s, as a result of increased home food production, farmers continued to enjoy popularity and political support for their efforts in saving the country increasingly expensive imports. At the same time, as has been noted in Chapter 2, the English have always retained an affection for the countryside and for the farming community and have developed a folk image of the farmer as a hard-working, thrifty and upright person. Farmers (the word 'yeomen' is often added by those who speak in these terms) were seen as the last representatives of the long tradition of independent, blunt-speaking, individualistic Englishmen who exemplified the moral and spiritual values of hard work, thrift, dependence on one's own exertions and the sanctity of family property. However, in a relatively short period of time, this image of the farmer has been totally changed. Today, he is not infrequently caricatured as a wealthy man, tilling the soil at public expense; a rich, greedy and arrogant exploiter of the environment; a destroyer of the countryside and its wildlife who needs to employ an accountant to reassure the tax office that he is not as wealthy as he appears. In 1973 Professor Colin Buchanan spoke of farmers as ' . . . the most ruthless section of the community', and ' . . . the real danger to the countryside'. The fact that official statistics have indicated that farming incomes increased by 24 per cent in 1981; 45 per cent in 1982 and 22 per cent in 1984 (there was a fall of 17 per cent in 1983) further reinforces this view. In 1970 only 15 per cent of farmers' income came from the public purse; today some sources claim that this figure has risen to 66 per cent. In 1982 it was estimated that the average farmer received £13,000 from public funds (though American farmers received double that figure). Furthermore, modern agricultural methods, particularly with regard to intensive livestock husbandry, the removal of hedges and increased field size, and the practice of straw burning, have all played their part in changing the public image of the farmer and have given rise to increasingly vocal demands for the erosion of that protection, both legal and financial, which farming has traditionally enjoyed, including the abolition of exemption from rates (since 1929) and the subjecting of all agricultural buildings to the normal planning procedures and restrictions.

Within the farming community, 'farmer bashing', as it is called, is seen as resulting from the widespread lack of knowledge which exists about modern farming and the over-sentimental and nostalgic attitude towards the countryside. Farmers are not inclined to treat seriously recommendations about the way in which they should conduct their business, from people who cannot distinguish between hay and straw. Farming organizations have responded with much emphasis on 'putting the farmers' case across'. However, the individual farmer knows that his income, which should be thought of as comprising management salary, interest on investment and reserve against a bad year, has remained at much the same level as in 1975, in real terms. His wealth, as reflected in the increasing price of land, particularly in the 1970s, exists only on paper and could only be realized if he ceased to be a farmer. The subsidies he receives support the processor and the consumer as much as the farmer, and agriculture is not the only industry which receives significant state funding. Many farmers view with increasing apprehension the rising level of criticism and feel that this will eventually be reflected in the degree to which politicians are willing to continue their support of the farming industry and will manifest itself in more significant constraints on farming practice than those that are contained in the 1981 Wildlife and Countryside Act.

In reality, the hostility which the farmers occasionally encounter relates to the new understanding of the countryside noted in Chapter 2. For the countryside, unlike the shopfloor of other industries, is both privately owned and farmed, yet at the same time it is publicly consumed as landscape and as a recreational area. In a society which increasingly sees the countryside as a place of residence, recreation and retirement, it is not surprising that farmers have found that their involvement in the countryside as a place of work and economic production, is being increasingly misunderstood and that their role is beginning to lack the social support it formerly enjoyed. In recent years, society at large has formed much stronger notions about many issues related to the countryside and agricultural practice. It is inevitable that this should be so, when more people are rediscovering the countryside through television and car ownership and rural recreation. In the 1960s and 1970s, countryside, heritage and conservation organizations began to attract a new, more concerned, more articulate and better informed membership. Many of these people now live in the countryside and are more than willing to express their views about the nature of farming in their immediate area. Thus, farmers have found that those who live in the contemporary village no longer share a common understanding about the countryside as a farmed environment, and their role in it. Farmers increasingly protest that they are seen by the new villagers as 'country wardens' rather than the managers of sophisticated agricultural enterprises. Many farmers find these attacks on the contemporary image of the farmer as rich and uncaring, particularly hard to countenance at a time when agriculture appears to be entering a period of decline. The average price of vacant agricultural land sold at the end of 1984 was £1,356 per acre, compared with more than £2,000 per acre in April of the same year. In real terms the price of agricultural land is now 12 per cent lower than in 1950. At the same time, the imposition of quotas for milk and the downward movement of cereal prices have produced a situation in which farmers are aware that profit margins will be increasingly squeezed in almost every area.

For the individual farmer in a particular village, the local impact of these changes in the social and attitudinal context of farming has been both difficult to understand and at times difficult to live with. In some villages the farmers and their families have retreated further into the self-contained world of the farming community and now have little contact with the other village residents. In other villages, by contrast, farmers and their families still play a full and central role in village activities; but in the main, farmers now play a noticeably less significant role than formerly in the life of the village and the local community. There is a tendency for them to find themselves physically, and in many other ways, outside the modern village. For them the countryside is the shopfloor of Britain's largest and most successful industry. It is clear that many of the new residents in the contemporary village do not see the countryside in that light, and that they are an increasingly powerful voice in shaping the future of rural Britain.

8

The Old Villagers

In the popular imagination villages are seen as inhabited by those whose forebears also lived there, and it is supposed that successive generations of the same family have crossed the same threshold to attend the baptisms, marriages and funerals which have marked the progress of the family's history. In reality, while it is possible to find some families with a long attachment to a particular village, or cluster of villages, their number is not great, even in the most remote areas. However, although in most villages there are only a few families with a long connection, nevertheless there is in every village a group of families who are regarded as 'the old villagers', as distinct from the more recently arrived commuters, retired people and weekenders, referred to as 'the new villagers'. One of the most distinctive features of modern village life is the division between these two groups; a division which is at one level economic and social, but at a more profound level is cultural and historic. For, as has been indicated in Chapter 6, the members of the old village community are the inheritors of the traditional understandings about village life, which date back to the time when the village was almost exclusively an occupational community. In a hundred years the village has changed from being predominantly a rural working-class settlement to being a mixed community of communities which is, in many places, dominated by 'the new villagers'.

The different attitudes between these groups can be noted at many points, but particularly with regard to employment and housing. The new villagers, who are predominantly middle-income earners, tend to be centrally concerned with the development of a career-line; for them the central point of stability is their job and they will change houses and districts according to the progress of their career. They are the 'colour supplement gypsies' whose roots do not lie in a physical but in an occupational community. By contrast, for the old villagers, who are predominantly lower-income earners, it is the house and the local community which provides the point of stability. For them, once they have found a house (whether rented, owned or tied) they tend to remain in the same house but change jobs according to local employment opportunities. Thus, it is common to find men, who once worked on a farm, in the construction industry, lorry driving or with the local highways department. For the old villagers the centre of their life is their home and the local community to which they are tied by membership of the local social network and in many instances by extensive kinship linkages. Put briefly, the new villagers are defined by their job, and the old villagers are defined by kinship and place. Clearly, this divide is becoming increasingly blurred in the contemporary village, but it is still important analytically in trying to understand the dynamics of contemporary rural communities.

Today, although the village has ceased to be an occupational community in the traditional sense, none the less those who live in the council houses and in the farm cottages still represent an unbroken continuity with the village's past. This group, whose pattern of life is essentially local, often feels itself to be under threat as the way of life which once supported it is gradually eroded, as are the local services and facilities on which the old villagers once depended. As a consequence the old villagers often have about them a sense of the past, a sense of loss and wistful regret that the cohesive family-based village community of their grandparents' generation has been dissolved into the modern village. But such regrets are often tinged with a realistic and thankful appreciation of the benefits which modern living has brought to village homes, and of the great improvement in their working lives.

If at one time the population of a village was comprised of those described as cottagers or villagers in Victorian books of instruction for parish clergy, today this group forms only a small part of the village population. Over the years there has been a steady movement of people away from the village either to seek a better life and employment in urban areas, or to move away from the harsh realities of village life in the 1920s and 1930s. In former generations, the farm worker was the archetypal member of the old village community and many of the attitudes of this group relate to the experiences of farm workers during the periods of agricultural depression. Throughout the decades of this century there has been a steady decline in the number of farm workers; one Cambridgeshire farm had forty-five farm workers in 1901, but by 1971 there were only six. In the late nineteenth century there were still 2 million farm workers, but the most significant period of decline has been since the Second World War. In 1948 there were 573,000 full-time agricultural workers in England and Wales; in 1984 there were 160,700*, which represented a 4.17 per cent decline since the previous year. (However, agriculture is characterized by the larger number of regular part-time, seasonal and casual workers who in 1984 totalled 156,000.) Perhaps the period of steepest decline in the full-time agricultural workforce was in the early 1970s; between 1971 and 1978 there was a 25 per cent decline. While, in the period after the First World War, it was usually calculated that one man was needed for every 25 acres, today there is no meaningful scale of calculation and 70 per cent of farms employ no labour. Immediately after the Second World War one Midlands estate employed eighty-five people, and employees' sons were automatically taken on. Today, while the group photographs of the assembled estate staff still adorn the estate office, the whole enterprise is run with a staff of ten.

While there is a sense in which the old villagers regret the passing of the days when the horse set the pace of farm work, nevertheless, for many these days have gone unmourned. Those who were accustomed to carrying a 2cwt sack of wheat from the threshing drum to the granary, did not need much encouragement to drive a combine harvester. The carter and the ploughman who used to get up at 4.30 a.m. to feed and groom their horses ready for a day's work, appreciate the luxury of starting a tractor at 7.30 a.m. A horseman might plough an acre a day, while today fifty or more acres can be ploughed with modern machinery. The constant reduction in the number of farm workers and the use of modern machinery have changed the nature of relationships within the farming community. In the old days, the farmer himself was a remote and authoritarian figure who gave his orders from his saddle on the back of a cob, and the farm worker was employed with a large group of other farm workers controlled by a bailiff or

* MAFF Statistics 1985.

charge-hand. Today the farmer and the farm worker have been brought much closer together and there is often a close personal relationship between them. On many farms a farm worker will be consulted extensively about the planning of the farm, and a family atmosphere develops between the farmer and the members of his staff and their families, as all feel themselves involved in the same enterprise. This is in marked distinction to the state of affairs which existed in the Victorian village. However, mechanization has also meant that the average farm worker now works predominantly on his own and loneliness has become a significant factor. The farm worker today in his tractor cab, in the middle of a large field, listening to the radio, is working in a totally different environment from that of his father or grandfather.

Farm workers have always been aware of the low status accorded by society at large to their job. While this has been slightly changed by the advent of mechanization, for the operator of a large and complex piece of machinery demonstrates to the wider world that his job is both skilled and responsible, nevertheless, in the main, farm work is still accorded low status. This is reinforced by the comparatively low wage which agricultural workers have traditionally received. The Agricultural Wages Board was established in 1917, but had to be abolished in 1921, at the beginning of the period of agricultural depression. The recovery in prices which marked the end of the First World War was followed by a collapse and farm wages which had risen to 40s per week in 1920 fell back to between 30s and 25s per week. It was this that provoked 'the great strike' in 1923, which started in Norfolk and preceded the General Strike by three years. The strike has an important place in the history of the trade union movement; yet, although it succeeded in halting the downward spiral in wages, farm workers were forced to return to work after the strike for 25s for a fifty-hour week. In 1927 wages fell again from 42s to approximately 30s, and it was not until 1929 that farm workers received Saturday afternoons off. In 1939 the basic wage of a five-and-a-half-day week with one week's holiday a year, was still under £2. By the end of 1944, after the attempted U-boat blockade of the North Atlantic had emphasized the vital strategic importance of domestic food supplies, the minimum wage was still no more than 65s per week.

Today it is less easy to generalize about agricultural wages, principally because few agricultural workers are on the minimum wage, and many, particularly those who manage livestock units, or earn considerable amounts of overtime on large arable farms, are, in relative terms, much better off than their predecessors. However, in the main, agricultural wages stay low. In April 1982 the Department of Employment listed 136 occupations in order of earnings; full-time male farm workers ranked 132 — fourth from the bottom. Reports from the Low Pay Unit in 1980 ('Poor Harvest') and 1982 ('Cold Comfort Farm') recorded that 40 per cent of farm workers were paid on or below the poverty line (i.e. the supplementary benefit level). In 1980, 6,500 FIS claimants were farm workers, who represented 17 per cent of the total claimants. Farm workers comprised the largest single group who claim family income supplement; this is regarded as a poverty wage supplement payable to full-time workers to increase their income. The benefits in kind which many farm workers once received, which included milk, potatoes, fuel and the use of a farm vehicle, are now of much less significance. In 1985 the basic rates of pay for farm workers were increased by 8.3 per cent by the Agricultural Wages Board, raising the minimum pay for a full-time farm worker to £82.80 per week; craftsman's rates were raised to £103.16 (30 per cent of the farm workforce earn this rate), and the two higher grades (which account for 10 per cent of the workforce) were raised to £112.13 and £121.10.

Low pay is one of many factors which determine the age profile of the agricultural workforce, which is weighted towards the older and younger age groups. There remain a significant number of elderly farm workers, who were once termed 'general farm workers', but whose traditional skills are now of less significance on modern arable and livestock farms. At the same time, agriculture attracts a disproportionately large number of school leavers in rural areas, reflected in the large intakes of agricultural colleges and the Approved Agricultural and Horticultural Youth Training Scheme. However, it is not uncommon to find that a sixteen-year-old will have moved from the farm by the time he is in his mid-twenties and married, attracted by the higher earnings in such industries as building, construction and road haulage.

The dispersed nature of the agricultural workforce, and the

particular relationship which exists between individual farm workers and a farmer, have always militated against trade union activity. It is estimated that only about a third of farm workers are union members, and although their union has an honoured and historical place within the trade union movement, from the days of the Tolpuddle Martyrs, it has never had the strength possessed by other unions in less fragmented industries. Union leaders believe that this accounts for the fact that skilled farm workers' wages have remained consistently 25 per cent lower than skilled industrial workers'. Such growth in union membership as there has been in recent years has principally occurred in intensive livestock units, slaughter houses, and packing and processing plants. After lengthy debate the National Union of Agricultural and Allied Workers became the Agricultural Trade Group within the Transport and General Workers Union in 1982, in order to enjoy the benefits of being closely associated with other workers on whom the agricultural industry depends, such as milk tanker drivers, and fuel and feedstuff delivery drivers.

In the early decades of this century, life was still relatively hard in many villages and today the attitudes of the old village community are still in part conditioned by this fact. In the nineteenth century, rural housing was often extremely poor for the farm worker and his family and much farm work was done on the basis of casual labour or hired gangs. As the competition from the industrial areas and the colonies made agricultural labour less easy to obtain, so farmers and estate owners built tied cottages for their workforce. In this century, with the shortage of rural housing, the number of farm workers in tied cottages has risen from 34 per cent in 1948, to 53 per cent in 1976. For many decades the problems surrounding tied cottages and particularly the distress caused to families by eviction when a man lost his job, have resulted in much bitterness and distrust within the village. This was compounded by the suspicion of many farm workers that farmers, who frequently dominated the old Rural District Councils, were often less than enthusiastic in supporting the building of council houses in their area, in order that they should continue to exercise control over a sizeable proportion of the rural housing stock. In 1976, the Rent (Agriculture) Act substantially altered the situation of tied cottages, and although many remain, an eviction can only be obtained if the farmer can prove that the cottage is essential to the working of his farm and the local authority is able to rehouse the evicted family.

But perhaps what has affected the farm worker more than anything else has been the fact that he is no longer a member of a large, cohesive, social and cultural group with its own codes and standards and its own means of according status and recognizing excellence. Most aspects of farm work are public activities, in the sense that bad workmanship is immediately exposed to public view. If the drill has a blocked coulter it is impossible to hide the result. A skilled ploughman or carter who worked in the fields around the village was accorded appropriate status in a community that appreciated and understood his skills. Today the village is no longer comprised of people who can appreciate such things and the commuting motorist, who drives past a well-ploughed field or a carefully tended flock of sheep, has no way of judging their excellence. It is this decline in the public support and appreciation of the farm worker's job which — as Howard Newby has pointed out — probably affects farm workers more profoundly than other aspects of change in recent decades.

In the early part of this century, life was still relatively hard for those who lived in the village. The cottages themselves varied enormously in comfort. Many had merely two rooms on the ground floor and two or three bedrooms upstairs, leading directly from one to another with no passage. Stairs were steeply raised, not infrequently coming directly out of one of the downstairs rooms.

There were no holidays as such, only the traditional week off after harvest for mops or Martinmas fairs, a legacy of the old hiring fairs, at which farm workers traditionally spent their harvest money on new boots, clothes and supplies for the winter. The work was physically demanding and many farm workers were glad simply to be dry at the end of the day. It was also dangerous, and accidents with horses, cattle, and drive belts from tractors and threshing machines often resulted in horrifying injuries. The diet was inadequate and monotonous with very little protein, and, as a consequence, poaching played a significant role in providing such meat as was seen in many cottage homes (in contrast to modern poaching which is largely carried out by town-based gangs). However, many farm workers could imagine no other life; they belonged to a homogeneous and purposeful community in which their skills were appreciated and understood. But increasingly their wives became impatient with conditions in the village, particularly as many had seen service in the larger houses in the district. The First World War changed the villages very little in themselves, but in the post-war period there was a new determination to improve living conditions for the villagers. Perhaps it was the wireless, or the widespread growth of the Women's Institute, which brought to village women new perspectives* and standards. Certainly, the Second World War changed the nature of village life much more dramatically, principally because large numbers of urban children were evacuated into the countryside and the arrival of the land girls of itself raised questions about the role of women in the countryside. It was not until the 1950s and 1960s that piped water, mains sewerage and electricity arrived in many rural areas, along with the television and a range of kitchen gadgets. However, in the 1970s, there were still clusters of houses in rural areas which were not supplied with electricity and which relied upon pumped water.

Even as late as the 1960s, the old village community, in many areas, remained culturally an identifiable group in which attitudes and understandings from the days of the traditional village were still preserved. The television has had a significant influence in lessening the cultural distinctiveness of the old village group and lowering the divide between the 'greater' urban culture and the 'lesser' rural culture, which still lingered in the homes of such families. Today there is a sense in which members of the old village community live in two worlds: they are a part of the old village culture, but the television in the home and the radio in the tractor cab link them into the mainstream urban metropolitan culture of our society. However, it is easy to underestimate how much of the old village culture is still perpetuated, not in the material dimension (with the possible exception of cooking), but more in terms of attitudes, disposition, modes of behaviour and values. It is still possible to speak of this constellation of attitudes as the remnant of the old rural culture, what the Americans call 'the rural mind-set'.

By its nature, the ethos and old character of the village community is elusive and difficult to describe, not least because of the great varieties between different areas. Nevertheless, the members of the old village community, to a lesser or greater extent, are the heirs of the old working-class solidarity, so characteristic of the primary industries, by which the village was welded together by its common history of poverty, hard work, danger, insecurity, disease and suffering. While the causes of much of this deprivation, as it was experienced in previous generations, have now been eradicated, nevertheless the hidden memory of the old village perpetuates and hands down attitudes formed generations ago. In a way, the old village community is dominated by a sense of displacement and loss: the residents feel that the village is no longer theirs, but that it has been taken over by newly arrived people who have no knowledge of the traditions, history and values of the old village. This feeling of displacement can often mean that the old village community appears aloof and restrained, for they know themselves to be the real villagers and their new neighbours are but temporary residents in a place whose history they cannot inherit. Inevitably, history becomes a matter of great importance and sanctuary for the old village community and this will often be focused in the church.

The old village community, impoverished by those who have moved away but enriched by its struggle to retain its own identity, echoes at many points the pre-industrial understandings and values of the village. Kinship is of particular importance, and, even where the old village community now forms a relatively small part of the total village, the kinship map, complicated by generations of cousin marriages, is still an important part of the reality of the village. This knowledge is often used by the old village community as a means of maintaining their distinctiveness and of excluding the more recently arrived residents. The old village community, even when it is reduced to just a few families, often retains a sense of being an alternative and hidden community, with its own leadership and its occasions and places of significance. Either the church, or the parish council, or the British Legion hut remains the preserve of the old village community who have, in a sense, retreated into a stronghold within which they can preserve something of their identity. Among the leadership of the old village community, often exercised by women, it is regarded as important that former glories and traditions should be maintained. There is a need to keep faith with the past and to fight off the sad and diminishing feeling which arises when long-honoured traditions and occasions within the village are forgotten or discontinued

Among the old village community the manners and mannerisms of the traditional village can still be found, and the instant intimacies of suburban society are resisted by a group of people who live so close to one another that a degree of social distance must be maintained. Social visiting, in particular the sharing of a meal in another person's house, still plays little part in the lives of the old village community who, in many cases, are only likely to invite near relatives, a clergyman and a doctor across their doorstep. By the same token, the division of the village into 'the man's village' and 'the woman's village' is still a reality in the old village community. While the old tradition of 'trousers churches' (where men sat on one side of the aisle and women on the other), has now all but disappeared, this distinction can still be found at other meetings. The belief that certain activities are exclusively for men and others for women still lingers in rural communities. If the deep division between the men's world and the women's world — the one centred on work and the farm, the other on the home and children — has blurred and in large part disappeared, nevertheless, something of this understanding lingers within the old village community. Among this group the strength of the obligation to look after elderly relatives should not be underestimated, and it is common to find a number of elderly people in a village who are almost entirely dependent on younger members of their family for a variety of needs including shopping, gardening, cleaning, cooking and elementary nursing.

If, in the early decades of this century, the majority of members of the old village community worked in agriculture, farming now provides jobs only for a small minority, although for the rest it still represents their cultural inheritance and they are likely to take a keen interest in what happens on the farms of the village. Many have found jobs away from the village and commute from a rural home to an urban job, sometimes at a considerable distance. Others have found jobs in the agriculturally related sector, driving milk lorries or doing contracting work such as drainage and hedging. For them the village is their home and they wish to remain there and find jobs within the locality. The lack of employment opportunities in many rural areas, particularly for young people, has become a serious concern and accounts for much of the out-migration from villages by young adults. It is noticeable that when major new developments are planned in a predominantly rural area (such as new airports or military bases), while others may complain on environmental grounds, members of the old village community are often primarily interested in the possibility of new jobs, within reach of their homes. For them the greatest tragedy lies in the fact that their children very often find it necessary to leave the village in order to find work and housing elsewhere. The recent rise in the cost of houses in rural areas has meant that in many cases it is now the council houses which have become the redoubt of the old village community. It is there, and on the allotments, that the traditional life of the village can still be found substantially unaltered by the many changes which have transformed other aspects of village life. However, since the 1980 legislation which permitted tenants to purchase their council houses, there is an increasing danger that even this element of the rented housing stock will be alienated from the old village community (see page 75).

In contemporary society people have come to regard deprivation as an urban phenomenon and to see poverty as something which exists principally in the inner city and the depressed industrial areas, despite the fact that statistics have always shown that income levels are higher in urban areas than in the countryside. There are various reasons for this, including the fact that poverty in the countryside tends to be both less visible and less concentrated than it is in urban areas. At the same time, those who are affected by the relative deprivation in the countryside are less in number, dispersed, unorganized and frequently relatively inarticulate. It is one of the paradoxes of social change in the contemporary countryside that the new villagers who have brought affluence to many rural communities, and have restored cottages that were once in an advanced state of decay, have also contributed to the cycle of decline in services and facilities in rural areas. Many of these people make almost no demands on local services; the possession of a car (and in many cases two cars) allows them almost exclusively to use urban facilities. While this is true of the urban shadow and the more accessible countryside, in the remote countryside the decline in the total population and the in-movement of second home and holiday cottage owners has had similar effects. This decline in the demand for rural services and facilities has occurred at just the time when expectations have risen significantly among members of the old village community. The existence of rural deprivation is often hidden not only at the level of public observation but also in statistical terms. Official statistics frequently take a district council area as the smallest unit, and within this area the presence of two or three market towns obscures the true position in the surrounding countryside. As a result English society (and the churches) have been noticeably slower to respond to the problems of rural deprivation than in America, where the existence of rural poverty has been well documented for several generations.

While, in essence, there is no distinction between urban and rural deprivation, nevertheless, as a social phenomenon, rural deprivation has markedly different characteristics. In the first place, it is noticeable that in the countryside even those on very low incomes are unlikely to think of themselves as poor. This is partly due to the fact that life in village homes has improved considerably in recent generations, with the advent of electricity and piped water which, together with other improvements in living standards, have made such homes very different from those of former generations. This, taken with the fact that until recently the number of wealthy people in the village was relatively small, meant that the village was a place of low expectations, where people were accustomed to accept standards which others would regard as unacceptable. It is common to find elderly people in the countryside, isolated by lack of transport, in communities which once had considerable facilities and services, who suffer from multiple deprivation yet do not regard themselves as anything other than much better off than their parents' generation. However, whatever may be true of the elderly, the advent of wealthy commuters and retired families into the village has had the effect of making some, particularly the young, aware of the wide differences between the lifestyles of the old village and new village communities.

As has been shown in Chapter 5, the principal problems of rural deprivation relate to the dispersed nature of the population and the high relative cost of providing services and facilities for small numbers of people in remote areas. As we have seen, the 1970s witnessed a radical change in the level of services available in the countryside, which resulted from a number of factors including the rising level at which services could be provided; with the higher standards now required, and changes in the social profile; and in some areas, the decline of the rural population. The combined effect of these changes has been to create areas which may look prosperous and affluent, but which contain within them pockets of considerable deprivation. As in urban areas, those who suffer most are the elderly, the disabled and young families, particularly those on low incomes, and young people in general. However, unlike urban areas, the low level of rented accommodation means that one-parent families and unmarried young people, including students, form a much lower percentage of the population than in urban areas.

In many areas the problem is not the provision of services; indeed, it can be shown that per head of the population there is often better overall service provision in rural areas than in urban areas. The basic problem is that of access. The real divide between the 'haves' and the 'have nots' in the countryside is the possession of a car or at least access to a car. The percentage of the population which own a car is significantly higher in rural areas than it is in urban areas, and families who for economic reasons would not consider owning a car if they lived in a town, find it necessary to maintain one. Any village street will bear witness to the fact that many relatively low-income families struggle to maintain an elderly car or van. This has given rise to a significant rural industry comprised of small garages or 'back garden' car mechanics who keep these vehicles on the road. Those who suffer from the highest level of multiple deprivation are those who have no access to private transport and have to depend on public services or taxis (another growth industry in the countryside). The influence of the key village policy, as noted in Chapter 5, has been such that most small villages today possess nothing more than a village shop with a post office, a public telephone box, and an occasional transport link. A significant number possess none of these facilities; in very rough terms, 50 per cent of rural settlements do not have a shop and approximately 30 per cent have no direct transport link. In such a situation there are inevitably pockets of isolation where small groups of elderly people are trapped without suitable services and facilities, access to which has now become extremely expensive. Despite the efforts of community transport initiatives, some locally based or organized within a cluster of villages by the Rural Community Council or the WRVS, there remain many elderly people in rural areas who suffer considerable deprivation.

The other principal deprived group in the countryside are young people. In the early decades of this century, most villages still had a school and the daily life of the village was punctuated by the noise of children assembling in the morning and playing in the playground at lunchtime, with the mothers arriving at the school gate at 3.30 p.m. Old village residents frequently comment on the silence and stillness that followed the closure of the school. As has been noted in Chapter 5, the decline in the birthrate and the changing social profile have meant that there are fewer children in many villages, and these are now collected by bus early in the morning and taken to schools either in neighbouring villages or to the nearest market town. The decline in the number of children in many villages has meant that a village child today does not grow up among a sizeable group of children of roughly the same age; an eight-year-old boy in a village may find that there are no other boys of his age. This degree of isolation can lead to considerable cultural and social deprivation and is one of the strongest arguments for a more centralized pattern of schools. It has been noted that the out-migration of young families from the village is often finally triggered by the involvement of children in a number of out-of-school activities at the secondary level. Village parents often find it extremely difficult to arrange for their children to be collected after sports matches, school-play rehearsals, choir practice or badminton club.

Many young people, particularly those with lower expectations and qualifications, find it very difficult to obtain suitable employment. While some youngsters leave the village for education and are unlikely to return, others leave later seeking employment away from the village, possibly following generations of young villagers who have joined the army or the police. The decline of agriculture as a major employer in the village has robbed it of just those jobs which many of the children of the old village community would have expected to fill. While, a few years ago, researchers were aware that school leavers were disinclined to take jobs in agriculture and still felt that there was a stigma attached to it coupled with low status among their peers, today there is great difficulty in finding jobs for all the youngsters who wish to go into farming, and courses run by county agricultural colleges attract large numbers. Many of the small high-technology industries that have moved into rural areas in recent years either bring their own workforce with them or fail to find, among the locally unemployed, people of sufficient skill or relevant experience. To be unemployed in Sheffield or Coventry is to be part of a sub-culture which, for all its difficulties, is supportive and in its own way personally affirming; to be unemployed in a small country village is not infrequently to be isolated and alone in a context where old-fashioned values of hard work and thrift are still honoured and where people are disposed to think of the unemployed as lazy, irresponsible and shiftless.

Young people in villages quickly realize the importance of personal transport and at the first opportunity they purchase a motorbike to get themselves in to the local market towns. Nothing reflects the young people's estimation of the village, as a place where nothing happens, so directly as the knot of youngsters that can be found on a Saturday afternoon in the centre of the neighbouring market town. These youngsters come, predominantly, not from the town itself but from the surrounding villages. They come simply to see if there is anything going on in the market town. Village youth clubs have a different history from those of urban areas, in that in urban areas youth clubs were organized to get young people off the streets, while in the countryside they owe their origin to the desire to get young people out of their homes. In the early decades of this century rural young people were regarded as essentially home based and worked very long hours. Rural youth clubs were established, not infrequently by clergy, in order to provide some recreational and educational opportunities in the village. Village youth clubs are notoriously transient affairs, dependent upon a reasonable number of young people coming into the appropriate age group at the same time, and the dedicated work of youth leaders and their assistants. In the past many village halls ran youth clubs or had youth clubs attached to them, which provided sporting, social and educational programmes. Today youth clubs in country areas are less frequently found, and young people are more likely to travel to a youth club in a local market town. The exception to this is the Young Farmers Club, perhaps the most successful of all youth movements in rural areas, and although its membership varies in character considerably from district to district it would in general terms be fair to say that it appeals more readily to the sons of farmers than to the children of the old village community.

However, not all the members of the old village community come into the categories described above, for the estate owners, or rather those estate owners who are members of the old county families, also come into this group, in their ancient gradations of aristocracy, gentry and squirearchy. As has been shown in Chapter 4, these families once played a dominant and all-pervasive role in the English countryside during the nineteenth century, but, by the end of that century, and in the early decades of this century, landowners suffered a series of political assaults which started with the imposition of estate duty on agricultural property in 1894. During the period of the agricultural depression, in the last quarter of the nineteenth century, many estates were forced to sell land and this series of sales was accelerated by Lloyd George's budget of 1910. Although the First World War gave a temporary boost to the fortunes of farming, it marked the end of a period in which the country houses dominated all aspects of life in the surrounding area. Perhaps the change was slower and more gradual than is sometimes suggested, but the First World War clearly marked a watershed in the social and economic life of the countryside, not least because many landed families lost almost all their menfolk in the trenches.

In the 1920s, when depression again engulfed farming, there were still country estates that were run on nineteenth-century lines, with large numbers of indoor and outdoor staff, by landowners who regarded it as part of their responsibility to provide employment for all young people in the village. Even at this late date many of the estates were essentially self-contained communities with their own timber and brick yards, the home farm and the gardens, and even a generator for their own electricity. As rising costs and lack of staff made this way of life increasingly unsustainable, many of the 'big houses' were abandoned or else sold for a variety of institutional usages, or, in extreme cases, dynamited as was Cassiobury House in 1927. Slowly a social revolution took place in the countryside, which was much accelerated in the period after the Second World War, and the old county families ceased to play such a dominant role as a more mixed rural community developed in which large owner-occupier farmers, together with the urban industrialists and city men who were purchasing many of the larger houses, played an increasingly significant role.

Certainly, in some estate villages the old, essentially paternalistic relationships were maintained well into the twentieth century; it is no exaggeration to say that the estate owner and his wife were treated almost as royalty within their own community. Church bells were rung on their return from staying in London for the season; the main street in the village was swept from end to end on Saturday afternoons before the party from the Hall made their way to church next morning. In those villages where all the houses and cottages were owned by the estate and almost all employment was provided directly or indirectly by the estate, the influence of the big house and of the squire's agent was all-pervasive, and whatever the villagers might have thought privately, it was necessary in public to adopt an attitude of deferential respect. In some villages the attitude of the big house was that of kindness, benevolence and a desire to protect members of the village from personal disasters, illness and other misfortunes, as well as the more general disorders which resulted from the periods of agricultural depression; in other instances the big house could appear oppressive, exploitative and autocratic. Certainly, in many villages few things could be contemplated and nothing decided without a nod from the big house which, well into the twentieth century, could be sure that most villagers would follow its lead.

The persistence of the influence of the county families and their continuing role in county and village affairs is a matter of surprise to many urban visitors to the countryside. While it is acknowledged that this influence is both significantly less in quantity, and markedly different in character, nevertheless through the chairmanship of the county council and its committees, through participation in many of the county activities and charitable and voluntary organizations, and through the leadership of the local village community, the old families still play a significant role in the life of rural areas, which their families have served in different capacities for many generations. In recent decades, many more large houses have been sold; some have become government institutions, schools, flats for time-sharing holidaymakers, and an increasing number have become old people's homes. Those houses which are still lived in have few servants, but the increasing post-war profitability of farming has rescued many from certain deterioration and possible sale.

While, in the pre-First World War period, many county families did not farm themselves, such families have now become prominent in the agricultural community. The pattern of landownership has changed considerably in recent years, as has been referred to in Chapter 4. In 1872 the Earl of Derby commissioned a survey (to prove that the land was not in the hands of a few nobles and gentry); however, to his embarrassment, the survey proved exactly the opposite. It showed that the Duke of Sutherland alone owned 1.3 million acres and it revealed that fifteen men had incomes from land of more than £100,000 per year. Today, institutional landowners predominate among the 'top ten' (the crown, conservation organizations, universities and colleges, the church commissioners, the nationalized industries, etc). Only one private landowner (the Duke of Buccleuch, who, through family trusts and companies, controls 250,000 acres), can be found on this list. Today, a county family is more likely to own an estate of between 500 and 5,000 acres, much, if not all of which, is farmed by the estate owner himself. Such estates, like large owner-occupier farmers, are much concerned with the problems of taxation and succession and with devising appropriate means of handing on the estate to the next or subsequent generations. One unexpected death can destroy the legacy of centuries through taxation. Though hunting and shooting continue to play a significant role in the countryside, hunting is by no means the prerogative of the old county families, as it was in the pre-war era. Joint masterships, city businessmen with a desire to hunt on Saturdays, have all considerably altered the context in which hunting takes place. Shooting is, on the whole, the favoured sport of estate owners (being more directly compatible with modern agriculture), though shooting on many estates is now part of the estate business and 'guns' (the right to shoot a certain number of days in the year) are sold for large sums of money. The days when the local squire could make a well-hung hunting gate or the planting of certain crops to encourage pheasants for his private enjoyment a condition of his tenancy agreement, are over.

In a sense, just as the big house lies outside the village and is surrounded and separated from the village by the walls of the park, so the landed families have always been outside the life of the village. However, at another level, in an estate village the family have played a central part in the life of the village community, with the squire as patron of the church, churchwarden, chairman of the village charity, the school governors and the parish council, and the women members of his family taking prominent roles in the Women's Institute, the village hall and the local flower show committees. This participation in village life and the ownership of many houses and all the land, has led to the forming of a close relationship, sometimes described as paternalistic, between the old village families and the big house. However, much as the village as a whole may criticize the life style, decisions and actions of those in the big house, it nevertheless remains a focus of their loyalty and affection. In turn, the family is expected to remember birthdays and anniversaries and to grace all village occasions, particularly weddings and funerals. Many villages are characterized by an ambivalent relationship between the village and the big house. At one level the old villagers deeply regret the changes that have taken place, as farming has become more businesslike and the management of the estate has been put on a more commercial footing. However, at another level there is a profound affection for the landed family and whatever the villagers may say themselves, they are unlikely to allow other people to criticize the squire and his family. The old days of deference, respect and 'knowing one's place', have given way to an era in which both sides know that the relationship has become a voluntary one. The squire and his wife retain the affection and respect of the village in so far as they encourage and foster village activities and take a personal interest in the families of the village. If the occupants of the big house are uninterested or uninvolved, this relationship soon evaporates.

Finally, there are a small group of people in the village notable today for their absence rather than their presence, who are part of the old village community by virtue of their role. In former generations the policeman, the schoolteacher, the doctor, the village nurse and the vicar formed a group of temporary residents who were accepted as part of the old village community by virtue of what they did rather than by virtue of kinship relations and length of residence. In many cases such people would remain in the village over a long period of time and integrate themselves thoroughly into the local community, but they always remained people from outside who had come into the village to do a particular job and could leave at any moment. Through the decades of this century the number of such residents has declined sharply. Stationmasters are now almost unknown in rural areas. Although some rural police houses have been retained, the policeman who lives there is likely to work from the police station in the nearest market town. In many areas schoolteachers travel in to their job at the village school, not least because of the high cost of local housing. Group practice has considerably changed the pattern of work for doctors and single-doctor practices in rural areas are now relatively rare. The village feels the loss of all these people who invariably made a considerable contribution to the life of the local community as office holders in village organizations and organizers of such activities as the youth club, the football team and the bell ringers. They had the particular advantage, like the clergyman, that although they belonged to the village by virtue of their office, they were not of a village family. Small rural communities, particularly in the days of limited mobility, needed these 'outsiders' in order to function more effectively as communities. The man from outside, whether he were the doctor, the schoolmaster or the clergyman, as will be shown below, had an important role to play in the village in providing leadership in situations which somebody from within the local community often found impossible.

Finally, account must be taken of a group who are not members of the old village community and have moved in recently, though they share many of the attitudes found in that community. In recent years a number of people have moved into the countryside to pursue some craft enterprise or small-scale industry. Those who have come into rural areas range from the self-sufficient smallholders practising wheelbarrow farming on a small acreage, to highly sophisticated computer-based services. There are those who practise a craft — such as potters, jewellers, woodworkers and other craftsmen. At the same time a number of highly sophisticated small industries have been developed in the countryside in recent years and although local residents often refer to these as 'chicken-hut industries', in fact many of them are highly sophisticated high-tech enterprises which use redundant farmbuildings as the base for their operation. These will be discussed further in the next chapter. The significance of this group is that they form another element of the contemporary village who share with the old village community the belief that the village should be both a place of work and a place where people live their whole lives.

9

The New Villagers

While, in the nineteenth century, some people were disposed to regard the village as in some ways similar to an open prison from which those who could made their escape to the city, by contrast, in the twentieth century, an increasing number of people wished to make the journey in the opposite direction. As a result, many villages have lost almost all vestige of the days when they were occupational communities and have become mixed residential settlements. The proportion of old and new villagers varies considerably in different parts of the country, but, in most areas, a process of population substitution has been taking place during the decades of this century, by which a variety of new villagers have taken the place of those who once lived and worked in the countryside. While, in the nineteenth century, the majority of villages were broadly similar in social composition, what differentiates villages today is the degree to which they have been affected by in-migration and the different in-coming groups who have favoured particular villages.

The work of rural sociologists in the immediate post-war period, such as the study of north-west Oxfordshire villages by C. S. Orwin and his team, was principally concerned to bring home to a wider public the degree of social disintegration which had affected the majority of villages. Such studies make pessimistic reading and they cannot be blamed for failing to anticipate the wave of migration into the countryside, as depopulation gave way to repopulation, in the second half of the twentieth century. As car ownership became a possibility for the middle-income earners, so it was no longer necessary to live within walking distance of the public transport networks. This factor, coupled with the improvement in the rural infrastructure encouraged many to move into rural areas and contributed to the transforming of the demographic structure of villages in this country, as in most European countries and the United States. By the 1970s, demographers were aware that a significant population shift was taking place, and that urban areas, which had recorded steady growth in population for many decades, were now declining.

By contrast, many rural areas, which it was assumed would continue to decline in population, now recorded steady growth, particularly in the more accessible and favoured areas. The population increased in areas defined as rural in the census, from 7.3 million in 1939 to 10.6 million in 1971. The rural population constituted 17 per cent of the total in 1939; 21 per cent in 1971. The British census of 1981 revealed that in the previous ten years the metropolitan areas had suffered the greatest population loss, and that London was below 7 million for the first time since 1901 (inner London lost 18 per cent of its population in the 1970s; Manchester lost 17 per cent and Liverpool 16 per cent). Conversely, Norfolk, Suffolk, Cambridgeshire, Hereford, Worcester and Shropshire all recorded increases in their population of between 5 and 10 per cent. The reasons for this change relate to complex push-and-pull factors, as well as to fundamental changes in attitude towards rural England mentioned in Chapter 2. In the 1960s and early 1970s (at least until the oil price rises of 1973/74), relatively cheap private transport and the development of the motorways opened up access to areas of the countryside which had previously been regarded as remote and relatively inaccessible. While those who moved into the countryside then, as now, do so at all ages, nevertheless it is possible to suggest that two groups predominated.

The first group are those with young families, who, having recently outgrown their urban or suburban first home, sought the countryside as a suitable place in which to bring up their family. Estate agents indicate that the critical time for this type of move is when the oldest child reaches the age of five. Many of the new families who arrive in the villages in the more accessible countryside are those with young children whose father has a managerial or professional job, who move into a new house on a private development at the edge of the village or who purchase and restore one of the cottages (possibly two cottages converted into one) in the centre of the village. The other group, who typically form a large proportion of the new households in the village, are those who have either reached retirement age or are anticipating retirement within the foreseeable future; many people move into the countryside in their mid-fifties or early sixties (what

the Americans call the 'empty nest move'). It is well known that
the period of bringing up young children and that of retirement are
both times in the life cycle when people have to adapt to new
circumstances, stresses and constraints. Indeed, there is a degree
of complementariness between the two groups, for under the
disposition of traditional society, it is the grandparents who play a
major role in the lives of the young children. It is possible to
suggest that among the many and varied reasons for making these
moves, people in these two groups are, consciously or
unconsciously, influenced by a view of the village as a warm,
accepting community which will act in some ways as a surrogate
extended family, in an age when the psychological need for the
extended family is still evident; but such families are often scattered
across the country. This in part explains the attitude of some
members of these groups (though clearly by no means all) to the
village of their adoption and their subsequent difficulties and
disappointments when the village fails to live up to their high
expectations. Many new villagers find that there is a considerable
mismatch between the reality of contemporary village life and
their expectations of what that village will be like. These
expectations often owe much to traditional attitudes to the
countryside described in Chapter 2 and to the rural 'soap operas'
on the television and the radio.

Dr Johnson may not have been thinking of commuters when he
expressed the opinion that heaven would contain the joys of the
countryside and the amenities of the town. However, there is little
doubt there are many people who believe in the desirability of
such a compromise. At one level, commuting has always been an
attempt to live in two worlds at the same time, but it is important
to recognize its significance in modern society. Those who choose
to live in the countryside and commute to an urban job are seeking
a quality of life for their home and family which they believe does
not exist in the city or the suburbs. For this they are willing to
make considerable financial sacrifices and to endure the problems
and the cost (not least in time) of long-distance commuting. They
value being part of a small-scale historic community and being
surrounded by the comforting symbols of the past: the church, the
pub, the village green and the old cottages. At the same time,
many place a high value on self-reliance, independence and privacy

which they believe to be more congruent with a rural rather than an urban life. The garden is a symbol of all these values and more British people have gardens than any other European nation. Socio-political analysts comment that when the outside world is threatening and depressing it encourages people to retreat into the secure fortress of their home and garden. Certainly, the 'home-centred culture' is a marked feature of the commuter's lifestyle. However, behind this lies the more fundamental desire of modern man to separate out the various compartments of his life and particularly to distance his work life from his family life. Commuting is a desired lifestyle for many because work and family are separated to the point where they hardly overlap at all. Such a lifestyle, which characterizes modern society, is markedly different from that of the old village community for whom work and family exist within the same social context.

In the mid nineteenth century, Surrey was a county of remote heathland and woods, less valued for farming than many areas, and, in consequence, one of the least populated of the home counties. The advent of the suburban railways, particularly in the Thames valley and to the south of London, allowed the relatively wealthy to choose the option of living in the country and commuting to the town. The term 'commuting' is derived from the commuted rate at which railway tickets for regular journeys were issued at this time. It was around the major conurbations that commuting developed in the late nineteenth century and early twentieth century, as an increasing number of people forsook the city and sought the peace and quiet of the traditional countryside, which could still be found within relatively easy travelling distance from central London. Such villages as Harrow and Pinner, still largely farming communities, were engulfed in the outward spread of the suburbs which followed the development of the suburban railway network. The period after the Second World War saw the development of the garden suburbs and an accelerating increase in commuting from those villages within easy reach of the metropolitan centres. Although, at this time, commuting was an option which was necessarily confined to the higher- or middle-income earners, the cost of travelling was still significantly less than the advantages to be gained by lower housing costs, rates and the general lower cost of living in rural areas.

While, in the first period, most commuters lived relatively close to a railway station, in the post-war period, with the more widespread availability of private cars, there was a surge of speculative building in villages at a greater distance from the urban centres. A major government initiative in the 1970s to decentralize industry and administration from the centre of London had a marked effect on villages in the hinterland of such towns as Swindon, Sheffield, Darlington and Workington.

Throughout the 1970s and 1980s, the number of commuters into London steadily fell by approximately 1 per cent per annum. Furthermore, high city rents and rates, the cost, discomfort and unreliability of suburban travel were factors which caused even more companies to relocate, especially in those areas where government incentives were available. In the twenty years before 1971, the rural population of England and Wales increased by 2.38 million. The greater part of this increase, both in that period and more recently, has been in the accessible rural areas such as the 'western corridor', bounded at its eastern end by the motorways (M4 and M3) and extending westwards to include Bracknell, Reading, Newbury and Swindon and eventually reaching the Bristol Channel.

In East Anglia, the packed carpark at Audley End Station, forty-one miles from London, which serves Saffron Walden and the surrounding country villages, proclaims that it is a typical commuter's railway station; trains take an hour to Liverpool Street (although electrification work will soon reduce that time). The one-hour isochrome (which estate agents call 'the golden circle') is regarded as the maximum desirable commuting distance for a regular daily journey. A recent programme of railway electrification has brought Oxford, Winchester, Brighton, Fareham, Colchester and Cambridge within this area. Such a journey would cost approximately £1,000 in fares (1984) though some of this can be offset against savings in rates. For some time, estate agents have been able to calculate the effect that improved communications links will have on house prices. The recently announced commencement of the Oxford to Birmingham M40 motorway link is already effecting house prices in south Warwickshire and north Oxfordshire.

In the literature of rural social change much has been written about the effects of commuting on villages; predominantly it has been assumed that commuters have destroyed village life, by forcing out the old village community and transforming the life of the village so that it resembles a discontinuous suburb. Certainly, the advent of such a large new population has changed many villages, but it would be more accurate to say that commuting has accelerated patterns of change which were already well established. In the years immediately after the Second World War, when many villages were still relatively unchanged, the arrival of a new, relatively affluent and articulate group did much to improve village life, for they demanded improved facilities and services, and invigorated and enlivened many aspects of village life. However, commuters see the village essentially as a place of residence (even a place of relatively temporary residence) and their effect on the village depends in large part on their numbers and the way in which they are accommodated within the village. If this has been done by a process of gradual infilling, with the addition of a few new houses each year, then there is the likelihood that these families will be relatively easily assimilated. Most villages like some development, for this is a sign of life and a hope for the future. If, by contrast, a new housing estate is placed on the edge of the village, doubling or trebling the population overnight, with all the new villagers moving in at the same time, then there is the likelihood that the new villagers will not be easily assimilated into the old village. It is probable that there will be little contact between the two and this division may well be formalized by the formation of a residents association for the estate, in opposition to the parish council. Both the physical structure of a village, and the rate at which new people come in, have a marked effect on social relations.

As has been mentioned, new villagers tend to have strong views, not only about farming and farmers, but also about what they like and dislike about the village. Characteristically, the new villagers are active and articulate in preserving and defending the village against changes which they regard as being at variance with their understanding of what the village should be like, and they know how to influence the public decision-making processes. A village which could boast only three graduates in the post-war period, may now have a significant number of company directors, barristers and chartered accountants, as well as retired diplomats and Services personnel. New villagers tend to see the village as a place of residence, retirement and recreational pursuits, not as a place of work. They tend to resist further development of any sort, frequently stating that the village has now grown to its optimum size; this tendency 'to pull the drawbridge up' after their arrival is noted by many commentators. But, at the same time, new villagers will expect the village to have amenities and services, including street lighting, litter bins and footpaths, and they will be active in lobbying for these and other improvements. However, their arrival may of itself have a detrimental effect on some services which are used predominantly by the old village community. The commuters, by virtue of car ownership (and in many cases second car ownership), the deep freeze, bulk purchase at the cash and carry, and in many cases private schools, do not create the demand which will support local transport, educational and retail services. It is often not realized by those who regret the disappearance of such services that, while a village might increase in size it does not necessarily follow that there will be a proportionate increase in the demand for these services. The new villagers see the countryside as a place of 'non-work'. They are particularly anxious that industrial and commercial developments should not take place in their village, which they believe should have an essentially residential character. New villagers find it difficult to understand that at certain times of year, field work has to continue into the late evening and tractors will be going up and down the village street throughout the weekend. New villagers are often particularly vigilant in monitoring local planning applications; in 1980 the new residents of a Midlands village successfully resisted planning application for a blacksmith's forge, on the basis that it would be detrimental to the essentially residential nature of the village.

Unlike the old village families and the farming community, the majority of whose lives are centred on the village, many commuting families actually spend very little time in the village and are often referred to by their neighbours as 'bed and breakfast residents'. Their lifestyles are dominated by journeys out of the village, to schools or to meet school buses, to work, or to the local station to collect their husbands from the train, to shop or to go to other centres for recreational pursuits. Many people never leave their homes unless they do so by car and old villagers often comment that they only get to know new villagers through a car windscreen. A recent survey has shown that some wives with children at different schools and a husband to take and collect from the station, can travel over 100 miles a day and a significant number travel over fifty miles a day.

With many families dependent on two wage earners, free time is limited to the weekends and such people tend to be part of the home-oriented culture which is a feature of the commuter's lifestyle. For them the enhancement of their homes and gardens is of particular importance and many villages have been transformed and old cottages rescued from the later stages of decay by the new villagers. One of the paradoxes of contemporary living is that while electronics and modern machinery have tended to de-skill people at their place of work, many people have learnt new skills in their domestic and leisure life particularly in gardening and home maintenance. It follows that this home-oriented lifestyle does not necessarily predispose commuters to become involved in the affairs of the local community. Furthermore, many commuters do not stay for any length of time in a village; their company moves them on, and commuter estates tend to be comprised of fellow residents in transit whom the old villagers regard in some respects with the caution and suspicion they once reserved for gipsies. It is noticeable that, in every age, the settled population has had a natural unease and fear concerning the nomads in their midst.

Some commuters seek to become involved in and to be part of the village to which they have moved, by joining in village activities and organizations. However, many find the local community difficult to get to know, clannish and distinctly unlike the warm, accepting community portrayed in rural 'soap operas'. Such newcomers often feel that it is necessary to be a part of the village for several generations before they are accepted. But all this is an indirect result of the different perceptions of what the village is and how it functions which are found among the new and old village communities. In fact, the old villagers find it difficult to relate to the newcomers, not least for fear that their village and its life will be taken over by their new, more affluent and articulate neighbours. The old villagers can appear to retreat into a hidden village life which is hardly visible to newcomers and from which the latter feel almost totally excluded. While the newcomers may take over the specialist activities such as the cricket club and the drama club, and may form a judo club in the village hall or seek to convert a nearby barn into a squash court, the old villagers tend to retain a hold over such organizations as the parish council.

The old villagers are the possessors of the village history and frequently they can be subtle in their use of it to mystify and, at times, even to outmanoeuvre those who have arrived in the village more recently. Also, members of the old village community are sensitive to the dangers and difficulties of certain leadership roles and are quick to support the election of newcomers as chairman or organizer of any enterprise about which they have reason to be doubtful. However, above all, there is a tendency among the old villagers to blame the newcomers and to make them the scapegoats for the cycle of decline in the life of the village. Those who come from outside are made to feel representatives of the hostile outside world and responsible for the remote public decisions, which, in recent years, have adversely affected many dimensions of village life. In many villages, new and old villagers relate well and benefit from the pooling of different insights and experiences. Particularly in the smaller villages, the interaction between the two communities can be beneficial and helpful to both; each respecting and acknowledging the contribution the other makes to the village. However, in other villages, particularly those where the commuters are in a position of numerical dominance, the old village community can easily feel that they have become strangers in their own village.

Finally, it may be noted that among some of the unhappiest newcomers are those young wives whose husbands take the one car to the station or to work; the young wife is left with small children, 'trapped' in a house on a new development on the edge of the village, aware that there is a community life to which she does not relate. The husband appreciates his rural home as a place of rest and recuperation at the weekends, but his wife can often feel isolated and alone. Sadly, depression, agoraphobia and alcoholism are the symptoms of this isolation. The playgroup, which meets in the village hall, has a most important role in helping young wives who find that the realities of village life, for the commuting family, are significantly different from their expectations.

If commuters are the typical new residents in urban shadow villages, then, among those who move to the more accessible villages, retired people predominate. Clearly, these two groups are not mutually distinct, and a number of people anticipate retirement by a few years and purchase a house in the country from which they commute for the last few years of their working lives (the 'three-day commuters'). It is widely acknowledged that the twentieth century has seen a change in the population structure, with the addition of a new generation frequently known as 'the fourth generation'. The old person portrayed in a Victorian novel or painting was likely to be someone in his or her late sixties or early seventies; today, such a person would be more likely to be the provider of voluntary services, rather than a recipient. While it is particularly difficult to generalize in this matter, it is possible to distinguish in the contemporary countryside between the active and recently retired (those aged between sixty and seventy-five) and the elderly retired (those aged over seventy-five). In 1901 when the total population of the United Kingdom was 38.2 million, the elderly retired numbered 0.5 million and amounted to 1.31 per cent of the population. By 1931 those over the age of seventy-five numbered 2.17 per cent of the population; by 1951 they numbered 3.56 per cent; and in 1981 when the total population had risen to 55.9 million, the elderly retired had increased to 3.1 million and constituted 5.55 per cent of the population. It is estimated that the number of elderly retired will reach a peak in 1991, when they will constitute 6.32 per cent of the population.

Retirement migration is the most significant factor in the changing demographic patterns of English society. While the desire to retire in a rural area has existed for many years (and it has been argued by some sociologists that it is socially necessary for retired people to move away from homes close to urban work places and make room for younger families), it was only in the middle decades of this century that retirement migration became a major demographic phenomenon. This was caused in part by the fact that retired people, with better pensions and larger sums of money saved during their working career, were able to afford to move to rural areas. No doubt the motorways and the wider availability of private transport also played an important part in opening up certain parts of the countryside for retirement migration. Between 1961 and 1971 the overall increase of persons over retirement age was 16 per cent; in rural areas the increase was 24 per cent. In certain counties, the percentage of persons over retirement age was particularly high: Devon 25 per cent; East Sussex 24 per cent and Dorset 22 per cent. Between 1971 and 1991 it is estimated that there will have been a national increase of 38 per cent in the number of persons aged over seventy-five. However, in Warwickshire it is suggested that the increase will be 57 per cent. These figures do not give any indication of the very localized nature of retirement migration. Such areas as the south west, the Cotswolds, south Dorset, north Norfolk and parts of the Lake District have become principal retirement areas.

It was once said by a retired bishop that when one had one foot in the grave, it was as well to have the other on a bus stop. Many retired people imagine that services and facilities are more readily available in rural areas than is the case. In the mid 1970s relatively inexpensive retirement bungalows were built in a number of areas (such as west and north Norfolk). While these homes were attractive to those who had visited the area in the summer and the remoteness was part of the attraction, those who purchased such homes for retirement soon discovered the reality of life in small settlements at some distance from the provision of services and facilities. In fact, many retired people now make a double move, moving first to a house with a garden and a view over the fields, for which they have saved during the latter part of their working lives. Possibly fifteen years later, when they become members of the elderly retired group, they find it necessary to make a second move into a flat or an old people's home in a neighbouring market town. It is noticeable that the number of complexes of small flats for the less active, elderly retired have been developed in such towns as Stratford-upon-Avon. Recently, figures from Cornwall indicated that in the three years prior to 1981, the number of private homes for elderly people had risen from forty to sixty; at that time twenty-five further applications had been registered and another thirty-seven inquiries were being processed. Local officials noted that in some areas premises that had recently been run as small hotels were now being run (it was suggested, more profitably) as old people's homes. Certainly, as has been noted in the previous chapter, in many rural areas large country houses have been converted to this use.

It is argued by some that it may soon be necessary to operate a policy, such as that in Newfoundland, where those who live outside certain designated areas do so in the knowledge that no services or facilities will be provided. Perhaps the point may be reached in the not too distant future, particularly in upland areas favoured for retirement, when local authorities may have to limit the area in which certain services can be made available. Certainly, the provision of domiciliary social services (particularly home helps) is increasingly difficult. It is suggested by some that the practice of limitation has already started to operate in an informal manner, and it is noted that there is a reluctance on the part of some doctors to place on their list those who live in very remote and inaccessible places.

There is a considerable debate about whether retired people are a burden or bring advantages to the areas in which they retire. For instance, it has been argued by the South West Economic Planning Council that retirement in Devon and Cornwall adds over £50 million to the economy of that region and that there is a sense in which retired people can be regarded as all-the-year-round holidaymakers, providing an additional source of local demand, similar in kind (and, in the case of the south west, similar in scale) to the tourist industry. By contrast, others argue that retired people have limited spending power and pose a considerable burden particularly on the medical and social services. Recent research has indicated that the vast majority of elderly people live and eventually die in their own homes and make no more than marginally extra demands on their doctor and social services. If the figures of Warwickshire may be taken as representative, only 7 per cent of the retired receive home help or 'meals on wheels'. At the same time, elderly people make relatively few demands on certain other services such as educational provision and the police force. However, the elderly retired do account for a significant proportion of the people who suffer from some form of handicap or disability. While the elderly retired (over seventy-five years) currently constitute only 5.55 per cent of the population, the elderly handicapped constitute 32.8 per cent of those severely or appreciably handicapped; (that is to say, that 15 per cent of those in the most senior age group are appreciably handicapped). An area which has a number of these people spread over a considerable distance may find it extremely costly to provide anything approaching adequate facilities and services. The problems of remoteness, isolation and high cost may be seen in their most acute form on islands. Alderney, for example, publishes a 'Guide for those considering settling in Alderney', in which it states: 'Persons in poor health, or of small means or advanced years would not find it a suitable place in which to retire.' It is clear that, to a degree, the same may be said for much of the remoter English countryside, but the problems of living in rural areas do not occur to those who have long dreamt of a retirement cottage far away from the disagreeable aspects of urban life.

Many retired people, who have little previous experience of living in the countryside, bring to rural areas a romantic and old-fashioned view of village life, coupled with a 'horse-drawn' attitude to farming. Frequently such people are shocked and alarmed when first they observe contemporary farming at close quarters and find that it bears little relation to the farming of their youth, fifty years ago. The estate agents' beguiling phraseology, ' . . . with pleasant southerly views over undulating farmland', gives no hint of the intensive nature of modern agriculture with large machines working day and night at certain times of the year. Recent research by farming organizations has indicated that retired people who have recently moved into the countryside are prominent in those groups which are most critical of modern agriculture. They also form a large part of the membership of conservation, preservation and wildlife organizations, and their views regarding what the village should look like, smell like and feel like to live in, bring them into conflict both with the farmers and the old village community. The retired, who have chosen to live in the countryside on account of its seclusion and peace are particularly watchful lest small industries should develop, either officially or unofficially, within the village. These they consider to be incompatible with a country village, which they imagine should have a residential and quiet nature.

Within the village itself, retired people vary from those totally absorbed in the 'home culture', and for whom the village is simply a place of residence, to those who throw themselves wholeheartedly into village activities. The active elderly are the group upon whom many voluntary organizations, including the church, largely depend for their most enthusiastic and committed members. Such people become involved in the various aspects of village life, including helping to run old people's clubs, 'meals on wheels', car rotas for visits to doctors and hospitals, prescription-collecting rotas, as well as the purely social, sporting and recreational aspects of village life.

At times, it appears that the old village community have a somewhat ambivalent attitude towards such enthusiasm. They appreciate what is being done for the village and are happy to benefit from it; on the other hand they may feel threatened as they see leadership roles, in many aspects of village life, taken over by enthusiastic, active retired people who come to the village not to gently fade away, but to be restored after an arduous working life. Many such people have held positions of responsibility and seniority, and are used to matters being conducted in a brisk and expeditious manner. At times, such people find the average village meeting slow, inconclusive and unproductive; they may be unaware of some of the subtle and partly hidden dynamics of such an occasion.

If commuters are the predominant new villagers in the urban shadow countryside and the retired predominate in the accessible countryside, then it is the occasional residents who form a significant part of the new village community in the less accessible countryside. Occasional residence takes a variety of forms which includes second-home ownership for weekend use; extended holiday residence; short-term summer holidays; and tourist visits. The urban population has always looked to the countryside for the provision of many of its primary needs, principally food, timber, building materials, fuel and water. Large numbers of rural people have always been employed providing these commodities to satisfy urban needs. Today the urban population, in addition to these requirements, looks to the countryside increasingly for recreational and tourist use. Occasional residents all regard the countryside essentially as a place of rest and recreation, where they can be restored and revitalized to face again the rigours and demands of an urban work life. Such people tend to see the countryside principally as landscape, as a backdrop to their leisure activities (or inactivities). If urban life is seen as essentially superficial, transitory, unnatural, and stressful; the countryside is seen as authentic, historic, stable and therapeutic. While urban life is regarded as energy depleting; country life is seen as restorative, and conducive to emotional and psychological stability.

Although second homes and occasional residence have a long history, it was the widespread availability of private cars in the post-war period, and the later development of the motorways, which precipitated the 'country cottage boom'. While for centuries the relatively affluent and aristocratic have possessed both town and country homes and have moved, according to the seasons, between the two, it was in the 1960s, in a period of growing personal affluence, that the opportunity to own a country cottage was extended to those of more modest means. In the initial period there were a significant number of houses and cottages surplus to the requirements of the local population which could be purchased at relatively cheap prices as second homes. In North Wales and Cornwall, former slate quarry and china clay workers' cottages were sold at very low prices as second homes, as were the cottages formerly used by farm workers in such areas as north Oxfordshire. Many of these were in the remoter settlements which were particularly favoured by the purchasers of second homes. While in the early period such cottages could be purchased for a few hundred pounds, it was not long before owners and estate agents realized the possibility of this new market. Today the sale of a three-bedroomed cottage in the Cotswolds can fetch from anything up to £70,000. Currently, a cottage in North Devon is being advertised for £30,000, though the estate agents add disarmingly, 'applicants are recommended not to attempt to examine the first-floor rooms since much of the roof has collapsed'. Cottages which have been 'modernized to a high standard' in exceptional cases can command three times this price, especially in the national parks. In most areas favoured by second home owners, surplus rural housing has long since been purchased and renovated, and attention has now turned to farmbuildings, no longer suitable for modern farming use, which are converted to second homes in those areas where the local authority is willing to allow this change of use.

A recent study has indicated that second home ownership in England and Wales has grown from 30,000 in 1950 to approximately 350,000 today. This figure suggests that only 2 per cent of householders (normally resident elsewhere) have second homes (including mobile homes and static, but not touring, caravans). This figure compares with 25 per cent in France, and figures in excess of 40 per cent in most Scandinavian countries. A part of the explanation for this lies in the fact that the early depopulation of the British countryside reduced the supply of suitable cottages and the significance of the greater proportion of flat dwellers in most European and Scandinavian countries. However, statistics of second home ownership may be depressed by the popularity of touring caravans in this country and by the fact that second homes are not necessarily registered in the name of the first home owner. Nevertheless, second home ownership is thought to be growing at a rate of about 25,000 per year and second home ownership levels may reach 10 per cent by the end of this century. For many people, especially those who live in city flats or houses, the possession of a country retreat is particularly attractive. There is some evidence to suggest that among the relatively affluent, when their children leave home, there is a tendency to sell a medium-sized suburban house in favour of purchasing a smaller house or flat and also a second home in the country. Country cottages are particularly popular purchases by those who live in tied or service accommodation (though technically these are not second homes). It is suggested that there may be a significant expansion in the number of second homes in rural areas including purpose-built developments comparable to the many lakeside chalet developments to be found in Scandinavia, Canada and parts of Germany. The number of static caravans continues to grow, and the concentration of caravans in the Mablethorpe/Skegness area is the largest in western Europe.

Clearly, the effect of second home ownership on villages is largely determined by its scale. While in the 1960s occasional residents tended to be highly localized in particularly favoured areas, today some level of second home ownership can be found in almost all rural areas. Needless to say, in the most attractive parts of the countryside and in the resort areas and national parks levels of second home ownership are particularly high. In the mid 1970s 80 per cent of the total housing stock of Yarmouth (Isle of Wight) was already in second home ownership. In the Lake District, approximately a third of the housing in Patterdale, Langdale, Grasmere, Rydal and Loughrigg are owned by occasional residents. Some individual Lake District and north Devon settlements are now wholly owned by people who are not continuously resident throughout the year. In Wales, second home ownership has assumed a cultural and political dimension which it does not possess in England, and second home ownership is particularly high in North Wales; in the Lleyn Peninsula over 20 per cent of the houses are in second home ownership.

Within the village, occasional residents have always caused some resentment, as a result of competition for existing housing stock. In a situation where those from outside, with greater financial resources, are able to buy up the available housing, with the effect that children of local families, at the time of their marriage, have to seek housing elsewhere, conflict is inevitable. This was exacerbated following the 1969 Housing Act, when improvement grants were available for all houses, including second homes; this was widely resented in rural areas and second homes were excluded in 1973. In response to the growing government awareness of the effect of second home ownership in certain areas, further changes were made in the tax position but this has had no perceptible effect on the increasing desire of many to own a home in the country. Such purchasers frequently choose the most attractive old cottages, often to be found around the village green or at least in the centre of the village. The fact that these cottages are empty for much of the year can make the village feel lifeless and depressing. Furthermore, second home owners tend to make minimal demands on local facilities and services, and not infrequently arrive in their cottages having made all the necessary purchases for their stay. An increasing number of second homes in any area has the effect of accelerating the cycle of decline in rural services and may trigger the closure of such facilities as the local shop and the local transport link.

Frequently, second home owners come to the village solely to relax and to be restored; as a result few play any significant part in the life of the community. The attitude of the old villagers varies from the feeling of flattery that affluent and important people have chosen to come and spend time in their village, to a feeling that second home owners are parasitic on the life of the village and have prevented a local family from living in a cottage (which is empty for a substantial period of the year). What may appear from a superficial glance to be a prosperous and well-kept village from the outside, may be for most of the year a half-deserted collection of buildings, which has a particularly depressing and sad effect on the few elderly permanent residents in such villages.

Finally, account must be taken of those who use the countryside for recreational and holiday purposes but who are urban, rather than rural, residents. Their influence on the countryside is more profound than might at first be supposed, particularly through lobbying and the shaping of public policy to take account of the recreational use of the countryside. As has been seen in Chapter 2, it was only when England became a predominantly urban and industrial nation that such issues were first debated, but since then the debate about access to the countryside has been seen as political, concerned as it is with such issues as freedom, restriction and private rights. In a sense, the campaign for the preservation of common land in the 1860s which culminated in the declaration of Epping Forest by Queen Victoria, on 6 May 1882, as for 'the use and enjoyment for all my people for all times', marked the beginning of an era in which the countryside was seen increasingly as a place where urban people took their relaxation and leisure. Increased access, principally by means of the new railways in the 1870s and 1880s, led many to avail themselves of the opportunity of visiting rural areas. Ironically, it was the proposed intrusion of the railways which provided a number of well-known campaigns for the preservation of the countryside. It was the proposed Buttermere and Braithwaite line, designed to carry stone from Honiston down the side of Derwent Water, which led Canon Hardwicke Rownsley to campaign in 1882 to preserve the Lake District environment from the intrusion of the railway. This led to his recognition that there was a need for a national body to hold buildings and land for the benefit of the nation. He was one of the three founder members of the National Trust in 1895. Canon Rownsley made clear that the purpose of the Trust was to hold land and buildings of historic interest and natural beauty so that they could be used and enjoyed by the public. In 1902 he was instrumental in raising money to purchase land on the side of Derwent Water.

At the same time the 1890s saw the high point of the cycling boom (the Cyclists' Touring Club increased its membership by 46,283 in the five years 1894—9). In the next decade the pneumatic tyre gave the bicycle both a wider range and a greater degree of comfort, and cycling expeditions, in the two decades before the 1914—18 War, were an increasingly popular Sunday occupation. At the same time walking tours and hiking became a significant popular pastime organized by a variety of societies and clubs such as the Order of Sunday Tramps founded by Virginia Woolf's father Leslie Stephen. The Youth Hostel movement, founded in 1930, had its origins in a similar movement which started in Germany in 1914, a country particularly affected by the contemporary European vogue for romanticizing rural life. The popular inch-to-the-mile maps of the Ordnance Survey, dating from the 1930s, with their cover picture of a resting cyclist wearing a floppy hat, Norfolk jacket and knee breeches and sitting on a hillside while contemplating the map and admiring the distant view in a detached way, captures this new attitude towards the countryside as a place of recreation. Since the nineteenth century, the conflicts of interest between ramblers and farmers have been marked by such events as the first proposed legislation to allow free access to upland areas in 1894; Canon Rownsley's march of 2,000 people along a disputed road at Latrigg in 1886; and the famous Kinder Scout trespass in 1932. Increasingly, urban people felt the need to be in the countryside and to enjoy free access to rural areas. In 1946 E. M. Joad published a book entitled *The Untutored Townsman's Invasion of the Countryside,* which among other things was an eloquent plea for more extensive footpaths. Following the reports by Dower in 1945 and Hobhouse in 1947, the National Parks and Access to the Countryside Act of 1949 brought into existence the National Parks and required county councils to draw up definitive maps of footpaths. The National Parks (now ten in number) represent the most extreme manifestation of the increasing influence of urban understanding about the nature of the countryside in rural areas.

Today, the growth of the desire to visit or to stay in the countryside is reflected in the membership figures of many of the country-based organizations. For instance, visitors to National Trust properties have increased from 1 million in 1960 to over 7 million in 1983. The membership of the Royal Society for the Protection of Birds has increased from 6,803 in 1952 to 385,364 in 1984; the membership of the Caravan Club has increased from 84,000 in 1970 to 250,000 in 1984; and overnight stays in Youth Hostels have increased from 1,487,010 in 1971 to 7,793,974 in 1984. In 1977 the Countryside Commission indicated that some 82 million day visits were made to rural areas and 54 per cent of the population of England and Wales made at least one journey each month, but the majority rarely went for more than 200 yards from their cars. In the tourist season over 2,000 people a day make the pilgrimage to the tiny six-bedroomed farmhouse in Cumbria where Beatrix Potter lived, and the degree of wear and tear on many of the footpaths in such places as Malham Tarn have become a matter of serious concern.

At the same time an increasing number of people participate in some form of country-based recreational activity, of which walking is the most popular. Farm holidays, as has been mentioned above, are of growing significance and some farms have developed farm walks, farm shops and a variety of other activities. At the same time tourism and rural holidays have created employment in service and craft industries in a number of rural areas. Other recreational activities including field sports, water sports and riding also create employment. The number of horses in Britain has doubled since the late 1950s and over 2 million people ride on a regular basis. In the urban shadow countryside this now constitutes a significant problem and 'horsyculture' has a considerable impact on land use patterns, with 20,000 acres of Surrey alone given over to this use and 10 per cent of all land in the Green Belt areas. Horses, many of which are kept in riding schools or livery stables, provide some rural employment, and one county agricultural college runs an extensive series of courses for those employed in this part of the rural leisure industry.

The effect on some villages of the transformation of parts of the English countryside into premier holiday areas has been considerable. Certainly, in the remoter areas where rural industries such as quarrying, farming and forestry are no longer major employers, the housing stock would have fallen into further decay had not second home owners purchased and repaired many cottages. The new occasional residents have brought with them much greater financial resources and have restored the fabric of many buildings in isolated and remote communities. But, at the same time, the new population has come in such numbers to certain areas that they have threatened to destroy much of what they came to enjoy. As a consequence, peace and seclusion in the English countryside have become increasingly expensive and people now have to travel to even more remote areas to be sure of finding that degree of remoteness and isolation which they are seeking. However, it has been the effect of this new element in the population on the community life of many villages which has been most marked. One village in Dorset, with a population of under 400 now boasts three antique shops, a luxury hotel and an international award winning restaurant. Such a village is clearly very different today from the occupational community of only a relatively few years ago. It is possible to tell a great deal about a settlement by looking at its shops; Stow-on-the-Wold has twenty-six antique shops, and the antiques industry, almost entirely oriented towards visitors, is now a significant feature of many rural areas. Clearly, such changes have transformed the most popular tourist areas, but the average village is not so radically affected by the sale of one or two houses to second home owners. However, while they may make a marginal contribution to the local economy, they may contribute little to the life of the community. The townsman when he visits and occasionally resides in the countryside is concerned principally with what the countryside looks like, while many of the old village community are surprisingly nonchalant about the physical environment of the village, but much more concerned as to what a village feels like to live in.

The previous three chapters have attempted to delineate the changing social profile of the contemporary village and to identify the various groups which form the population of a typical modern village. Those involved in any aspect of village life, and particularly in local government or the representative bodies of the countryside, know that there is a measure of conflict between these various interest groups, as each tries to make the countryside and the village conform to its dominant understanding. Farmers see the countryside as the shopfloor of Britain's largest industry; the old village community see the countryside as their home, a place where they need the facilities and services to sustain an acceptable lifestyle; the commuters and the retired see the countryside as a place of residence, retirement and relaxation; and, finally, the second home owners and the occasional residents see the countryside predominantly as a refuge, a place of recreation and rest away from the pressures and stresses of modern urban living.

Clearly, such views of the contemporary countryside are not compatible and much of what happens in the modern village is the result of the interaction between the different understandings. Behind all the more pressing and acute problems concerning employment, settlement patterns, transport, land use, housing, education, social and welfare provision, changing agricultural practices, conservation, landscape and heritage protection and the future of the village as a community, lie these different models and understandings of the village. This question is itself a part of a larger question concerning the role of the countryside and the rural community in a society which is now predominantly urban and metropolitan. It is evident from the above that the various groups have fundamentally different understandings and mutually exclusive conceptions and models of what the village should be like. Much of what happens in village life today is a result of the interaction between these groups, and their relative strength in particular parts of the countryside will determine the outcome of this interaction. In a country which has no government ministry directly responsible for co-ordinating rural affairs and no coherent policy for the countryside, there is a tendency for the loudest voices to prevail.

Perhaps the most fundamental distinction in the contemporary countryside surrounds the attitudes of the various elements of the social profile towards the place of work. It can be seen from the above that the farming community and the old village community see the countryside as a place of work; a place where people live their whole lives, including their family and work lives. On the other hand, the commuters, the retired and the occasional residents see the countryside predominantly as a place of residence, retirement and recreation, and regard it essentially as a place of 'non-work'. This has profound implications for the countryside. But although this division ramifies into every aspect of village life, it should not be concluded that the average village is in a state of constant conflict. In the majority of villages new and old residents relate to one another well, and are happy to work together for the good of the community or at least to coexist without major difficulties. However, it is useful for those who work in the countryside to have some understanding of the changes which have taken place in the social profile and the dynamics of the contemporary village, for this forms the context of all activity in the countryside and particularly that of the churches.

The Parish Church in the
Distant Past

The history of the development of the village and its parish church is by its nature specific rather than general, for the history of no two villages is the same. In attempting to trace the development of the country parish church it is inevitable that the author will have in the front of his mind the churches which he serves in south Warwickshire. While no church could claim to be typical, these three churches in the Stour valley, south of Stratford-upon-Avon, bear witness to the individual religious, social and economic changes which have left their mark on the parish church in every generation.

St Mary's Whitchurch stands isolated by the river in the middle of a 'lost village'; it contains some pre-Conquest stonework; the tomb of a priest buried in 1442 upon which is incised a cross, chalice and Bible; glass, reputedly from Evesham Abbey; a Jacobean pulpit; and a magnificent Norman doorway. By contrast, St Mary's Preston-on-Stour, a parish first owned by Deerhurst and then Tewkesbury Abbey, bears all the marks of being in an estate village. The church was substantially altered by James West between 1752 and 1764, and the work was done by Edward Woodward of Chipping Campden: he rebuilt the chancel and restored the tower for under £2,000. The chancel contains a remarkable collection of thirty-five stained-glass medallions, the product of the Grand Tour, and the family memorials of the West family. All three parishes have a population of only 300, and the third parish, St Mary's Atherstone-on-Stour, has never been more than a small hamlet. Its medieval church was demolished and a new church, built for approximately £5,000, was opened by the Bishop of Gloucester on 23 May 1876. The church was poorly built with inferior materials and it is now unfit for use.

In many villages the parish church is not only the architectural focus but also the oldest building. It is a potent symbol of the village's identity and the former generations of the village are buried in the churchyard around its walls, or beneath its floor. Any visitor to the village is likely to be taken to the church, for nothing symbolizes more powerfully the history and continuity of the community. The church provides a continuous link with the earliest days of the village's settlement and it is part of its contemporary role to be a guardian of the village's history and a remembrancer of its past. It is said that a people without a past are like a man who has lost his memory and become bewildered, impoverished and lost. The church is for many people in the village one of the principal means by which they keep in touch with the past. It provides villagers both with a physical reminder of the continuity of the generations and also with occasions in the year when the past can be remembered and the interelatedness of the past, the present and the future can be felt and understood.

So dominant has been the tendency to write the history of the Church as if it were the history of the upper echelons of the institution, the bishops, cathedral dignitaries and Oxford dons, that there are few published works on the development of the country church, and such as there are tend to be anecdotal rather than analytical. The Church is an enigmatic institution and no account of its contemporary role or significance can be complete without extensive reference to its history. This is particularly the case in the village, where the church is so intimately bound up with the history and development of the community as a whole.

In the mid seventeenth century, road conditions were still so bad that it may have taken several days for the villagers in south Warwickshire to hear that on 29 May 1660, Charles II had reached London amidst universal acclamation. The restoration of the monarchy marked the end of the Church of England's formative period and the beginning of what may be regarded as the modern history of the parish church. The long shadows of the Civil War and the King's execution provoked a determination to build on the foundations that Elizabeth I had laid, and, with the Act of Uniformity of 19 May 1661, and the edition of the Book of Common Prayer the following year, the Church of England was firmly re-established. These events gave the inhabitants of Whitchurch sufficient confidence to rebuild their church, which had been largely destroyed as a result of a gale in 1649 — an event which many may have seen as a judgement of the times. The steeple and the roof were completely destroyed, and the new roof and bellcot bear the date 1666. At that time the Bishop of Worcester gave permission for the ruins of the old steeple to be removed, the bells sold and a new west wall to be built. However, when these repairs were undertaken, Christianity in England was already nearly a thousand years old and much of the shape of local church life had already been determined.

The term 'parish' was unknown in pre-Conquest England and does not occur in the Domesday Book, where the word 'manor' was commonly employed. In the sense in which the historian Bede used the term 'parish', it denoted the sphere of authority of a bishop; the term 'diocese' (which is derived from the secular nomenclature of the Roman Empire) came later. While the Celtic missionaries, who were essentially itinerant preachers, worked from monastic settlements in the northern and western parts of the country, the mission of Augustine landed in Kent in AD 597. By the mid seventh century the kingdom of Kent had been parcelled out into parishes by Archbishop Honorius but it was Archbishop Theodore who is usually credited with the creation of the parochial system. He encouraged Saxon landowners to erect churches on their estates and granted the right of perpetual patronage. In other areas, away from the more populated south east, minsters were established (as at Sturminster, Wimborne Minster, Kidderminster, Minsterley and Minster Lovell). In the surrounding villages stone crosses marked the assembly point for religious services, which were held in the open. But, certainly by the end of the eighth century, local landowners were being encouraged to erect churches in place of, or alongside, the old stone crosses. The status of the priest, who officiated in the church, was that of a private chaplain to the landowner; he was not infrequently one of the landowner's servants who had been sent to the bishop for instruction and ordination. Priests were in short supply and the rights and interests of the established minsters in some areas stood in the way of that village-based ministry which Bede was among the first to call for, as early as the first decade of the eighth century. The local priest, in addition to his glebe (which literally means soil or 'clod of earth'), also received a range of dues payable at appropriate times and festivals. At first it appears that the tithe was a voluntary gift by the faithful, but the Church sought to have this regarded as an enforceable tax, though this was not achieved until the tenth century.

The earliest stone towers were not built in the Midlands but in the areas adjacent to the east coast, and were erected during the Scandinavian invasions. Originally there were forty-one in Suffolk and 129 in Norfolk; all had high doorways that had to be reached by ladders which could be withdrawn in times of danger. As has been shown in Chapter 3, the early development of the village was brought to an abrupt halt by these invasions which started in the eighth century. In the first period the raids were principally for plunder and the monastic houses and the minsters were plundered, many beyond hope of recovery. Crowland Abbey, founded in AD 716, was sacked by the Danes and its abbot, Theodore, was killed before the altar, praying for his assailants. By the ninth century, raiding and plunder had given way to conquest and occupation, as one after another of the ancient kingdoms succumbed. In 870, only Wessex remained, where Alfred fought for eight more years until the Battle of Edington, after which Guthrum, the Danish leader, was baptized at Aller near Athelney in 878, and a treaty divided England in two. Alfred, who saw this invasion as a visitation of God's judgement, set about re-establishing the Church. He saw the Church as an important instrument of national and cultural unity, and much in English religious life owes its distant origins to Alfred. By the time of his death in 899, the Danish invaders had begun to be absorbed into the life of the English countryside and the Church had rapidly recovered its position. Five new dioceses were created and, later, bishops were appointed for Cornwall and East Anglia.

On the eve of the Norman conquest, when the first stone church was built at Whitchurch, many of the parochial clergy would have been local men, who, it may be assumed, were similar in many ways to other members of the village. At that time the clergy were married, though already this was looked upon with disapproval by reformers seeking higher standards. The parish churches were mostly of wood (of which one survives at Greenstead, in Essex). The church itself was the property of the Saxon thegn and was both essential to his status and part of his capital worth; the village church could not exist outside seigneurial jurisdiction. Not only did the builder of the church, and his heirs, retain the right to appoint the priest, but they also acquired an interest in the tithe and offerings.

Anglo-Saxon England failed for lack of strong leadership, and William, Duke of Normandy, himself the descendant of Norwegian Vikings, marched into the resultant political vacuum. In order to precipitate the surrender of London, William devastated large areas of the countryside and in a relatively short time the Norman takeover was effected. Such resistance as there was, particularly that of Hereward the Wake in the Fens, was shortlived, as the Normans consolidated their hold on England as a Norman colony. In a relatively short time the old Saxon Church and culture disappeared; the senior clergy, with two exceptions, were replaced; the English language went underground; and Norman styles in art and architecture predominated. At Whitchurch, the Saxon landowner Alwin was deposed by William in favour of Robert Beaumont, who was a commander of the legion in the invasion of England and was knighted on 14 October 1066. He eventually became Baron of the Exchequer of Normandy; Chief Minister to William II in 1090; Privy Councillor in 1100; and Commander of the Second Division in Henry I's army at the Battle of Tenchebrai in 1106, having been created Earl of Leicester in 1104. This longlived nobleman rebuilt the church at Whitchurch which was for a long time of classic Norman proportions.

From the Domesday survey it is not possible to estimate with any accuracy the number of parish churches in the countryside as a whole. The number of churches actually mentioned in the survey is less than 2,000, of which half are in the counties of Norfolk, Suffolk and Lincolnshire. In some counties the only churches named are those liable to pay dues to the Crown, and in two counties (Cornwall and Middlesex) no churches are mentioned at all. However, the record is sufficient to allow it to be seen that in many areas, particularly in Suffolk where over half the villages had their own church, the notion of a parish church and a resident priest (*ibi ecclesia et presbyter*) had become part of the fabric of the English countryside.

In the early medieval period three processes of change can be identified: first, the continuing development of the parochial system as new rural settlements became parishes in their own right. There was once a small chapel of ease, in the parish of Whitchurch, at Crimscote, which in all likelihood was built in this period. Perhaps not until the thirteenth century was this process complete and new churches, which were initially dependent chapels, were built at the expense of those who used them. They were not endowed with tithe, and the mother church retained rights over baptism, marriage and burial fees. At certain festivals the worshippers were expected to attend the mother church. As might be expected, the tendency was for these chapels to be made parish churches by bishop's licence. The period of church building reached its zenith between 1150 and 1250; large numbers of churches were built and almost every church received some addition or improvement. It has been calculated that in the small county of Rutland alone there were fifty churches at this time; that is, one church for every 250 people. The network of parishes now brought every member of the 2.5 million population into close relations with the church and the parish priest. More than 8,000 parishes were registered in a survey of 1291 and further evidence suggests that there were possibly as many as 1,500 more. Although some parishes, particularly in the north, were extensive, it is estimated that, on average, parishes contained approximately 300 people. It is possible that there were as many as 23,000 priests, assisted by 10,000 clerics in minor orders, serving in the parishes at this time.

Second, it was in this period that the clergy became an increasingly separate and independent group in English society. Gradually the Church became a great feudal power, and at the local level the parish priest was no longer the servant of the local landowner. At the national level the Church became increasingly independent from the state, symbolized by the Act of Benefit of Clergy (by which an accused man in orders could claim exemption in a lay court), which Thomas à Becket so firmly defended before his martyrdom in 1170. The first line of the Magna Carta (1215) read: *quod anglicana ecclesia libra sit* (that the Church of England may be free).

Third, the development of monasticism in twelfth- and thirteenth-century England lies outside the scope of this chapter, although it was in many ways a rural phenomenon. However, as its development accelerated in the twelfth century, it had a particularly deleterious effect on the parish churches. In the early period, the village clergyman was styled 'rector'; he was appointed by the landowner, instituted by the bishop and enjoyed his benefice as a freehold. As the monasteries developed, many landowners desired to give their churches (and the income associated with them) to a monastic house to ensure that prayers were said for themselves and their families. In this way, the monasteries were able to acquire considerable wealth from the rectorial income of the parishes. It was at this time that the parish of St Mary's Preston-on-Stour was appropriated by Tewkesbury Abbey. Eventually, approximately half the parishes were appropriated by the monastic foundations, who instituted vicars in the parishes. It is not uncommon in the countryside today to find that the market towns and large villages have vicarages while the small hamlets and villages have rectories, for the monasteries were given only the wealthier benefices.

On the eve of the dissolution of the monasteries, of the 622 parish churches in the county of York, 392 were the property of monastic or collegiate establishments. The Lateran Council of 1123 had forbidden monks to serve as parish priests and had encouraged the monasteries to present priests for those parishes which they controlled. The fourth Lateran Council of 1215 regularized the position regarding vicars and instructed all rectors (whether corporate or individual), who did not reside, to institute vicars, not as employees in receipt of a wage but as benefice priests with the freehold and specific endowments. The reforming Archbishop, Stephen Langton, whose appointment had led to a four-year period of excommunication when the churches were closed and Masses were not said, enacted at the Council of Oxford in 1222 a measure which required a vicar's income to be no less than 5 marks (£3.33). The survival of hundreds of documents bears eloquent witness to the endeavours of the diocesan bishops to safeguard the village churches and their vicars at this time. A further problem faced by the parish clergy was the sudden rise in power and importance of the friars. Not unnaturally, the local clergy resented the friars, who usurped their right to act as spiritual counsellors, to hear confessions, and to minister to their parishioners at death. Deep hostility developed between the secular parish clergy and the friars, not least because they represented a financial threat to the local church. This problem, which troubled all Europe, particularly the universities, was settled in 1300 by a Papal Bull, which brought into being the system of licences which in a changed form still exists.

Fourteenth-century rural England was increasingly polarized between the landless poor and vagrants, and wealthy farmers, landowners, wool merchants and staplers, as a result of changes in land use and the development of sheep farming. It seems that much of this new money was used to build not only country houses but also the magnificent parish churches of the period in the perpendicular gothic style, that essentially English style that originated at Westminster and was perfected after 1331 at Gloucester. The expression 'as sure as God is in Gloucestershire' was coined to account for the great multitude of churches, dating from this period, in that county. The new wealth and the piety of individual parishioners led to the rebuilding of large numbers of churches in this period. In the county of Norfolk there are 650 medieval parish churches; in Suffolk, 550. The largest churches are to be found in Norfolk, the richest county in England in the fourteenth and fifteenth centuries, and in those areas such as the Cotswolds which benefited most from the wool trade.

But in the late medieval period, as has been noted in Chapter 3, the villages suffered from disease, civil war and the debilitating effect of weak government and heavy taxation. After the splendours of the 'age of faith', the Church seemed to fall into a malaise. Certainly, the Black Death caused high mortality among the clergy who, in the course of their duty, were inevitably brought into contact with the dead and dying. Some authorities suggest that up to 60 per cent of the parish clergy perished. In the fourteenth and fifteenth centuries inflation, high taxation and oppressive legislation provoked a variety of outbursts of revolt. These were aided and abetted by village clergy and poor friars, such as John Bull, who were motivated, at least in part, by their hatred of the wealthy bishops, monks and church dignitaries. Although Protestant apologists have concentrated attention on the gross superstitions of the late medieval Church and their 'purification' in the post-Reformation period, the literature of the period provides many examples of idle absentee clergy and rich worldly monks which, although they may not be all individually true, point to a commonly accepted view of the Church. At another level, the relative income of the parish clergy was falling and the situation of many poorer parish clergy was certainly deteriorating at this time. It was the most conscientious of the parish clergy who died in the various outbreaks of disease and their place was often taken by men whose wives had died in the plague, of whom a significant number were reputed to be illiterate. By the early sixteenth century it was reckoned that an income of £16 would be necessary to meet the expenses of a parish clergyman, yet less than a quarter of the parishes in England provided an income of this size.

In the second and third decades of the sixteenth century, anti-clerical feeling in England had been transformed in scale, temper and conviction. Wolsey's reforming legislation of 1518 made little difference and even the subsequent legislation of 1529, aimed at curtailing clerical absenteeism, trading and farming and introducing higher standards for ordination, failed to improve the situation radically. Anti-clericalism paid a large part in the English Reformation. Certainly, the views of Zwingli and Luther were relatively unknown in England before the late 1520s, and while the Lollards had built up some following in such rural areas as Buckinghamshire, Oxfordshire, Essex and Kent, their numbers were small and, in the main, restricted to urban centres. However, their continuing attack on the wealth of the Church played on the feelings of many contemporaries, who, in the sixteenth century, had come to believe themselves to be particularly oppressed by the Church and to feel uncertainty about the jurisdiction of the ecclesiastical courts and resentment at the size of fees and tithes. All these factors played a significant if not a decisive role in bringing about the Reformation in England.

The breach with Rome in 1533—4 was principally a constitutional change which declared that the Bishop of Rome had no more jurisdiction in England than that of any other foreign bishop. But the temper of the times was more clearly shown in a bill of 1535 which opened with the words, 'For as much as manifest sin, vicious, carnal and abominable living is daily used and committed among the great and small abbeys, priories . . .' The Reformation made the King in Chancery (the Court of Delegates) the highest ecclesiastical court and, in a relatively short period of time, saw an enormous amount of wealth pass from the Church via the Crown to local landowners, who were the ultimate purchasers of the monastic estates. The continuity between the pre- and post-Reformation period is well illustrated at Preston-on-Stour where, in the late sixteenth century, Robert Wakeman, nephew of the last Abbot of Tewkesbury (who was made first Bishop of Gloucester), farmed much of the land. (The modest wealth of the Cromwell family came from church land which had belonged to the monks at Ely.) In all this upheaval, perhaps what is surprising is that there was so little revolt or protest during the period when 825 religious houses in England and Wales were suppressed. However, at the local level, many villages would have experienced merely a change from a religious to a secular landowner. It is recorded that at Evesham Abbey where the monastery was suppressed on 30 January 1540, the monks and choir were not allowed to complete the psalm they were singing at Evensong. It is reputed that the local people, after years of oppression from the monastery (as the major local landlord) tore down many of the buildings, grateful for a free supply of superior building materials. Many fixtures and fittings from monastic churches can now be found in parish churches and some of the glass from Evesham Abbey found its way to St Mary's Whitchurch

In 1534, the *Valor Ecclesiasticus,* a survey of the revenues of parish churches, had convinced many clergy that the wholesale appropriation of the clerical revenues of the parishes was now being contemplated by the Crown. While this did not happen in Henry VIII's reign, it contributed to the growing uncertainty, and from 1536 onwards there was a further decline in the number of ordinands: this contributed to the acute shortage of suitable clergy for the parochial ministry, which was one of the major problems the Church faced during the next 120 years. The old King remained loyal to the Catholic faith and there were few changes in the appearance of the liturgy during this time. However, chained Bibles made their appearance, and in 1537, Thomas Cromwell ordered that proper registers be kept of baptisms, weddings and burials. In this period it appears that many parishes economized and used the cheapest paper. A further Act of 1597 ordered that parchment be used and that entries going back to 1558 should be copied out.

On 28 January 1547 Edward VI came to the throne. Within a few months royal injunctions were published ordering that such images in the church as might lead to superstition be removed; the number of candles on the high altar were to be reduced to two; the ringing of bells during Mass was to cease, and a copy of the Book of Homilies and the paraphrases of Erasmus were to be placed in every parish church. It may be assumed that vast quantities of church furniture and ornaments were removed at this time in conformity with the new ordinance, and it is known that many churchwardens held sales of church furnishings which were no longer required. In 1549 Cranmer's new prayer book was ready and was imposed as a schedule to the Act of Uniformity. From then on all clergy were obliged to use the new book on pain of imprisonment. In a relatively short period, the old religion had become proscribed; the practice of generations and the devotions associated with them were supplanted. It is hard to imagine that the suddenness and the ruthlessness of these changes did not affront the consciences of many people. Certainly, 'the German doctrine' as Protestantism was called, remained virtually unknown to the conservative people in rural areas, and even in the towns and the more sophisticated south east, passionate Protestants often complained that they were treated as madmen. It is hard to imagine that the suppression of much medieval spirituality and particularly the vast cult of prayers for the dead, which had worked its way deep into the hearts of many country people, was not deeply offensive to many. Some commentators have suggested that its suppression has had a permanent effect on popular religion in rural areas.

Under the presidency of the Duke of Northumberland, the Privy Council decreed on 3 March 1551 that the treasures that had been amassed in the parish churches should be confiscated. Commissioners were despatched to ensure that these temptations to superstition which the churches had amassed over the centuries were sent to London for sale by the government. However, enterprising churchwardens in many cases had secreted these treasures or sold them off. Within four years almost all parish churches in England had been stripped of all that was worth stealing, and although the commissioners sought to make churches respond as quickly as possible, there can be little doubt that many rural churches kept to the old ways for as long as they could escape detection, particularly in Lancashire, home of the

Pilgrimage of Grace, and in Cornwall where the only rebellion against the 1549 Prayer Book took place. At the same time, legislation allowed priests to marry and Cranmer, among others, took advantage of this permission. Steadily the pace of change quickened and on 1 November 1552 another prayer book appeared and legislation was enacted which threatened lay people absent from church with imprisonment (the third offence carried imprisonment for life). Bishops such as John Hooper set out on energetic tours of inspection of their parishes to insist on the new Protestant worship, to inquire into the morals of the laity, and to test the clergy on their knowledge of the Bible and the New Testament. Shortly after becoming Bishop of Gloucester in 1550, Hooper examined some 300 clergy in his diocese and to his dismay discovered that 168 could not repeat the Ten Commandments; thirty-nine did not know that the Lord's Prayer appeared in the Bible; and thirty-four could not say who was its author. There is no record of how the incumbent of St Mary's Atherstone-on-Stour (then in the Gloucester diocese) fared in this examination. It has been estimated that in the course of Edward VI's reign, crown land with a capital value (calculated as equivalent to twenty years rent) exceeding £400,000 was granted away, mostly to members of the council or senior government officials. The land yielded more than £320,000 when sold by the Crown, and almost all of it (about 1,000 manors) had come from the suppression of monasteries or endowed chantries.

Mary's accession to the throne on 19 July 1553 brought a reversion to Catholicism and saw churchwardens hastily attempting to buy back furnishings and fittings which had only recently been sold, or restoring to the church those that were in their own possession. Mary succeeded in returning English religious life to the state it had been in during her father's reign. No doubt many in the villages welcomed the return to the old religion, which had been so suddenly overturned. It is hard to believe that Edward VI's commissioners were wholly successful in suppressing the cult of prayers for the dead, which formed such a large part of late medieval spirituality, and many must have been pleased to return to old and familiar patterns. On the grounds that they were married, 800 clergy were deprived of their livings, as were seven bishops. During Mary's reign 300 English men and women were executed as

Protestants, and though outwardly the counter-Reformation quickly succeeded in restoring the Church to its earlier period, in numerous other ways it was a total failure, for many people instinctively recoiled from the accompanying brutality and tyranny.

It is well known that Elizabeth I kept her religious views to herself — a fact that may have played a part in establishing English reserve in these matters — but her preferences were displayed in the appointment of Matthew Parker as Archbishop of Canterbury, a man of moderate reforming views who had taken advantage of the permission to marry given in Edward's reign. Though monarchs changed, Parker remained very much his own man, capable of both compliance and opposition, and he spoke out against further expropriation of church property. Much of the ethos and the shape of the Church of England is owed to his energy, tact and moderation. In January 1559 the second Prayer Book was reintroduced with some important additions and alterations. In a Church where so much had changed in the previous twenty years, it is hard to imagine that there was not much disobedience, but only 200 clergy, mainly in the north and west, were removed from their parishes by the Elizabethan commissioners despatched to enforce the new laws. The chronic problem of the parish churches during Elizabeth's reign, which had been building up since the middle of the fourteenth century, was that of the shortage of suitable clergymen. In 1559 fewer than half the parishes in the diocese of Canterbury had a resident clergyman. The Church, like other sectors of society, had been severely affected by the influenza epidemic of the late 1550s, and the uncertainty of the times also served to depress the number of ordinands. At the same time, whereas in the pre-Reformation Church the quality of the individual priest had mattered less in the final analysis than the due performance of his formal round of services in the church, in the Elizabethan Church, where greater emphasis was placed on the pastoral and preaching aspects of the clergyman's role, personal qualities mattered much more. What was now required was a literate, learned and articulate ministry.

The Henrician reforms had proved a financial catastrophe for the Church, and no serious thought was given to the problem of clergy incomes which had been further depressed in a period of inflation. In some measure the conservatism of the reformers is reflected in their preservation of the tithe and the profits from glebe land as the principal basis of the parish economy. Thus, the ministry was poorly rewarded; graduates remained in very short supply; and the prestige of the clergy was persistently low, particularly as other professions such as the law and the army now offered more promising alternatives to the able and ambitious. An experiment in the use of lay readers as 'lectors', on the Lutheran model, was instituted to supplement the diminished ranks of the clergy, so that the parishes without a priest could have Morning and Evening Prayer. The Anglican Church under Elizabeth I, as it was shaped by such as Hooker, was not without its tensions, but its middle-of-the-road conservatism and deliberate ambiguities suited all of a more gentle, moderate and hopeful temper. Slowly the beauty of the Book of Common Prayer began to find its way into people's hearts and command widespread loyalty. Of the thirty priests removed in Essex at the beginning of Elizabeth's reign, eighteen were granted their benefices again after agreeing to use this prayer book.

In Edward's reign, and that of his father, the country gentry had come into possession of much of the former ecclesiastical property, and even Mary's advisers knew that this situation could not be reversed. In Elizabeth's reign lay control over many aspects of church life was restored, and as the new arrangement settled down, there was a notable and natural tendency for the squire of the village to again become the patron of the living. Within the churches nothing short of a revolution had taken place, both in their appearance and in the form of worship. The church walls were whitewashed in order to obliterate the medieval paintings. The minister now occupied the desk at the top of the nave or just inside the chancel screen, facing the congregation, who could not only see him but could hear him speak to them in their own idiom and might join in what Archbishop Cranmer had especially designed as a biblical and congregational service. Cranmer had originally envisaged that the Holy Communion Service should be attended by a large number of communicants and form the central act of Sunday worship, to which Morning Prayer would be an introduction. This hope and expectation was defeated by the Englishman's conservative determination not to communicate more than a few times a year (as in pre-Reformation practice). On the walls of the church could be found inscriptions of the Ten Commandments, the Lord's Prayer and the Royal Coat of Arms, as at Preston-on-Stour and Whitchurch. Few new churches were built during this period, but many were re-ordered internally; pulpits appeared in increasing numbers and the old chantry chapels were converted into family pews. But in many parishes matters improved only slowly, and in the 1580s Archbishop Whitgift suggested that half the livings in England were worth less than £10 a year. In some areas there were almost no graduates, and the Archbishop thought that there were only 600 'learned' men in Holy Orders.

During Elizabeth's reign the Puritans had gained in numbers, and, as James I had come from Presbyterian Scotland, they imagined that he would be sympathetically disposed towards them. As he journeyed south, he was presented with a petition signed by 1,000 Puritan clergy seeking his support against certain practices in the Book of Common Prayer. The King referred the matter to the Hampton Court Conference in 1604 which seemed to favour the Puritan point of view, but eventually James, like Elizabeth, came to regard the Puritans, who were in fact his most loyal supporters, as intent on the ultimate destruction of the monarchy. But the Conference did commission the Authorised or King James version of the Bible, which was eventually published in 1611 and placed in every parish church. Neither the Bishops' Bible nor the Geneva Bible, both of which were widely used, were free from inaccuracies and the revision went far beyond the light revision of the Bishops' Bible which had been originally planned. However, sufficient of Tyndale and Coverdale's English survived to give the 1611 Bible a style which was already old-fashioned and majestic. The new Bible, like all new departures in church life, did not immediately recommend itself and it is known that Lancelot Andrewes and William Laud continued to use the Geneva Bible while preaching. However, the Authorised Bible was the only Bible printed in a suitable form for use in the parish church, and for that reason, if for no other, it soon supplanted the other two. Even the original hearers of this translation would not have recognized it as being in everyday language, and as Edwards comments: 'St Paul's theology as translated in the authorised version can never have been entirely and immediately plain to all churchgoers.' However, the Authorised version and the Prayer Book quickly became the two pillars on which the worship of the English country church was firmly settled.

During the reign of James I, few clergy failed to conform and only ninety out of 10,000 were deprived of their parish because of open refusal. Even of these, it appears that the majority were eventually reinstated. However, in the more remote areas many of the clergy received only meagre stipends and the practice of placing adjacent parishes together, in order to achieve a better living, was widely adopted. In the reign of Charles I, particularly under the influence of Archbishop Laud, greater ceremonial was encouraged in the parish churches and Holy Communion was received with greater frequency, customarily once a month. It was at this time that, in the lives of such as George Herbert, Nicholas Ferrar, Alice Thornton and Lancelot Andrewes, Anglicanism can be seen emerging from its formative period, not so much as an ecclesiastical compromise but as a way of life with its own character and ethos, characterized by reason, discipline and propriety embodied in a Church solidly based on Scripture and the Book of Common Prayer.

George Herbert was born in Montgomery Castle on 3 April 1593. He was descended on his father's side from the earls of Pembroke and on his mother's side from a Shropshire landed family. His mother, a woman of great devotion and serenity, and a friend of John Donne, watched carefully over his education as he made his way under the guidance of private tutors from Westminster School to Trinity College, Cambridge. In 1620 he was appointed Public Orator of the university, a position which brought him to the attention of King James and of Bishop Lancelot Andrewes. The position of Public Orator was an acknowledged stepping stone to a prominent career in public life, but in 1624 and 1625 he suffered, in quick succession, from the death of his three benefactors, the Duke of Richmond, the Marquis of Hamilton and the King himself, and from the serious onset of the tuberculosis from which he eventually died. The course of Herbert's life changed dramatically and he reaffirmed his early resolve to seek ordination. From John Donne's patron, Bishop Williams, he received the preferment of Prebend of Leighton Bromswold in Huntingdonshire, which he refused to accept simply as a sinecure, but, with the help of John and Nicholas Ferrar and financial contributions from Lord Pembroke, he set about restoring the church.

In 1630, after considerable hesitation, he accepted from Charles I the rectory of Fugglestone with Bemerton near Wilton, outside Salisbury. There, for a little over two years, this tall emaciated man of such lovable gentleness and dignity, lived the life of a country parish priest and created a pattern of virtue and good practice which has done much to shape the Anglican parochial ministry. 'Holy Mr Herbert' is no invention of Izaak Walton, writing thirty-seven years after his death, and without firsthand knowledge, but it was a contemporary estimate of his character. His brother, Lord Herbert of Cherbury, wrote: 'His life was most holy and exemplary, in so much that about Salisbury, where he lived . . . he was little less than sainted.' His book *A Priest to the Temple, or the Country Parson: His Character and Rule of Holy Life* was, as he wrote, 'a mark to aim at' and an accurate reflection of his own practice. It is remarkable for two features: first, for Herbert's insistence on the authority of the country clergyman. The book begins, 'A pastor is the deputy of Christ for the reducing of man to the obedience of God'. Elsewhere he writes: 'It hath been formally judged that the domestic servants of the King of Heaven should be of the noblest families on earth; and although the iniquities of late times hath made clergymen meanly valued, and the sacred name of the priest contemptible, yet I will labour to make it honourable by consecrating all my learning and all my abilities, to advance the glory of that God that gave them . . . And I will labour to be like my Saviour, by making humility lovely in the eyes of all men.' It was an authority grounded in a holiness which country people could understand, a holiness which was born of temperance, prayerfulness, humility, hospitality and courtesy. George Herbert remained very much a gentleman: at his death his household contained six servants and two curates, and he was chaplain to the Earl of Pembroke, whose remarkable second wife, Lady Anne Clifford, restored and rebuilt many churches in Cumberland and strengthened the Anglican cause during the period of the Commonwealth. That such a man should turn his back on a career at court after so distinguished a time at Cambridge, and should serve a country parish of 300 people, deeply impressed his contemporaries.

Second, as *A Priest to the Temple* bears eloquent witness, George Herbert called the clergy to higher standards of devotion and parochial practice. Izaak Walton, in his *Life,* devotes four pages to Herbert's detailed rationale of Morning and Evening Prayer, which he read daily 'at the canonical hours of ten and four'. He was joined by 'most of his parishioners and many gentlemen in the neighbourhood, while some of the meaner sort would let their plough rest, whenever Mr Herbert's saint's-bell rang to prayers'. He writes: 'The country parson is exceedingly exact in his life, being holy, just, prudent, temperate, bold, grave in all his ways.' Not only did he call the clergy to prayer, but also to visiting and to taking up the concerns of their parishioners both as their doctor and lawyer. Also he advised them to gain a knowledge of tillage and pasturage, and to make use of it in their teaching, 'because people, by what they understand, are best led to what they understand not'. In short, he made all the affairs of his parishioners 'his joy and thought'. Herbert's gift lay in his close touch with ordinary life; his was a saintliness of a practical and domestic nature, unlike the ascetic austerity of Nicholas Ferrar or the fashionable intellectualism of such as Lucius Cary, Viscount Falkland, around whom the 'Great Tew circle' formed. Apart from his poetry (sent from his deathbed to Nicholas Ferrar) he gave the clergy a model of parochial ministry, both in his life and in his writing, which was 'a mark to aim at' and which has had a profound influence on the Anglican parochial ministry in rural areas in all succeeding generations.

It is hard to imagine what were the effects of the Civil War on these three parishes in south Warwickshire. Certainly, it is almost possible to see Edgehill from some places in the village, and the route of Charles I's escape after the Battle of Evesham lies very close (and is the subject of numerous plays and projects in local village schools). The Civil War began in August 1642 and as the scene of war moved about the country, there was much devastation especially of churches and church property. Many churches bear the marks of axe or bullet, or record that Cromwell stabled his horses there. Certainly, the Cromwellian troops thought themselves to be fighting against the Church and made the churches and their ornaments a natural object of destruction. Many works of art which had escaped the attention of earlier generations, or had been placed in the churches during the Laudian period, were now destroyed. Hammerbeam roofs were peppered with Cromwellian shot, the more accessible statues were mutilated or decapitated, stained glass was smashed, books were torn up and vestments cut to pieces. The scars of this period can be found in both Whitchurch and Preston-on-Stour; in the latter church the only figure that remains is the inaccessible head of Mary, carved on a stone which supports the main beam of the nave roof.

Following Cromwell's victories, the Westminster Assembly of 1643 framed the Solemn League and Covenant of February 1644 which was imposed on all those over the age of eighteen. In January 1645 Archbishop Laud was executed, and a new Directory of Public Worship compiled at the Assembly was introduced in place of the Book of Common Prayer. By this stage, many clergy were either Puritan at heart or at least willing to sign the covenant and continue in their parishes as Presbyterian ministers. Of the clergy of approximately 10,000 only 2,425 were evicted and replaced by 'intruded' ministers. The number of clergy removed varied from diocese to diocese; in the diocese of Ely, of 121 parishes, forty-five incumbents were deprived under the Commonwealth. Among the deprived clergy a few went overseas into exile, as their predecessors had done a century before; some were committed to prison, but others were given posts as tutors or chaplains in private houses. It is recorded that Viscount Scudamore helped more than seventy ejected clergy including Thomas Fuller and Robert Herrick. Lady Anne Clifford, Countess of Pembroke, was another noted patron during the period of the Commonwealth, and had seven places of worship restored on her estate.

The King's execution on 30 January 1649 outraged the deepest feelings in the country and alienated many who had been, and might have continued to be, supporters of Cromwell. In the same year the tower of St Mary's Whitchurch fell, and it is easy to believe that parishioners would have connected the two events in their minds. The execution, in a sense, made the Restoration inevitable, and from 1662 to 1859, a special service was held in parish churches to mark the day of the King's execution. In the local community the distress of 1649 was great; bad harvests, high taxation and the general dislocation caused by the war, bore heavily on the families of the village. The use of the Book of

Common Prayer continued to be prohibited, though there is evidence that Anglican services were held discreetly up and down the country, especially baptisms, weddings and funerals (even the Lord Protector's daughter was married in the chapel at Hampton Court according to the Prayer Book service). Some attempt was made to tackle the perennial problems of the poverty of the clergy by supporting the lowest paid ministers with some of the land that once belonged to the bishops and the cathedrals. But a more radical restructuring was not carried through; Cromwell had at first promised to destroy the tithes, but later changed his mind. However, it is easy to overestimate the degree of disruption that occured during the period of the war; two-thirds of the English parishes had no change of minister under the Commonwealth.

From this period the origins of religious plurality in the village can be traced. While the Presbyterians were staunchly Erastian, the Congregationalists and Baptists were of a more independent mind. The Congregationalists developed and grew in great numbers during the Civil War and were particularly strong in the army, in London, in East Anglia and in the towns of the south west. The Baptists had broken away from the Brownists, early in the seventeenth century, when John Smith had left London for Holland where he baptized himself and formed the first English Baptist church. A party came to England in 1612 and a number of local congregations grew up. These came to be called General Baptists, to distinguish them from the much stricter Calvinists, who constituted the Particular Baptists from 1633 onwards. After the Restoration, the Baptists were much persecuted and John Bunyan spent twelve years in Bedford jail. Though many Catholic families continued in secrecy and obscurity, they obtained a bishop in 1623, when Dr William Bishop from Brailes in south Warwickshire was consecrated titular Bishop of Chalcedon with jurisdiction in England and Scotland. The Catholic population tended to be located in those areas at greatest distance from London.

Oliver Cromwell died in 1658; his son resigned as Protector in 1660, and Charles II arrived on 29 May amidst universal acclamation. The clergy exiled on the Continent had prepared the ground well and the Church of England was restored as the only legal and established Church in the land. The Book of Common Prayer was used in the King's chapel; Anglican bishops were appointed and they set out, with the vigour of men long kept waiting, for the task of revitalizing the Church. Within a few months 700 Puritan clergy had been ejected from their livings and St Bartholomew's Day (24 August) 1662, the day the Act of Uniformity became law, was long remembered by the ejected clergy, and those who followed them, as 'Black Bartholomew'.

In 1661 the elections to Parliament produced a House of Commons eager for revenge on the rebels and this spirit was taken up at the Savoy Conference. At the second session, in 1661, the 1552 Book of Common Prayer, with some alterations (especially the Baptism for those of riper years, for those who grew up unchristened during the Commonwealth), was included in the Act of Uniformity. However, the Book of Common Prayer was accepted in the House of Commons by a majority only of six, and they, believing reforms should be more radical, insisted on the right to debate further changes. The prohibition of Anglican practices in the fifteen years previously, had a profound effect on the character of the settlement of 1662 and gave it a hint of intolerance which troubled Church and State for long after that date. There followed a series of Acts, known as the Clarendon Code, which among other things required all in public office to be communicant members of the Church of England and made non-Church of England religious services illegal. In 1666 the Five Mile Act further forbade all non-Conformist ministers to live or visit within five miles of any place which they had previously ministered. Such legislation led to a further 1,000 ministers being expelled and had the effect of permanently dividing England between Conformists and non-Conformists. Although Puritan power was eclipsed, the Puritan legacy lived on, for, as J. R. Green has written, Englishmen were 'what Puritanism had made them, serious, earnest, sober in life and conduct, firm in their love of Protestantism and truth'.

The solidity of the Restoration settlement was tested by James II, who was not only a Roman Catholic, but had made it clear that he wished to install his co-religionists in positions of authority and influence, particularly in the army and the universities. The birth of a son to his wife precipitated the events which led to his flight from London on 18 December 1688, and the arrival of the Anglican Mary and her Dutch Calvinist husband, Prince William of Orange, in the city on the same day. The Revolution of 1688 achieved what Civil War had failed to achieve, both in the name of religion and of civil liberty. It was in the years after the restoration of the monarchy, when the Church of England was so firmly re-established, that the people of Whitchurch reroofed their church and finally carted away the rubble from the spire which had fallen in 1649 and built the new west wall and bellcot.

11

The Parish Church in the
Recent Past

While St Mary's Whitchurch was repaired in the mid seventeenth century, St Mary's Preston-on-Stour was radically altered in the mid eighteenth century. In 1747 the Marriott family moved from Alscot Park (which they had inhabited since 1614) and the estate was purchased by James West. The church was substantially altered by him between 1752 and 1754, in a style which matched the 'Strawberry Hill Gothic' additions which he made to Alscot Park. The medieval tower and nave remained, but a typically mid eighteenth-century chancel was added which contains both the glass brought home from the Grand Tour and the family memorials. The work of constructing new pews in the nave and rebuilding the chancel was completed by Edward Woodward of Chipping Campden for the sum of £2,000.

However, even if the churches in the Stour valley were in relatively good order, the early eighteenth century saw the Church as a whole emerging from a period of 200 years of change and conflict, during which its constitutional status had been significantly altered by the Act of Toleration. Both locally and nationally the Church was dependent upon the patronage, wealth and support of the landed interest and the state. The once powerful ecclesiastical courts were now devoid of independent coercive power, and convocation, which had been prorogued in May 1717, following a conflict with the state over the question of ecclesiastical authority, was not to meet to conduct business until 1852. At the parochial level, the clergy were once again dependent on the landed interest which had been so firmly re-established by the Glorious Revolution. When, in 1671, Viscount Scudamore built a rectory for the previously homeless vicar of Hempsted in Gloucestershire, the second occupant caused this Te Deum to be carved:

> Whoe'er doth dwell within this door,
> Thank God for Viscount Scudamore.

When James West was still resident in London, but carrying out alterations to Alscot Park, the Revd Joseph Green, incumbent of Preston-on-Stour, acted as his clerk of works, and from his correspondence it appears that he oversaw the work in the house and generally acted as a steward of the squire's property.

The Church of the eighteenth century is customarily seen through the eyes of Victorian writers, who have portrayed it as uniformly decadent and lethargic. Certainly, the Church was weakened by the loss of the Puritans; the sudden collapse of Calvinism, as a factor in English religious life, is one of the most significant changes in the English religious tradition. There is no doubt that in the late eighteenth and early nineteenth centuries the ministry of the Church was in considerable disarray. There was an acute shortage of suitably qualified candidates; clergy stipends were low; many vicarages and rectories had fallen into disrepair. Historians have portrayed the clergy of this period as of low social status on account of their humble social origins, their lack of education and the poverty of their benefices, the rusticity of their lifestyle, and particularly the socially degrading tasks they were forced to engage in to supplement their meagre stipends. The curate of Lastingham in the early eighteenth century had thirteen children to support on a stipend of £20. His wife kept a public house and he was able to convince the archdeacon that his indirect clerical management (and his fiddle-playing) caused the parishioners to be 'imperceptibly led along the paths of piety and morality'.

In 1704 the establishment of Queen Anne's Bounty was a means by which some of the Church's revenues were used to create a fund for the relief of the ill-housed and poorly paid clergy. This followed a survey which had revealed that half the benefices were worth less than £80 a year and that many of the curacies were worth less than £20 a year. The plunder of the Church which resulted from the impropriation of livings had left many benefices below subsistence level, and the practice of impropriation had taken place in approximately 4,000 of the 9,284 livings by 1603. In practice the lay rectors took the lion's share, as in Hornchurch in Essex, where at this time the benefice income amounted to £800 but the vicar's stipend was £55. At Hogsthorpe in Lincolnshire the benefice income was £80 but the vicar received £10. Ruefully an early eighteenth-century vicar remarked that clergy got 'leavings not livings'. Impropriation led directly to non-residence, absenteeism, pluralism, unqualified and otherwise unsatisfactory clergy and the general demoralization of the Church at the local level. By this time the incumbent of Preston habitually lived in Stratford-upon-Avon, and it is unlikely that there has been a resident clergy in the parish since the Reformation. The attempts of the Bounty to augment the income of the poorest parishes did not prevent widespread non-residence, which was allowed automatically for graduates (so long as their livings were within thirty miles), and for those who taught in schools (the vicar of Preston customarily taught in Stratford grammar school) or universities, or were chaplains to the nobility. In practice, it was possible for almost any clergyman to obtain a nominal post which would entitle him to be non-resident. In the county of Oxford in the 1780s, approximately 100 of the 165 incumbents were non-resident; in the diocese of Exeter, 159 out of 290 were non-resident.

It was assumed that the conscientious clergyman in the early eighteenth century would read both Morning Prayer at 10 a.m. (which comprised Morning Prayers, the Litany, and ante-Communion and a sermon) and Evening Prayer, frequently at 3 p.m. so that people could return home before dark. The two-hour interval between the services was filled with performing baptisms, churchings, marriages and burials, and the clergyman would often be in church for the whole day; if non-resident, he would eat his lunch in the vestry. However, in practice, double duty on Sunday had been steadily declining. In the Forest deanery of Gloucester diocese in 1750, of thirty-five churches twenty-three had single duty. Church attendance had clearly declined sharply, and the clergy who replied to Bishop Secker's Primary Visitation in 1738 regularly reported habitual non-attendance among the 'lowest ranks'. One of the striking aspects of these reports was the implication that religious practice had fallen off alarmingly within the lifetime of those replying. There is a tendency to overlook the fact that the alienation of the working class from the Church, which was observed by so many nineteenth-century writers, had its origins in the practices of rural communities in the previous century; habits of indifference stretch back over several generations and corresponding attitudes towards the Church had become embedded in the local culture.

In those areas where clergy were largely non-resident, such clerical work that was done was performed by 'gallopers': curates who were known for their dexterity in speeding from one church to another, to serve as many churches as they could on a Sunday for a fee of half a guinea per service. The procession of curates leaving Oxford over Magdalen Bridge on a Saturday afternoon to serve the parishes of Oxfordshire was considered one of the sights of Oxford in the mid eighteenth century. On 9 December 1775, James Woodforde records that snow stopped the curates leaving the city. The various effects of this system were that single duty became the rule; that the curates were forced to hurry through the services, and that the Sunday service was at no fixed time. Charlotte Yonge recorded that at Otterbourne, at the end of the eighteenth century, there was only one service and that the bells were rung when the curate could be seen riding towards the church. Numerous anecdotes point to the careless performance of the services and they bear witness to what must have been a common experience. Dr George Horne (later Bishop of Norwich) wrote in 1787 of his visit to a country church. Having described the dilapidated state of the church and the churchyard, he continued:

> The minister of this noble edifice was answerable to it in dress and manner. Having entered the church he made the best of his way to the chancel where he changed his wig; put on a dirty, iron-moulded, ragged surplus; and after a short angry dialogue with the clerk, entered his desk and began immediately without looking into the book. He read as if he had ten other churches to serve that day, at as many miles distance from each other. The clerk sang a melancholy solo — neither tune nor words of which I have ever heard before.

Since 1750, penal coercion to attend church had almost disappeared; the diocesan correction books for the reigns of William and Mary, Anne and George I, include a number of cases of presentment of non-worshippers and non-communicants, but they contain no record of any action having been taken. The clergy themselves, finding the procedure fruitless, gave up the prosecution of habitual non-attenders. One of the last references to an attempt to exercise ecclesiastical discipline of this nature occurred in 1778. The neglect of church attendance had caused concern before the last quarter of the eighteenth century, but there seems little doubt that it had now reached much larger proportions. John Butler, shortly after his translation from Oxford to Hereford in 1788, sent out visitation queries and compared the results with the diocesan survey last made in 1747. The decline in church attendance was so distressing that he was unwilling to divulge the figures. The church attendance figures had been by no means high in 1747, and, when the increase in population was also considered, the results must have been even more alarming. The report of a group of clergymen in Lincolnshire published in 1800, revealed that in seventy-nine parishes with a population of 15,042, the average number of members of the congregation was 4,933. Edward Stanley recorded that when he took over the family living in 1805, the established practice was for the clerk on Sunday mornings to stand in the churchyard and only call the vicar if someone came to church.

When the clergy of the mid and late eighteenth century are compared with the parish clergy of the Caroline period, it can readily be seen that as a group they were more wealthy, lived in better houses and were in every respect more significant figures in rural society than had been their seventeenth-century predecessors. At Whitchurch, little is known of the early eighteenth-century clergy but in the middle years of that century the living belonged to the Smith family, and father and son ministered to the parish for a period of sixty-nine years. The rectors followed the example of the rest of the village; the old rectory by the church was demolished and a new purpose-built rectory with a commanding view of the valley, seventeen rooms, stables, coach house, pigsties, laundry and all other facilities was built by Edward Kenwrich in 1789. (At this time money could be borrowed from Queen Anne's Bounty for such a purpose, against the security of the benefice.) John Clare observed that the poor clergy, who worked and prayed alongside their flocks, went out when pauperism and enclosures came in; but such clergy were affectionately remembered in the countryside.

A number of diaries of eighteenth-century parish clergy have been edited, and they allow a composite picture of that century's parish clergymen to be presented. The tendency to see the eighteenth-century church through the eyes of Victorian writers has partly obscured the fact that by their own lights many of these clergy were conscientious and endeavoured to fulfil the duties of their office according to the understandings of the time. However, the rising price of agricultural goods, the enclosures and the consequent commutation of the tithe for a block of land (which comprised a farm of seventy-five acres in Whitchurch), had the effect of making the clergy, both individually and corporately, significantly more wealthy. This fact was reflected in their houses, which in the eighteenth century more commonly resembled the hall than the farmhouse, and in the adoption of new modes of dress and recreation suitable to their new status. Benjamin Newton, Rector of Wrath, combined the duties of rector with the interests and occupation of a moderately well-to-do country gentleman. He hunted with all the neighbouring packs; he shot over the manor for which he had the deputation of sporting rights; he fished; he kept greyhounds; and he attended the race meetings at Richmond and Catterick, as well as the local balls. He farmed, on a considerable scale, his own glebe and rented land; he bred horses; he sat on the county bench; and he visited and entertained his friends in a constant round of hospitality.

It is estimated that of the 3,128 Enclosure Acts between 1757 and 1835, in 2,220 instances the tithe was commuted and in the overwhelming number of cases commuted for land. The conditions of commutation were remarkably generous to the clergy and the value of benefices increased accordingly. At Long Melford the income of the benefice rose from £460 in 1790 to £1,220 in 1819. Inevitably, as benefice incomes rose, at a time when respectability was gauged in acres and the owners of the soil derived from it not only wealth but also high social status and the right to govern, the Church attracted men of a higher social status, particularly the sons of the lesser squires who were severely hit by the inflation of the eighteenth century and the development of the large estates. In 1756, Lord Chesterfield wrote to a father who asked his advice: 'I entirely agree with you in your resolution of bringing up all your sons to some profession or other.' He went on to suggest 'general rules by which I would point out to them that profession which I should wish them to apply to; I recommend the army or the navy to a boy of warm constitution, strong animal spirits, and a cold genius; to one of quick, lively and distinguished parts, the law; to a good, dull, decent boy, the church . . .' A glimpse of the clergy of this period is caught in the novels of Jane Austen, who was both the daughter and the sister of a clergyman; and it seems clear that many did not see the clergyman's role as a sacred order at this time. John Skinner wrote of the Revd Mr. Gunning of Farmborough, a recently arrived neighbour:

> He seems an open-hearted man, but I do not think exactly calculated for a clergyman, as he keeps his hounds and having no other pursuit, thinks more of the hare than he does of hunting out what may benefit his parishioners.

But whatever low estimation the clergy may have had of their duties, there is little doubt that those who were resident were deeply integrated into the lives of the local community. They shared a common interest in farming and were looked to by that community for many things beyond traditional clerical duties sanctioned by the ordinal. A series of entries in the diary of Benjamin Rogers, who was in correspondence with many eminent doctors, recorded the last days of a parishioner and the clergyman's efforts on his behalf.

> (25 March) Order'd William Allen of Bridgend to be blooded for the Pleurisie. (2 April) Order'd him to be blooded again. The first time about 11 ounces was taken away; the second about 9 ounces. (3 April) He was blooded again, 10 ounces being taken away as before. (4 April) He died.

It appears that James Woodforde in his early days at Castle Cary had a considerable reputation for veterinary work, for which he received fees. In his Norfolk diaries he records the cases of sickness among his servants and parishioners and the attempts he made to cure them. 'My boy Jack had another touch of ague about noon. I gave him a dram of gin at the beginning of the fit and pushed him headlong into one of my ponds and ordered him to bed immediately.'

However, nothing symbolized the rising significance of the clergy in rural society more clearly than the degree to which the clergy fulfilled the role of magistrates in late eighteenth-century England.

It has been shown that in the county of Oxford, of convictions recorded at Quarter Sessions in 1790, 86 per cent bore the signature of a clergyman. The diary of Benjamin Newton reveals that he was an active magistrate not only in his attendance at Petty and Quarter Sessions, but also in the smaller matters of a magistrate's duty in the local community. Blomfield (later Bishop of London), when at Dunton, wrote in June 1813:

> My time will be somewhat more occupied than formerly as I am now a commissioner of Turnpikes and a Justice of the Peace: and the county business will never get on without me. I must study Burn with diligence before I can indifferently minister justice . . . I shall moreover probably be a commissioner of the Property Tax, all of which offices will a little interfere with Greek.

Certainly, not all clergy agreed with this union of ministerial and magisterial offices, but in the absence of others willing to undertake the work, the resident clergy were often the only suitable candidates. The clergy were also active as politicians and although it is difficult to assess the degree of their influence, none the less, at a time when the franchise was restricted, it was agreed by many (particularly the Whigs, who called them 'the black recruiting sergeants') that the influence of the clergy was extensive. Lord North's Tory triumph in 1770 was regarded as 'greatly owing to the exertions of the clergy'.

The mid eighteenth-century restoration of St Mary's Preston-on-Stour resulted in a church which articulated values and understandings different from those of the traditional medieval building. The bareness and sparseness of the décor, the clear glass in the nave windows, the plain white walls, the plain oak pews with elmboard seats, the family pew in the chancel, the hatchment and memorials on the walls, and the prominent position of the pulpit: all were eloquent of new and different understandings of the nature of the Church and the faith.

Throughout the eighteenth century non-residence and the use of curates meant that the amount of Sunday duty performed by the clergy steadily declined. Single duty, as has been mentioned, now became common in as many as 40 per cent of the churches, so common that in the early nineteenth century, in visitation inquiries by the Bishop of Exeter, he omitted the words 'twice every Lord's Day'. James Woodforde, although he was constantly resident, had only single duty. Even this occasionally had to be cancelled, when the church was being cleaned or the weather was bad; or Woodforde, being ill or away, was unable to find a substitute.

However, the service itself was essentially an offering of the whole community in which many people played a direct part. The clergyman's duties were those of reading the service and preaching the sermon, which came at the end of the service, unless it was a Sacrament Sunday. It was inevitable that the educated clergyman, who took pains to express himself as a scholar, in carefully composed literary exercises, spoke only to the educated members of his congregation. The clergyman who took the university disputations as his model, or who composed, with the aid of references from Greek and Hebrew texts, a sermon which occupied him for a considerable part of the week and took more than an hour to read; or the clergyman who simply read his father's or grandfather's compositions, would have had some difficulty in holding the attention even of the educated members of a country congregation. For the rest, the sermon could often have had little meaning, particularly when clergymen such as the Revd John Coleridge of Ottery St Mary introduced lengthy Hebrew quotations into their parochial sermons: Coleridge regarded Hebrew as the 'immediate language of the Holy Ghost'. Clearly, Hogarth's cartoon of the sleeping congregation recorded an experience with which many could identify, and a large part of the appeal of non-conformity lay in the more energetic and colloquial preaching of ministers whose social and educational situation more closely approximated that of the congregation.

In the eighteenth century, preaching was dominated by the example of Archbishop Tillotson. His sermon 'His commandments are not grievous' typified an age in which the doctrine of the divine wisdom and God's beneficence achieved pre-eminence. Tillotson established a school of preaching which was markedly different from the medieval school; his preaching was centrally concerned with morality and made its appeal to reason and commonsense (natural wisdom) rather than to divine revelation. Many clergymen did not compose their own sermons but read those of eminent divines, or patronized the ingenuous Dr Trusler, who, in the 1770s, established a business in abridging the sermons of eminent divines, and printing them in copperplate, so that if the pulpit was overlooked by a gallery, the occupants would think that the clergyman was reading his own composition. Later attacks on the clergy constantly drew attention to their being content to read from the pulpit sermons that they had not written.

At the same time the musicians and singers were responsible for the music and, in the eighteenth century, they were usually accommodated in a west gallery. The gallery in St Mary's Preston-on-Stour was built for the purpose at this time. During the service the congregation stood and turned west during the musical parts of the service (hence the expression 'to turn and face the music'). The musicians had a considerable reputation for independent action and were liable to meet any interference by the clergyman with a demonstration of their disapproval, often during the service. A large number of clergy had 'trouble with the musicians', as did Woodforde on several occasions. The standard of performance was often low and Oxenden wrote of the Barnham musicians: ' . . . the singing was almost ludicrous, provoking laughter rather than an expression of praise'. However, in other places high standards were aimed at. Arthur Gibbs wrote of the Chedworth band, 'these musicians are the descendants of the village musicians who, to quote from the *Strand Musical Magazine* of September 1897, 'led the Psalmody in the village church sixty years ago with strings and wind instruments'. Mr Charles Smith of Chedworth remembers playing the clarinet in Handel's *Zadok the Priest* performed there, in 1838, in honour of the Queen's accession.'

In addition, the parish clerk, whose liturgical functions customarily included leading the responses, reading the notices and briefs, and reading over the psalm before it was sung by the congregation, played a major role in the service. The office was freehold (and in many parishes hereditary). The Revd George Woodward identified a fellow traveller in a stagecoach as a parish clerk by the peculiar way he said 'Amen'; clerks were often known as 'Mr Amen'. It appears that the clerk was often a source of considerable mirth and irreverence in the eighteenth-century church, being on occasion quite unequal to his duties. James Woodforde, recording in his diary on 14 April 1791; wrote: 'Poor old John Smith my clerk made a shocking hand of it singing this afternoon in church, much laughed at.' Whatever may be said about eighteenth-century Anglican worship, and there are many testimonies to its dullness, it was in a real sense the offering of the whole community in an act of worship, which included the village choir and band, with fiddles, bass, viol and serpent, the charity children in blue uniforms under the eye of the parish beadle, bell-ringers in the tower, and the parish clerk. In many churches, scenes such as that depicted in Thomas Webster's picture of the village choir must have taken place regularly every Sunday. This was all to change in the mid nineteenth century.

Certainly, no eighteenth-century Church of England clergyman had more lasting effect on the English countryside than John Wesley. It is estimated that in thirty-five years, on his preaching journeys, he covered 250,000 miles by horse and preached 40,000 sermons. He frequently preached four or five times a day, and could persuade thousands of tired country men and women to asemble and hear him preach at the beginning and end of a day's work. Those who were 'lost' and were little valued or esteemed in eighteenth-century society, found a new identity through Wesley's teaching, as souls deserving of salvation. By their pennies they founded Friendly Societies, Co-operative Societies, Sick Clubs and, of course, chapels. The Church of England was based on the parochial system; from the day that Wesley declared that 'the world is my parish', a break with the Church of England was inevitable. In thousands of villages there sprung up chapels, which were the religious expression of other divisions and stratifications which had become evident in eighteenth-century society. It is hard to underestimate the Methodist contribution to village life, for it gave to the village that sense of working-class solidarity which took pride in independence and honest poverty, but had a horror of destitution and charity. The thrift, sobriety, hard work and earnestness of much Victorian working-class village life had its origins in Wesley's preaching and the churches that he and his followers established.

By the second and third decades of the nineteenth century, changes were taking place which were radically to alter the nature of the clergyman's role. Society was no longer disposed to accept the combination of rich rewards with minimal duties which had marked the eighteenth-century church. As William Cobbett observed after completing his tour of Hampshire, Berkshire, Surrey and Sussex in 1823: 'I cannot conclude my remarks on this Rural Ride without noticing the new sort of language I hear everywhere made use of with regard to the parsons, but which language I do not care to repeat.' The mounting wave of agitation broke heavily on all ancient institutions and they were subject to every sort of attack, including physical violence. The unreformed Hanoverian Church found itself assaulted on every side, in an age which would no longer tolerate the abuses and privileges which it harboured. It was widely agreed that a sizeable proportion of the national wealth could no longer be set aside for the maintenance of the clergy. The Ecclesiastical Commission, established by Peel in 1835, was the means by which it was hoped by laymen and progressive churchmen alike, that the obviously archaic structure of the Church of England could be remodelled, so that it could more effectively discharge its pastoral duties. The Church (unlike Parliament and the universities) proved a difficult institution to reform, not least because of its localism, and the achievements of the Commission were principally to improve the administration and the use of resources. A series of Acts were passed by Parliament in 1813, 1817, 1828 and 1836, which sought to compel clergy to reside in their parishes; to limit their extra ecclesiastical activities; to encourage them to pay curates properly and to keep the parsonage house in good repair. In 1827, approximately half the benefices had non-resident incumbents; by 1850 this figure had dropped below 10 per cent. In Cornwall in 1831 there were only eighty-nine resident incumbents; by 1869, the year of Bishop Henry Phillpotts' death, 219 out of a total of 232 incumbents now resided in their parishes.

The congruity of the clergyman's role with traditional society made it particularly vulnerable to the changes brought by industrialization and urbanization. While the parliamentary reforms, as much desired by energetic clergy as anyone, served to improve standards, so did the teaching of the Evangelical and Tractarian movements, which were of such influence in this period. Both movements sought to present the clergyman's role in a more spiritual light, and to encourage new standards among their ranks. 'The young lady', wrote one clergyman, 'will scarcely care to recognize as her proper spiritual guide and friend, her partner at

221

last week's ball; and the dancing priest may well find it difficult to assume at once his ministerial character towards those with whom he has shared the small talk and trifling things of a cricket or archery club ball . . .' A mid nineteenth-century layman wrote:

> You must remember that the tone of feeling which existed in the Church even five-and-twenty years ago, both with respect to duties and amusements, was very different from that which is to be found among us at present. At that time a person in Holy Orders might have been seen at Ascot or Newmarket without any very great scandal. But were a clergyman now to be seen on a racecourse he would, even by worldly people, be considered to have disgraced himself and his profession.

Bishop Blomfield's biographer wrote:

> In character, habits, attainment, social position, and general reputation, the ordinary clergyman of 1860 is a very different being from the clergyman in 1810 . . . Speaking generally, the remark of Mr Thomas Grenville, who died in 1846 at the age of 91, may be taken as true, that no change which has taken place in his lifetime was so great as the change in the clergy of the Church of England.

In the eighteenth century, as it has been seen, the clergyman's role had included many elements which were derived from his position in rural society rather than his ordination. However, in the mid nineteenth century, the clergyman was called to meet new expectations of his pastoral and spiritual role, and other functionaries such as the Poor Law administrator, the political agent, the teacher, the registrar, the doctor, the policeman and even the sanitary engineer, came to administer functions which the clergyman had previously been content to perform, in an essentially amateur capacity, in the country village. In Warwickshire in the early 1830s Sir J. E. Eardley-Wilmot, Chairman of the County Quarter Sessions, declared himself in principle against the appointment of clergy as magistrates, but conceded that, in some areas, it was a necessity in the absence of other suitably qualified men. His successor, the Earl of Warwick, was equally opposed to the appointment of clergymen and, by 1868, the clergy constituted only 7 per cent of the Warwickshire Bench.

In many places country doctors were often selected to replace the clergyman on the magistrates' bench.

In the mid nineteenth century the residence legislation meant that in many country parishes there arrived for the first time a resident clergyman, trained at one of the new theological colleges and determined to introduce higher standards into parish life. Many of these resident clergymen started in the church building itself and attempted to improve the conduct of church services. They were unwilling to put up with the rustic standards, particularly of the clerk, whose activities were often fatal to the new sense of reverence and decorum at which they were aiming. One such clergyman wrote of his clerk: 'He can read but little, he can sing but one tune of the psalms, he can scarcely write his own name or read.' The dismissal of the clerk frequently caused less trouble than that of the musicians and singers, and many diaries record the struggle which the clergymen had to achieve this end. However, by the late 1850s and early 1860s, hymns which had not been common in the 1840s were widely introduced and the old musicians were often incapable of meeting the new demands made upon them. In many parishes the musicians had to make way for a new harmonium and a choir of the children from the parish school, both placed in the chancel and under the clergyman's eye and immediate direction (or that of his wife). Implementing these reforms was not easy, and they were often undertaken against a background of bitter opposition from the displaced musicians. T. T. Carter describes the removal of the gallery and the breakup of the choir at Clewer as 'a terrible grievance'. Thomas Hardy in his novel *Under the Greenwood Tree* described the last days of the gallery musicians and singers in a Dorset village, and the introduction of an organ into the chancel, played by the schoolmistress. He wrote in the preface to his story:

> Under the old plan, from half a dozen to ten full-grown players, in addition to the numerous more or less grown-up singers, were officially occupied with the Sunday routine, and concerned in trying their best to make it an artistic outcome of the combined musical taste of the parish. With the musical executive limited, as it mostly is limited now, to the parson's wife or daughter and the schoolchildren, or to the schoolteacher and the children, an important union of interests has disappeared.

At the village of Stanguard, near Peterborough, a newly erected barrel organ was installed in time to celebrate the Treaty of Paris, signed on 30 March 1858 at the end of the Crimean War. It played twenty-four psalm tunes and six chants. The case was handsome and the tone was reported to be rich and powerful; it was paid for by subscription, with the vicar himself subscribing more than half the cost. These changes had a profound effect upon the nature of worship and were indicative of the new understanding of the role of the church in the village. Reluctantly one of the musicians (in Hardy's novel) was forced to concede that in changed times new ideas had replaced those of former generations. 'Parson Maybold, every tradesman'd like to have his own way in his workshop, and Mellstock church is yours.'

Increasingly, the worship in the parish church ceased to be the offering of the whole community, many of whom participated in different ways, but became something which was organized and performed almost totally by the clergyman himself. Influenced by his new professional understanding, worship tended to become a professional service offered to the village by a qualified practitioner, rather than the offering of the whole community. As Hardy noted, while the quality of church services had improved, this was achieved at the cost of an important 'union of interests' between the clergyman and his parishioners. This transformation of public worship in the mid nineteenth century may be regarded as indicative of a more fundamental change in the way in which the clergyman perceived his role, and, as a consequence, his relationship with his parishioners. In brief, while in the former period the parishioners were customarily participants in the worship and life within the church, in the late nineteenth century they tended merely to be 'consumers' of a service provided by professional personnel. Like the services offered by other professional men, there was a marked tendency, which persisted, to regard the public aspects of religion as essentially something which is done to and for individuals by professional personnel.

Country life in the early nineteenth century was often portrayed as boorish and uncultured, if not wild, savage and brutal. It must have appeared even more so to the newly ordained clergyman who had left the seclusion of Oxford to take up family or college living and found himself in the midst of a community at best indifferent and frequently hostile. In a letter of 1828, the incumbent of Checkendon advised Samuel Wilberforce, his successor, not to allow his man to sleep in the village. He said it was his practice to have his man on guard at night, carrying a gun loaded with a ball, and a swordstick. The whole period was pervaded by the atmosphere of war, revolution and social instability, certainly until the late 1840s. Even ten years later, the new rector of Ilmington, in Warwickshire, the Revd J. C. Young wrote: 'The attractions of the rectory house and grounds were somewhat neutralized by the accounts which reached me from all quarters of the depraved condition of the parish.' By this he meant 'deplorable attendance at church, drunkenness, bastardy, poaching and even serious riot'. Apparently the previous incumbent, 'a man of amiable and retiring disposition', had even had his life threatened; 'his nerve was so shaken as to render residence elsewhere essential to his health and peace of mind'.

Along with all his fellow clergy, the Revd J. C. Young sought to solve this problem by founding a range of parochial institutions which included provident clubs, penny readings, magic lantern shows and, most important of all, a village school. Village schools are the enduring monument to the work of the parochial clergy in the mid nineteenth century, for neither their system of provident institutions nor their elaborate restoration of the church have survived subsequent changes in taste and local demand. However, the system of parochial primary education, which was largely established through their efforts, and, in many cases, financed from their private resources, has remained unchanged in many of its essential features. The primary school, with its separate entrances for boys and girls, its prominent foundation stone (in all probability bearing a date between 1840 and 1870) and the schoolmaster's house attached to it, was considered an essential part of the parochial machinery in the mid nineteenth century, and many incumbents considered that their most important work was done within its walls. Between 1811 and 1833, 7,000 schools were built or assisted by the National Society (the Churches' organization for financing schools) which educated 500,000 children. By 1842, the number had more than doubled to seventeen thousand.

As the clergyman sought to concentrate on the work of the church and the school, so his involvement in many other aspects of country life contracted, and his role was marked with a new professional character which allows us to speak of the 'Victorian rural clergyman' as a recognizable figure. Within the church the removal of the village musicians and band and the parish clerk, and the new emphasis on sacramental worship (full eucharistic vestments were used for the first time in 1849 in Wilmcote in Warwickshire), altered the way in which both the clergyman and the church were regarded. At the same time, while in the eighteenth century, pastoral work, as it later came to be understood, seemed to be neither practised nor looked for, in the nineteenth century the active clergyman busied himself in a constant round of visiting the homes of his parishioners and organizing social and recreational activities (often aimed at drawing them away from the public houses).

But as the clergyman went around his parish he often found himself separated from his parishioners by an unbridgeable gulf, for he was no longer indistinguishable from the yeoman farmer clergyman of the early eighteenth century. He had become a professional man and a member of the professional upper middle class. Edward Monro, himself a country clergyman, found it necessary to write in a handbook for clergy advice aimed at helping them to 'get alongside' the working men in a country parish. Monro wrote in 1850:

> The visits of a clergyman to his poor must lose very much force unless he lays aside the magisterial air, so very commonly used. He has no right to cross the poor man's threshold with a covered head, nor in any degree to demean himself as a superior within the walls of the cottage.

While the owners of the large houses, and the majority of the farmers were likely to attend church, increasingly the villagers themselves attended the Methodist chapel. The chapel was outside the village in the sense that it was beyond the reach of the formal power structure of the Victorian village and was often physically outside it, because the landowners were unwilling to allow a chapel to be built. Here many of the artisan and working families found that not only were their religious needs met, but also there was for them a significance which the formal structure of the village denied them — perhaps most important of all, an education.

It is no coincidence that most of the leaders of the agricultural unions came from the Methodist chapel congregations.

One effect of the residence legislation was to place many clergy in close proximity to the lives and working conditions of the rural poor. Numerous clergymen submitted evidence to the Poor Law Commission, and to inquiries into the sale of beer (1833) and the employment of women and children in agriculture (1843). They deplored the harsh conditions under which women worked in the fields; the gang system; and the immorality, brutality and drunkenness of village life. In *The Spectator* of 23 November 1872, a letter from a country clergyman recorded how his congregation had been deserted by many of the farmers because of his consistent campaign against women, especially when pregnant, being made to work in the fields. Dr Arthur Wade, the Vicar of Warwick, had led a procession of 50,000 people in protest against the transportation of the Tolpuddle 'martyrs'. Sanitary reform and bad housing conditions became a predominant concern of the clergy in the 1850s and 1860s. The clergy knew that 'low fever' was almost constantly present in areas of poor housing and little sanitation, and that infectious, fatal diseases were common in such areas. Archdeacon Fearon, in his charge of 1865, encouraged the Leicestershire clergy to make representations to the landlord when they found cottages that were particularly bad and did not answer 'the requirements of health . . . , self-respect and decorum'. Henry Moule, Vicar of Fordington, wrote eight letters to Prince Albert between September 1854 and October 1855, about the insanitary state of many of the houses of the poor on properties in his parish which were owned by the Duchy of Cornwall. William Butler at Wantage was much concerned with such matters in the town and was a member of its sanitary committee. Eventually, he purchased a row of cottages, had them demolished and rebuilt them as model homes. The Revd Lord Sidney Godolphin Osborne, Rector of Durweston in Dorset, wrote many letters to *The Times* on behalf of the agricultural labourers; they form an interesting account of what many rural clergy knew at first hand about conditions in the countryside. The Revd Edward Girdlestone, of Halberton in Devon, was a campaigner for sanitary reform and a fairer wage for rural labourers. He organized a mass migration of labourers from that area to counties where wages and conditions were better.

Between 400 and 500 labourers and their families were said to have left the district, and the Halberton farmers were forced to raise wages from 8s to 17s to keep their remaining men.

Some clergy were found among the early supporters of those who attempted to form a trade union for agricultural workers. An early union was helped by the Vicar of Leintwardine; it claimed a membership of 30,000 and had twenty clergymen as vice-presidents. However, Joseph Arch's National Agricultural Labourers Union, established following a speech to Wellesbourne, Warwickshire in 1872, was strongly anti-clerical in many of its early pronouncements. It accused the clergy of being deeply implicated in agricultural capitalism and the changes in land tenure which had pressed so heavily on country people.

No doubt some clergy would have agreed with Bishop Ellicott of Gloucester's suggestion that the union leaders should be thrown in the duckpond, but Arch was not without supporters among the clergy and these included Bishop Fraser of Manchester and Dr Percival, President of Trinity College, Oxford (later, Bishop of Hereford). There is little doubt that many parochial clergy, from their intimate knowledge of the countryside, saw the justice of his demands. The Revd and Hon. J. Leigh of Stoneleigh was a remarkable supporter of the strikes. He met Arch on several occasions and attended his meetings. Archdeacon Holbeche of Banbury proposed the workers' motion on their behalf at a meeting of landowners. The south Warwickshire clerical meeting formally recognized the right of combination put forward in Arch's manifesto of April 1872. In the same year the Revd J. A. Lawrence, Vicar of Chalgrove in Oxfordshire, became secretary of the local branch on 2 June 1874. He not only chaired a union meeting in the village, but gave permission for it to be held on the vicarage lawn. At the meeting he expressed 'willingness to help in any way he could'.

However, in 1874, the union suffered defeat over the strike in Suffolk and Norfolk and the membership rapidly fell away. It can be assumed that the majority of clergy were reluctant to take sides or to antagonize the farmers, whatever they may have felt. The Revd Mr Jenyns, Vicar of Hitcham, wrote: 'It is not every clergyman that will boldly stand up against a body of farmers, who have long had their own way in everything . . .' Certainly, at Halberton and Chalgrove the incumbent met with implacable opposition, not only in respect of his political activities, but in every way.

The last decades of the nineteenth century and the early years of the twentieth century, before the First World War, are often portrayed as the Golden Age of the Anglican rural clergy. Certainly, in many rectories where the income was sufficient to employ servants, the clergy were able to sustain a style of life which, though less grand, approximated in many respects that of the manor and the hall. They were able to send their sons to public schools and to professional careers in the army, the Church or the empire, and to provide a comfortable and appropriate lifestyle for their wife and daughters. However, the residence legislation, which had done so much to awaken the clergy to the nature of their duties, had settled many in parishes which were too small and too poorly endowed. The decline in agricultural prices in the last two decades of the nineteenth century had resulted in a sharp decline in clerical incomes, particularly for those dependent on the letting of their glebe: in certain areas some clergy had to face a number of years when their fields were untenanted. The Revd E. B. Rutherfield recorded that the value of his benefice fell from £1,500 per annum in the high farming years of the 1860s, to £300 per annum in the depressed 1880s. At Ansley in north Warwickshire the value of the living fell from £236 in 1884 to £160 in 1904, by which stage the practice of making Easter Offerings as a gift to the incumbent, had already become widespread throughout the Church. Less income led directly to the dismissal of the curate, more modest contributions to village charities and organizations, and less support for the school — indeed, for the work of the Church at home and abroad.

But poverty may have been easier to bear than the vague presentiment of a life passing by, which many rural clergy were beginning to feel. Richard Jefferies provided a touching vignette of a country parson in the 1870s, as seen through the eyes of his wife:

> But the work, the parish, the people, all seemed to have slipped out of her husband's hands . . . But surely his good intentions, his way of life, his gentle kindness should carry sway. Instead of

which the parish seemed to have quite left the Church, and the parson was outside the real modern life of the village.

In an age characterized by activity and achievement, success and boundless opportunities for the energetic and determined, there was increasing concern for the loneliness and stagnation of clergy ministering in small country parishes. At this time Atherstone-on-Stour, Preston-on-Stour and Whitchurch all had their own incumbents, even though it is unlikely that the total population of the three villages was above 500, and, certainly, the two smaller hamlets (which both had resident incumbents) were unlikely to have had a population of above 100 each. Naturally, many of the clergy found other interests to occupy their time and Whitchurch's incumbent at this period, the Revd Harvey Bloom, became well known as an antiquarian and historian. He catalogued the libraries in Warwick Castle and Worcester Cathedral.

It was no coincidence that the first criticisms of the patronage and freehold system should date from this time, when H. Rider Haggard wrote:

> In the future, although it may be distant, I believe that all will be changed; priests will not be pitchforked into livings by the arbitrary decision of the owners of the advowsons, which in practice often means their own decisions, but will be selected by proper authorities in consultation maybe with representatives of the parishioners, for their quality and nothing else. Also, perhaps, the revenues of the church will be paid into a general fund and portioned out according to its local need, to be supplemented, if need be, by the contributions of the laity . . . Of one thing I am certain — if the church does not, or cannot, reform itself ere long, the laity will lose patience and take matters into their own hands.

In a country where farming was depressed and new life was centred on the urban and industrial areas, country clergy suddenly became increasingly aware that they were left in a backwater. Some asked for no more and pursued faithfully a lifelong ministry in a small village; but others found this deeply frustrating, as did Dr A. Jessopp, Vicar of Scarning in Norfolk. He wrote, in 1890:

When the rector on his induction takes the key of the church, locks himself in and tolls the bell, it is his own passing bell he is ringing. He is shutting himself out from all hope of a future career on earth. He is a man transported for life, to whom there will be no reprieve . . . for the day he accepts a country benefice he is a shelved man . . . once a country parson, always a country parson.

But of all their troubles, the poverty of the benefices was perhaps the most significant, as Rider Haggard wrote in 1899:

The poor parsons, how will they manage to live, I wonder? It is undoubtedly to the advantage of this parish that a clergyman should be able to keep up a modest position; that he should not at least be notoriously struggling with debts or visibly out at the elbows. Yet in eight cases out of ten, how is he to do so in these days . . .? There are very many benefices in these counties [East Anglia] that do not return £300 clear per annum.

Indeed, seven years later, the average income of a clergyman was revealed to be only £150 per annum.

The First World War was a crucial time for the Church of England in particular, and for the countryside in general, and it marked a period of abrupt change. It saw the erosion of many of the social conventions which had previously sustained church attendance, notably the English Sunday, and in the village the clergy became aware of the competition of other leisure activities. Bishop Randall Davidson devoted part of his charge to his clergy in the diocese of Winchester, in 1899, to observing that the bicycle was having a particularly deleterious effect on Sunday church attendance. In the last quarter of the nineteenth century the number of clergy continued to rise until it reached a peak of 25,235 in 1901. In 1873 there were 429 parochial clergy in the Hereford diocese in addition to twenty full-time clergy on the cathedral staff. In the Norwich diocese in 1880 there were 1,140 priests ministering to 600,000 people. But from the turn of the century the number of clergy began to decline, and almost every rural area which now comprises a rural deanery has lost approximately one clergyman every fifteen years during this century. By 1931 the total number of Anglican clergy had already

231

fallen by over 6,000. While, for a short time in the late nineteenth century, it appeared possible to provide one clergyman for almost every parish no matter how small, already by the 1920s it was acknowledged that this policy had to be abandoned, and neighbouring parishes were linked together under the charge of one clergyman. Pluralities, one of the abuses in the eighteenth century, became again a common feature of the countryside, but caused in the twentieth century through lack of clergy.

At the same time many clergy, particularly the 3,030 commissioned as chaplains in the First World War, were determined to see changes in the Church's structure. In 1918, the Enabling Act was passed, followed by the Parochial Church Councils Measure in 1921. At the Service of Thanksgiving, Archbishop Cosmo Lang said: 'For the first time, the laity in every parish throughout the land are offered voice and vote in the management of the church.' The long period of clerical absolutism which, as Owen Chadwick has noted, had existed since the end of 1868, came to an end. From now on, the vicar could not run the church without reference to anyone else. The Measure declared: 'It shall be the primary duty of the councils in every parish to co-operate with the incumbent in the administration, conduct and development of church work, both within the church and outside.' The councils established themselves as the administrative and financial committees of the parishes, responsible for such matters as finance, money-raising, fêtes and jumble sales, and finding teachers for the Sunday schools and leaders for the Cubs and Brownies.

In the inter-war years there was renewed agitation for the abolition of tithes. In 1836 the Tithe Computation Act was passed, and payment in kind was superseded by a cash payment called the tithe rent charge which was assessed on the average price of corn for the previous seven years. Opposition to the payment of tithe always intensified during periods of agricultural depression, and during the 1880s there was widespread agitation. However, this died down as a result of the Tithe Act of 1891, which transferred liability for these charges from the tenant to the owner of the land. As the large estates were broken up in the period after the First World War and there was a consequent increase in the number of owner-occupier tithepayers, once again agitation mounted against the payment of tithe. In 1930 a Tithepayers Defence Association was formed in Kent, and in the following year in Suffolk, Norfolk and Essex. Ultimately there were fifty such county organizations in England and Wales, and a National Tithepayers Association was established which fought against what its members regarded as the major injustice against the farming community, in that they were expected to pay a charge which other sections of the community did not meet. In one year alone, because of default in payment, 16,000 applications were made to the courts, mostly by the ecclesiastical authorities, for the distraint of goods. Effigies of the Archbishop of Canterbury and Queen Anne were burnt on a bonfire at Beachbrook Farm, Westwell near Ashford in Kent, on 5 April 1935, following an abortive auction sale of nine cattle seized for tithe arrears. In 1934 a Royal Commission was set up to inquire into and report on the whole question of the tithe-rent charge in England and Wales. The resulting Tithe Act of 1936 provided for the termination of the charge in 1996. Under the new arrangement the Government paid the church and lay tithe owners — such as Oxford and Cambridge colleges — large amounts in compensation for the abolition of tithes, but sought to recover the money from the farmers over a sixty-year period. Tithe collection was now a much quieter matter and compulsory redemption was carried through when land came onto the market. In June 1976, Parliament was informed that from October of the following year the collection of this charge would be suspended; the cost of collecting it had become too great. Thus ended the historic system of supporting the Church and its ministry in rural areas; perhaps the most remarkable feature of this system is that it has not left behind a legacy of bitterness.

The problems of many country clergy were exacerbated by the fact that the benefice houses, built in a period of limitless fuel and many servants, were now increasingly inappropriate and many of them had not been maintained to a sufficient standard for several generations. One clergyman's wife told the Church Assembly in 1933 that a brass band playing in the kitchen could not be heard in the drawing room of her twenty-one-roomed rural rectory. The Ecclesiastical Dilapidations Acts of 1871 and 1882 had led to the appointment of diocesan surveyors, who were required to produce a schedule of repairs and to issue certificates when these were completed. This ended the period in which the claims and counter-claims of outgoing and incoming incumbents had often to be settled in the courts. Almost the first act of the new Church Assembly was to pass the Ecclesiastical Dilapidations Measure, which enforced a single compulsory system by which incumbents were charged an annual payment and their houses were inspected on a five-year basis. This system worked well until after the Second World War when there was a formidable backlog of dilapidation and the annual assessments had become very high (though they were increasingly met by the parochial church council). The Dilapidations Commission was established in 1958, and a new Measure came into effect in 1972 whereby the diocese took over from the incumbent all responsibilities for the repair of the parsonage. By this time many dioceses were well advanced in the process of selling off the older and larger houses and building rectories and vicarages in villages which were more appropriate to the circumstances of clergy and their families in the second half of the twentieth century. Though many parishes have regretted the loss of what has become 'The Old Rectory', few clergy had sufficient income to live with even moderate comfort in these large houses, and the Church was unwilling to keep them in repair.

In this period the parishes of St Mary's Preston-on-Stour and St Mary's Whitchurch, were served by the Rector of Whitchurch; Atherstone was linked to a parish in the Gloucester diocese. Increasingly it was recognized, as has been noted in Chapter 4, that villages were suffering from a variety of factors and that the Church could make a real contribution to overcoming these problems. Many far-sighted clergy did, but as Robertson Scott wrote in the 1930s, 'If you would rouse the village you must first rouse the priest because the churches have the chance of doing so much for the rural district'. A survey in 1943 of a group of villages in north Oxfordshire commented on the isolation, demoralization and inadequate stipends of the clergy, and suggested in effect that a deanery team ministry should be set up, with salaries paid out of pooled endowments. It recommended also the use of retired clergy and arrangements for laity to be much more heavily involved in parochial work. This far-sighted report anticipated many of the changes which have taken place in the rural church in recent years.

12

The Parish Church in the
Contemporary Countryside

In recent years no part of the Church, not even in the inner city, has experienced such dramatic changes as the church in the countryside. Within the memory of many of the older members of the congregation the church had an acknowledged place in the life of the village, of which its resident clergyman was a conspicuous and respected member; well-attended services were held every Sunday; there were a Sunday School, a youth fellowship, uniformed organizations and a Mothers' Union, and much of village life seemed to focus naturally around the church and its annual programme of activities. Today, in many places, the clergyman responsible for the church lives as much as five miles away and is consequently rarely seen in the village; services are held at fortnightly intervals and the small congregation is oppressed by the financial burden of maintaining an ancient building. Of the annual programme of activities there is now almost no trace.

There are many who now doubt how much longer it will be possible to maintain such situations, which could be multiplied many times over, particularly in the remoter rural areas. Some commentators, as Wilfred Browning has noted, have argued that 'in England the parochial system as it has been known since the early Middle Ages, is at last on the point of breakdown'. It is in the inner city and the remoter countryside that this breakdown is most apparent; and many would maintain that it has already occurred. Reviewing a recent report on the Church in Suffolk, the religious affairs correspondent of *The Times* wrote: 'The Church of England faces extinction in the countryside in the next twenty years . . . It is a picture of almost unmitigated hopelessness' (7 June 1985). However gloomy the situation may look in places (as undeniably it does), such a comment fails to acknowledge that many people in numerous villages are searching with faith and imagination to find new ways to make the ancient parochial system work in very changed circumstances. For none would deny that the circumstances in which the country parish now operates have changed radically in recent years. Changes in ecclesiology, principally reflected in modern liturgies; and changes in the understanding of ministry, together with changes in the nature of the village itself (which have been examined in previous chapters), have radically reshaped the context in which the modern rural church operates. But perhaps nothing has had so far-reaching an effect as the decline in the number of stipendiary clergy.

In 1961 there were 15,488 full-time clergy in the Church of England. Leslie Paul, in his report of 1964, predicted that there would be 18,940 in 1971; in fact, there were only 15,223. In the next ten years there was a further sharp reduction of 4,000 clergy, to 10,922; and in 1984 there were 10,749 full-time diocesan clergy. However, it is the local effect of this contraction in clergy numbers which is of most significance. The South Hereford deanery had a population of 10,700 in 1871 and was served by twenty-six clergy; exactly 100 years later, the population had risen slightly, to 10,894, but the number of clergy had fallen to fifteen. As a very rough guide, it may be suggested that most rural deaneries have lost one clergyman every fifteen years during the decades of this century up to 1970, though the pace has been by no means even. Since then, however, this decline has accelerated, not least because in the mid 1970s a compulsory retirement age of seventy was fixed, though in fact the provision of better pensions allowed the majority of clergy the option of retiring at the age of sixty-five. In effect, between 1973 and 1984 many dioceses have reduced the number of their clergy by approximately one-third. Possibly the steepest decline has occurred in the Hereford diocese which had 320 clergy in 1932, but only 148 in 1985. However, in some areas the real decline in stipendiary clergy has been masked by the number of active retired clergy.

It is difficult to generalize about the rural church, because the extent of the decline in clergy numbers has varied from one area to another, although it has been felt most acutely in the remote and inaccessible areas. As early as the post-war period there was considerable difficulty in filling vacancies in these areas, and such vacancies tended to become longer. It is no coincidence that the experiments in group and team ministry occurred first in the remote Lincolnshire Wolds and the Norfolk Breckland. By contrast in the accessible countryside, until relatively recently, there has been little difficulty in filling parishes, and vacancies were relatively short. Many clergy have seen themselves as spending the last period of their active ministry in a rural area, and, as the 5,000 clergy ordained in the period immediately after the Second World War approached retirement age, so there was a steady supply of applicants for rural parishes. As late as 1969 Bishop Frank West (then Bishop of Taunton), wrote in the *Church Times:* 'There is no shortage of clergy anywhere in the rural dioceses.'

However, by the 1970s, the declining number of clergy was having an effect on church life in every area, both urban and rural. None the less there remained, at least in percentage terms, a much larger proportion of clergy working in the countryside. This was one of the principal conclusions of the Paul Report (1964), which had shown that whereas there was one clergyman per 1,000 of population in rural areas (such as Hereford), there was one to every 6,000 of the population in urban areas (such as London and Birmingham). According to his yardstick, Paul suggested that a quarter of the clergy were overworked, while a third were underemployed; the latter group were almost exclusively in the countryside. One of the respondents to his questionnaire had a parish of only 220 people; another wrote: 'The parish is not a full-time job . . . it is very easy to find oneself gently rotting away.' At the same time Paul was able to show that half the benefices of the Church of England contained only 10 per cent of the population (in the rural areas), while less than one-tenth of the benefices contained one-third of the population (in the cities). Paul reported that, in 1961, 15 per cent of the clergy (1,566) served single parishes of under 1,000 population.

In 1974 the Church sought to take tentative steps to rectify this imbalance between the urban and rural deployment of the clergy, and the Sheffield Report of that year suggested a formula for the deployment of clergy which sought a gradual reduction of their numbers in some rural areas. This further accelerated the decline in clergy numbers, and in some rural deaneries there was a 50 per cent reduction in the number of clergy between the mid 1970s and the mid 1980s. At the same time, for a variety of reasons which included the fact that clergymen's wives found it difficult to obtain jobs in rural areas, the countryside became a less attractive place for younger clergy. Consequently the practice, which had long been condemned, of encouraging elderly and sick clergy to accept rural livings, had to be continued.

By the 1970s the Church was beginning to be aware that it was faced with considerable problems in many rural areas, and solutions were canvassed with a new urgency. Different dioceses adopted different approaches but, gradually, three distinct pastoral strategies emerged. The idea of a collaborative ministry, in which a number of clergy and parishes co-operate together to form a single unit, has a long history in the Church. One of the best summaries of its aims was given by the Vicar of St Mary's Portsea, Cosmo Lang, in his annual report to the parish in 1900. He said: 'It secures a large district from the local jealousies and controversies of small isolated parishes; it keeps a large area in touch with a fuller and wider church life; it prevents a clergyman sinking into dullness and depression under the weight of isolated responsibility; it maintains an atmosphere of freshness and readiness to make new ventures.' In the previous century, the Vicar of Andover and Bishop John Wordsworth had contemplated such an approach for the revitalization of the churches in rural Hampshire, but the constraints of the ecclesiastical law prohibited any experiment of this nature.

In rural areas, collaborative ministry dates from 1949 when Dr Harland, Bishop of Lincoln, established the South Ormsby Group, which came into full operation in 1952. Twelve small parishes with a total population of 1,100, in approximately seventy-five square miles, previously served by six elderly clergy, were welded together to form a single group served by a rector, two assistant clergy and a deaconess. In 1961 nine parishes, then totally without pastoral care, in the northern part of the Breckland area of west Norfolk, were formed into the Hilborough Group. In many respects this was modelled closely on the lines Archdeacon Smith had drawn at South Ormsby, with ten parishes, a rector, a senior assistant curate and a deacon. The area of the Hilborough Group, while large, was less than that of South Ormsby, being forty square miles with a total population of 1,800. In the next ten years seventeen groups were established in Norfolk, and by the time of the retirement of Launcelot Fleming in 1970 appoximately a third of the parishes and a third of the clergy in that diocese, were involved in collaborative ministries. In operation, the groups varied considerably, as did the nomenclature. Some referred to themselves as groups, others as teams, while others described themselves as 'a team of clergy ministering to a group of parishes'. However, each group sought to provide, for a wide area, a pastoral ministry which combined on-the-spot local pastoral care with centralized planning of services and other activities such as youth and children's work, adult education and conformation classes. Like the Methodist circuit system the groups were seen as a means of allowing the strong to support the weak and permitting the clergy to work together, as a team, to their own and the parishes' mutual advantage.

Leslie Paul, writing of the rural clergyman in 1964 said that it was statistically the case that he had more cries of despair from incumbents in the countryside than in the towns. The debilitating problem of raising considerable sums of money from small communities to repair historic buildings, coupled with indifference, isolation, poverty, large houses and gardens, non-payment of clerical expenses, the feeling of being ignored and irrelevant, appeared to dull the faith and encourage despair in the hearts of many caring and able priests. One such clergyman wrote: 'The amount contributed for all church purposes last year was £23. I have had five confirmation candidates in seventeen years. There is no parochial church council, no organ, no choir, no verger, no heating in the winter.' This seems an extreme case, but the report cites others which are equally depressing and Paul finishes this section of his report by saying: 'one conclusion presses itself; the inflexibility of the existing parochial system is an impediment to the exercise of the church's pastoral ministry . . .'

The Pastoral Recommendations Committee set up by the Church Assembly as a result of Leslie Paul's report, endorsed with enthusiasm the notion of collaborative ministry, and the terms 'group' and 'team' were invested with legal connotations in the Pastoral Measure 1968. This consolidating measure embodied many of the proposals contained in the Paul Report and had a considerable effect on all rural areas. The Measure, the purpose of which was 'to make better provision for the care of souls through the re-organization of parishes and ministries', gave considerable powers to the diocesan pastoral committee. The Measure amended the law relating to pluralities and the union of parishes and benefices, and enabled parishes to be created without a parish church. It provided for the alteration of ecclesiastical boundaries, for the preservation or disposal of redundant churches, and for the setting up of group and team ministries. A team was defined as a single benefice (often formally comprised of a number of benefices), served by a staff of clergy, one of whom was the team rector. A group was defined as a federation of independent benefices, with a number of clergy working together and commissioned 'to assist each other so as to make the best possible provision for the cure of souls throughout the area of the group ministry'. The basic unit of both these forms of ministry is the benefice (and not the parish). A simple distinction between the two is that a team is a single benefice and a group is comprised of several.

Gradually, throughout the 1970s, the number of groups increased, as did the number of dioceses in which they were established, despite the fact that collaborative ministry has always suffered from being regarded as a regrettable necessity rather than a hopeful and effective way of developing the ancient parochial system. By the late 1970s, the continuing decline in the number of clergy sharply increased the number of dioceses which were prepared to regard collaborative ministry as part of their strategy for rural areas. By 1983, in the Church of England as a whole, 10 per cent of the clergy worked in collaborative ministries, comprising in total 333 teams and eighty-one groups. Such ministries, by pooling the resources of an area and by allowing the clergy to work together as colleagues, have brought new life and vigour to many rural areas, and have encouraged younger clergy to work in the countryside. However, such ministries are not spread evenly across rural dioceses, and a number of dioceses, including Salisbury, Bath and Wells, and Exeter, together account for a significant number of the rural collaborative ministries.

A second strategy, which recommended itself to many dioceses, was that of attempting to concentrate the resources of the Church on the larger villages and market towns, from which the smaller villages and hamlets could be served, as was recommended in the north Oxfordshire report mentioned in the previous chapter. One of the effects of the Pastoral Measure 1968 was to establish in every diocese a pastoral committee. In the early 1970s many of these committees produced strategy documents which were, in a real sense, the ecclesiastical equivalents of the county structure plans. These documents (Hereford 1971; Coventry 1972; Bath and Wells, and Worcester 1973; Exeter 1974) were, in effect, a management plan for the diocese, which in many cases involved the establishment of a management structure, the centralization of resources, and the pruning of the extensive network of country churches. The Pastoral Measure 1968 had introduced the possibility of declaring a church to be redundant as a regular place of worship. There were many who believed that the large number of rural churches, particularly in some of the remote areas, was one of the major hindrances to the effectiveness of the Church's ministry. In some dioceses plans were adopted to prune selectively the Church's rural network, and lists were compiled of churches designated for redundancy. Many dioceses found that when a village discovered that its name was on the list, this had a galvanizing effect on local church life. However, a number of rural churches have been declared redundant (between 1969 and 1984 the national total was 1,002). Eighty churches have been declared redundant in the Lincoln diocese which, together with Norwich, has a very large number of medieval churches many of which are situated in small hamlets.

A second element in this planned approach to the rural church concerned the rural dean, who was frequently portrayed in such documents as the Church's 'middle management'. Leslie Paul had laid much stress on the deanery and had called rural deans 'bishops in little'. John Adair advocated the adoption of the deanery as the basic pastoral unit of the countryside, saying: 'Central to my proposed policy is the concept of a team ministry based upon the deanery unit. The Dean should be the leader of the ministry team in this area.' Others saw the Saxon minster, with its college of canons, as providing ancient legitimation for this strategy. However, in practice, deaneries have proved themselves to be too large an area to constitute a meaningful pastoral unit in rural areas. Historically, deaneries have never been considered in this light. They were established by Samuel Wilberforce, Bishop of Oxford, in the mid nineteenth century in their recognizably modern form.

He wrote, in a letter of 1846: ' . . . my great objective is that the rural dean should form an easy and accurate medium of communication between me and the clergy of the deanery.' Wilberforce's 'medium of communication' understanding of the deanery was steadily developed, through the Ruri-decanal Conference, and further defined when the deanery became an integral part of synodical structure in the early 1970s. Clearly, an organization as complex as a modern diocese needs appropriate means of internal communication, but the deanery remains an artificial construct within the Church, designed principally for this end, rather than to serve a pastoral purpose. To suggest that the deanery should fulfil a wider and essentially different role as the principal pastoral unit of the Church is to alter considerably the Church of England's traditional understanding both of its local ministry and of its own nature.

In practice, the planned approach to the problems of the rural church, as exemplified by the diocesan strategy documents of the mid 1970s, was only implemented on a limited scale in the Church of England. By contrast, in the Methodist Church, a parallel policy was widely adopted: many small chapels were closed, and the ministry was centralized in such towns as Downham Market. While there are a few examples of deanery teams in rural areas, some of which are focused on market towns, on the whole the particular nature of the Church of England, and its essentially local commitment and involvement, made it resistant to the implementation of a planned diocesan policy. In some dioceses, aspects of the mid 1970s strategies have been implemented, but in all cases this has had to be done on a piecemeal basis, as a result of the constraints which freehold and patronage impose on any attempt to plan the rural church from the diocesan centre. However, centralist policies are advocated by a significant number of country clergy today who have come to regard the large number of church buildings in their case as liabilities which absorb their time and energy. Such clergy often advocate the closing-down of many of the church buildings, and encouraging people to travel on Sundays to a small number of central churches in the towns and larger villages.

Today, in all the predominantly rural dioceses, the vast majority of country parishes are served as part of a cluster of parishes under the care of a single stipendiary clergyman, a form of ministry often called multi-parish ministry. A glance at the *Church Times* appointments column will reveal many incidents of a clergyman, who is already serving three or four country parishes, also taking responsibility for two or three neighbouring parishes. As a result, in some areas multi-parish ministries of between four and six have become the general rule, and eight to ten are not uncommon. In the Golden Valley in Hereford one clergyman had thirteen parishes; and there is one example of a multi-parish ministry of seventeen in Lincolnshire. In the Lincoln and Hereford dioceses six parishes per clergyman is now the norm. A typical large multi-parish ministry will involve ten parishes and may stretch twelve miles in each direction and include 3,000 people. Clearly, the differences between this form of ministry and a collaborative ministry, though real, are at best artificial. Some multi-parish ministries are organized as if they were a centralized ministry; some collaborative ministries appear to be a number of adjacent multi-parish ministries. Many multi-parish ministries have suffered at their onset from being brought together in a piecemeal and random way, as a result of the timing of vacancies in neighbouring parishes, and with little or no regard to the social geography of the area. Some individual parishes have been linked in various combinations with their neighbours over the last twenty-five years.

Multi-parish ministries are the third and least radical strategy, for they are at one level merely a means by which the available clergy can be spread more thinly over the countryside. Many parishioners expect the clergyman to continue to exercise a traditional ministry, even though he now has six parishes, while within living memory the parish was served by a resident clergyman responsible for that parish alone. As a consequence of this situation, multi-parish ministries highlight one of the basic problems of rural ministry today: the tension between the desire of the clergy to centralize church life and the desire of the people that it should remain essentially local. Some multi-parish ministries are run as if they were a number of adjacent but essentially unrelated parishes; this is probably only possible when the numbers are confined to under four. However, certainly above six, a threshold is passed above which it is no longer possible for the clergyman to treat the parishes on an individual basis and he will find it necessary to develop a more centralized approach to some aspects of parish life. It is not hard to sympathize with the desire of the Lincolnshire clergyman who, in 1984, presided at twenty-one annual general meetings of church or church-related organizations for some degree of centralization. But village identity, and the significance of the church as a potent symbol of that identity, is a strong force. In practice, some compromise has to be achieved which recognizes the limits of what a clergyman working on his own can reasonably hope to achieve, and what people in the individual parishes actually want.

In considering the rural church today, account has to be taken of the fact that the majority of rural churches are small in terms of the size of the regular congregation. There is a tendency in all denominations to underestimate the number of small churches, and as a consequence denominational literature and material often implies that the normative church is larger than in reality it is. The Methodist Constitution, for instance, assumes that a church will have a membership of 150. However, among the 8,000 Methodist churches there are only 800 (10 per cent) with a total membership of more than this number, and 4,000 (or 50 per cent) of all Methodist churches have a membership of under thirty. What is true for the Methodist Church, that it is predominantly a denomination of small churches, is true of all other denominations. In the Baptist Union, of 2,041 churches three-quarters have a membership of less than 100, and half have a membership of less than fifty. In at least one United Reformed Church province, 30 per cent of the churches have a membership of below twenty-five. In the Church of England, the concept of membership is not so strongly articulated, but in many rural dioceses the proportion of churches with an active participating membership of under twenty-five appears to be of the same order (as was indicated by a recent survey of part of the diocese of St Edmundsbury and Ipswich). Another recent survey has indicated that, nationally, 30 per cent of Anglican churches attract twenty-five or fewer worshippers on an average Sunday. Thus, rural congregations are characteristically small in number and this is one of the most important single facts concerning the rural church.

However, it should be noted that the majority of rural settlements have a population of under 500, and many are much smaller. In such communities, a congregation of twenty-five represents a more significant engagement with the community than a congregation of 250 in a large suburban parish of 20,000. In fact, as Leslie Paul noted, there appears to be an inverse relationship between the number of people in a parish and the proportion of that population which attends church. That is to say, that the proportion of people who attend church increases as the size of the settlement diminishes. On average (though there are significant regional differences, particularly between the western and eastern sides of the country) in a small rural settlement of 500 or below, approximately 10—15 per cent of the population is likely to attend worship on a regular basis; in medium-sized rural settlements, with a population of approximately 1,000, the proportion falls to between 8 and 10 per cent. (The national average is approximately 3 per cent.) The small size of the typical rural church accounts for many of its characteristic features. In many rural churches there tends to be a nucleus of people who are in a real sense 'the church'. Small numbers can give rise to a sense of failure and defeat (even if in proportional terms the church is relatively successful in its engagement with the surrounding community). For instance, the dioceses of Guildford and Lincoln have approximately the same population, but the latter has four times as many churches. As a consequence, one diocese is characterized by large congregations which are planning to increase the size of the church building; the other is characterized by small congregations coping as best they can with the maintenance of an historic church.

In the view of many, the rural church passed through a particularly 'low' period in the mid 1960s and early 1970s, before the impact of some of the reforms to the structure and finances of the Church (especially the Pastoral Measure 1968 and the Synodical Government Measure 1969) was widely felt. None the less there persists in many churches a sense, however historically inaccurate, that things have been and are declining and such churches tend to be pervaded by a sense of unexpectant, dogged heroism rather than one of confidence and hope. This is often allied to a conservatism which is itself an expression of insecurity and fear. Whatever happens, the congregation, that small nucleus of people, are determined that the church will not close in their day, and church life can easily be dominated by a feeling that the current congregation are the last adherents of the old tradition. It is important to appreciate that the strength and vigour of the rural church cannot be determined by statistical means; the most important aspects of the rural church are not readily accessible to sociological inquiry. A small church is not a failed large church; it has its own character, structure and dynamics which need to be understood and appreciated. In a small church there can be a deep feeling of fellowship, a quality of caring that is absent elsewhere, as well as a high degree of integration into the local community and a directness and simplicity in worship. As Carl Dudley has written: 'In a big world, the small church has remained intimate; in a fast world, the small church has remained stable. In an expensive world, the small church has remained plain. In a complex world, the small church has remained simple. In a rational world, the small church has kept feelings. In a mobile world, the small church has become an anchor. In an anonymous world, the small church calls us by name.'

The fact that rural churches are small membership churches dominates the central activity of the Church, which is worship. Indeed, in some country churches with very small congregations, it is almost impossible to sustain what might be termed public worship, for inevitably the services begin to feel like a private act rather than a public occasion. There are many churches in which, when a certain group of people arrive, the start of the service need no longer be delayed, for no one else is expected. The empty rows of pews and the weakly sung hymns serve only to reinforce the private and closed nature of such an act of worship. In the post-war period, and in some areas until relatively recently, it was still customary to find country churches where there was an expectation that Sunday services would take place at 8 a.m., 11 a.m. and 6.30 p.m., possibly with a Sunday school either during the 11 a.m. service or in the mid-afternoon. Each service tended to have its own following and to be marked by a different character. For example, the particular atmosphere of the 'early service' was for generations almost the defining characteristic of rural Anglicanism; for others, choral Matins, which was solemn, unemotional and majestic, and had about it something of the atmosphere of the public school chapel in the era of Empire, was what characterized the country church. In the evening the service tended to be sung, with the choir again present, but the sermon was shorter and the service was less formal than in the morning.

However, this pattern of worship was already breaking down even in the inter-war years, and certainly in the post-war period a number of churches dramatically altered this traditional pattern. First, the decline in the number of clergy, and the linking together of parishes, inevitably led to an overall decline in the number of services. Only the larger villages and market towns were able to maintain a three-service Sunday pattern, and increasingly, the smaller country churches had only a single service on Sunday. The loss of Evensong, according to some contemporary sources, was particularly regretted and had the unintended consequence of tending to unchurch some people who had previously been attenders only at evening worship and never became part of the morning congregation.

Gradually, in the 1960s, the parish communion movement, which had taken firm root in suburban parishes, began to make an impact in rural areas. In a different age, and when one service per Sunday was becoming the norm in many country churches, it seemed to many that Matins was no longer suitable or appropriate as the principal morning service. Many country clergy sought to change the pattern of services so that a service of parish communion became the regular Sunday-morning worship, partly for reasons of theological preference, partly for more practical reasons. Such a service aimed at a different atmosphere for, among other things, the service had to be 'child-worthy'; in many places it was both brighter and obviously a congregational service. At the same time as liturgical revision progressed, so the various new orders of service were adopted in village churches. These services, which led to the publication of the Alternative Service Book in 1980, contained a subtly different theology of the Church from that found in the Book of Common Prayer. The theology of the Church in the new service books, which was that of the Lord's people gathered round the Lord's table, tended to supplant older understandings of the nature of the Church as the offering of the whole community to God in prayer.

Some critics have seen in these changes the impact of suburbanization on the rural church in this period. Certainly, while a century before, many Church of England clergy were born and bred in the countryside, the number of such clergy rapidly diminished. In previous generations, many clergy brought to their ministry an instinctive understanding of the nature of country villages and their churches. Today, the picture is totally different; the overwhelming majority of ordinands come from urban and suburban parishes and naturally bring to rural ministry urban assumptions about the nature of community and of the Church, which are reinforced in their theological colleges and early ministerial experience. Thus, some have suggested that the parish communion movement, advocated by such clergy, has had the unintended consequence of distancing the Church from the mainstream of village life. As a result of this and other changes, the rural church in many areas has come to assume the character of a eucharistic sect as opposed to that of a community church. Certainly, as Canon Charles Smyth once observed, the spirituality of country people 'has never been naturally sacramental, but was in the early period mystical and more latterly moral'. However, it is undeniable that the adoption of the parish communion as the single and only service in many country churches has altered the nature of the rural church at a much more profound level than merely altering the service book and the form of worship.

If it is possible to speak in such terms, an average multi-parish ministry has a combination of parish communion services, family services and evensongs (though the latter are not found everywhere). Family services recognize the reality of church life in many villages in which it is families, rather than individuals, who attend church; and worship needs to be structured in such a way that there is something to engage the interest and commitment of all age groups. Family services range from those which have a fixed order and are in a sense a modern version of Morning Prayer, to those that are unstructured and in which there is much congregational participation; indeed, some are taken entirely by members of the congregation. Such services allow the less committed relatively easy access to the worshipping life of the church where a greater commitment can develop. Evening services have been severely hit by competition from television and other entertainments, and the general decline of 'the English Sunday'. It is customary to say that the television serial of *The Forsyte Saga*, which was shown in 1967 on Sunday evenings, decimated Evensong, and at the same time the popularity of religious television ('Stars on Sunday' started in 1969) had a contributory effect.

In any part of the countryside it can be seen that there are a variety of approaches to multi-parish ministry today; the distinction between these approaches shows particularly clearly over the provision of Sunday services. In some multi-parish ministries there is an attempt to provide a service in every church on every Sunday, though as the number of parishes rises this can become increasingly difficult for the clergyman. Others attempt a monthly scheme of services which gives the larger churches a service on every Sunday, but the smaller ones have services either fortnightly or at greater intervals. Others pursue a more centralized plan, based on a monthly parish communion in one church for the whole area, which gives shape to the month's work and is something to work towards, to visit towards and prepare for. Whatever policy is pursued, at some level there has to be a compromise between the clergyman's desire to centralize and concentrate church life, and the desire of many people in the villages for it to remain essentially local. Achieving this compromise is one of the major areas of tension in contemporary rural ministry, and the problem is considered in the next chapter.

Many commentators have observed that there are essentially two Churches of England. Certainly, in many country parishes, there are in effect two distinct congregations. One is the smaller congregation whose members attend the regular Sunday-by-Sunday worship, know each other intimately, feel themselves to be responsible for the life and administration of the church, and are in effect 'the Church' in the village. At the same time there is a much larger congregation, sometimes including a sizeable proportion of the whole community, who regard themselves as members of the church but who attend relatively infrequently, sometimes only on the major church festivals or other special occasions. The tension between these two congregations and their different expectations and understandings will be considered further below, but on major church festivals the second of these congregations is usually present in considerable numbers. Special occasions play a particularly important role in country churches and the year is centred around the celebration of Christmas, Mothering Sunday, Easter, Harvest and Remembrance Sunday. Of these special occasions Christmas is by far the most significant, and many country churches have their largest congregations at this period, when carol services, nativity plays, special services for the old people's club and the Women's Institute augment the regular pattern. By contrast, Easter tends to coincide with considerable activity on the farm and often the first spell of warmer weather, when many people go on holiday; attendance at Easter services often fails to come up to expectations. After a long summer gap, Harvest Festival is another occasion of large congregations and is usually accompanied by harvest suppers either in the village hall or in the church, sales of produce, and other harvest events. Remembrance Sunday is celebrated both in the church and at the war memorial on the village green and marks the last of the principal village occasions. Much can be made of the traditional festivals such as Plough Sunday, Rogation Day and Lammas, though all of these need some considerable reinterpretation, as they reflect farming patterns that have long since ceased to exist.

The most significant consequence of recent changes in the pattern of worship in rural churches, and particularly the emphasis on parish communion, has been that the provision of services is now even more closely tied with the availability of clergy. The coincidence of the sharp decline in clergy numbers and the emergence of a pattern of worship increasingly dependent on the presence of a priest, has led to a situation in which the availability of clergy increasingly shapes this and other aspects of church life. The need for rural clergy to service the largest possible number of churches on any particular Sunday, has led to a situation in which it is now normal for the clergyman to arrive from a previous service at the last minute, and sometimes to disappear during the last hymn (the singing of which is partly drowned by the roar of his departing car). It is practices such as this that have led many to advocate more centralist solutions, with fewer services at strategic points.

However, there is much to be said for adopting patterns whereby each parish in a multi-parish ministry has its Sunday service at the preferred time, irrespective of neighbouring parishes. The clergyman comes to celebrate Holy Communion occasionally; readers come to preach more frequently; but, when neither is available to come, the congregation itself takes responsibility for the worshipping life of the church. This is well within the bounds of possibility for almost all rural parishes. While not wishing to deny the centrality of Holy Communion, nor the significance of preaching, it is important above all things that the local congregation should meet for worship and that the worshipping life of the church should be regular and continuous. If stipendiary clergy numbers decline further, and if the pattern of worship remains tied to the availability of a clergyman, many parishes may find themselves in a situation of having only one service a month. One of the most encouraging features of many country parishes in recent years is the fact that people have come forward who are willing to take the service, or parts of the service, so that an authentic local church life, based on regular worship, can be maintained even in the smallest community.

A further aspect of worship in a country church is that of finding an acceptable compromise between the different preferences of various groups that can be found in the contemporary village. One group may prefer the 1662 Prayer Book and a formal approach to worship; while another may prefer the Alternative Service Book and a more relaxed and informal style of worship that can absorb noisy children in moderate numbers. Differences in preference can be extreme, as between those who prefer a Christmas carol service led by a village choir accompanied by the American organ much damaged by mice, to those who would rather listen in silence to taped music from King's College Chapel, Cambridge. Such contrasts between local involvement and supreme excellence are only one dimension of these differences. Furthermore, it should be noted that in some congregations Sunday may prove to be the least convenient day, particularly in those areas with a large number of retired people (for whom Sunday is the day when they either visit or are visited by their young families); those who participate in sporting events (many of which take place on a Sunday); and members of the local farming community (who, if they have stock to feed in the winter months find the timing of Sunday services difficult). Midweek evening services, often in a private house, can provide an important addition to the pattern of services in a country parish, particularly in the winter months.

Finally, baptisms, marriages and burials are simply extreme manifestations of the general proposition that people in the village still, in the main, expect the church to be a means by which they find significance and meaning in life; and they expect their local clergyman to preside at these important family events. Many of the families who do not attend church regularly, still expect to bring their babies to baptism and their children to marriage in the church, and will be puzzled and mystified if they are met with anything other than a welcome and by attitudes which tend to exclude all but the most dedicated. For the village church is not a gathered church, in the sense that that term is used of suburban churches, but is the symbol of the presence of Christ at the centre of a community. Such a church needs to be inclusive rather than exclusive; it needs to be welcoming and to have thresholds which are easily crossed by the less committed on their journey in faith.

In the nineteenth century the abundance of clergy meant that even the smallest country parish, such as Atherstone-on-Stour, was served by a full-time resident clergyman. Indeed, the three parishes of the Stour valley mentioned in Chapters 10 and 11 each had its own clergyman until the 1920s, although the total population was never more than 500. Particularly in the late nineteenth century, when new understandings of the clergyman's role decreased their involvement in the civic and administrative elements of village life, the clergyman and his family became responsible for every aspect of church life, however small. At that time the pastoral strategy of the Church (in so far as it is possible to speak of it in such coherent terms) was that of Nelson's navy: to appoint the best man available and give him total power and responsibility. In the late nineteenth century, in marked distinction to the eighteenth century, attitudes of dependence and deference developed which accentuated and perpetuated this situation. All church life became dependent upon the activity and attitudes of the clergyman, and even those who were willing to take some part in the life of their parish church saw this in terms of 'helping out the vicar', for he and his family often ran the church almost as if it was their private chapel or an extension of their family prayers, a view which had been encouraged by many of the Victorian writers on pastoral practice. There can be little doubt that the contemporary reluctance of many church people to become involved in the life and ministry of their parishes is a consequence of the form in which the church leadership was shaped in the nineteenth century. The presence of a highly trained man whose role is to promote the goals of the organization, encourages those around him to leave matters entirely in his hands. It has been argued by some that the presence of a professional man inhibits the growth of a shared and corporate ministry even in those places where the clergyman is willing and able to share with his congregation functions which were previously understood to be exclusively his preserve.

Today, expectations formed in this period have lingered on; still in many places the view that the church belongs to the vicar and that he alone is responsible for its life and activity, is deeply ingrained. Many local people in the countryside find it difficult to conceive of church life without a resident clergyman directing it and being responsible for every aspect of its life. It has become common to say that, in structural terms, the country parish has a 'parson-shaped hole' in the middle. When this hole is filled, the church is somehow complete and functioning properly but when it is unfilled, there is a profound sense of incompleteness which, because of the strong expectations formed in previous generations, many people find disturbing and disorientating.

In recent years the decline in the number of clergy has meant that it has not been possible to fill all vacancies as they have arisen and the 'parson-shaped hole' in the middle of many country churches has not been filled with a resident stipendiary incumbent. The majority of parishes have had to share a clergyman who may reside in the next parish, but, more recently, may live several parishes away and as much as ten miles from the village itself. There are still many people who regard this as an unfortunate and essentially temporary state of affairs, which an upturn in the number of ordinations will rectify. On that day, 'the Bishop will then allow us to have our own vicar again'. However, there is nothing in contemporary church life to encourage the belief that this will be either possible or desirable.

However, despite the sharp decline in the number of clergy, the traditional parish system has received only minor modification in recent years. Claims that it is on the point of breaking down have been made for the last hundred years, but the parochial system has proved a very flexible instrument of church strategy. None the less, in recent years, it has been acknowledged that this strategy has been stretched to the utmost, particularly in the remoter countryside, as stipendiary clergy have been called to serve an increasing number of parishes. As a result, where it has proved impossible to fill the 'parson-shaped hole', a number of schemes to provide a substitute or supplementary ministry have come to the fore. The first of these was the development of non-stipendiary ministry which traces its roots back to the work of Roland Allen, who was a country clergyman in Buckinghamshire before the First World War and for much of his life a missionary in China.

Non-stipendiary ministry was authorized by the bishops in 1970 (as auxiliary pastoral ministry). Under this scheme a man is ordained but continues to earn his living in his secular job. There are now a considerable number of such ministers working in the rural church, though their distribution is uneven (800 non-stipendiary ministers now work in the Church of England as a whole). In one rural diocese, one in seven of all the clergy are non-stipendiary. Yet in some areas it has not been easy to find recruits and a variety of reasons are offered for this. Some suggest that while in an urban area a non-stipendiary minister will join other clerical colleagues as an assistant, in the village, where he is alone, the mantle of the former stipendiary clergyman is difficult to inherit. Inevitably, the non-stipendiary clergyman finds himself subjected to the same expectations and valuations as his stipendiary predecessor. Others have made the point that village residents know in their bones a good deal about the social dynamics of small-scale communities. Traditionally, part of the ethos of villages has been that 'one keeps one's head down'. The reason for this has to do with the nature of social relations in a small-scale community, and to fail in this is to invite the operation of some of the subtle and not so subtle manifestations of community sanction. For these reasons, although people will help in any way they can, many are reluctant to resume the type of role among their neighbours which non-stipendiary ministry envisages. Such things should not necessarily be accepted at their face value by the Church, but neither should they be denied, for they are part of the pattern of constraints in which local ministry has to operate. The fact that the stipendiary clergyman is 'a man from outside', is still of significance in the dynamics of small-scale rural settlements.

More recently a localized form of non-stipendiary ministry (variously called local ordained ministry, or local non-stipendiary ministry) has been developed, principally in the dioceses of Hereford and Lincoln, and it is hoped that it will make a significant contribution in rural areas. In this form of local ministry the onus is on the local congregation to select and present a candidate to the bishop for training and subsequent ordination. The training is local and it is envisaged that the ministry will be confined to the locality which originally initiated and authorized the appointment. Celebrating the Eucharist and leading worship will form a primary element in the clergyman's role, in those areas where there are few clergy, though the tendency to see his ministry exclusively in these terms must be resisted. Such a development is a further extension of the traditional pattern but with a significant change: that the initiative lies with the local church, whose members are in effect taking responsibility for their own ministry.

In some areas, for both practical and theological reasons, the attempt to fill the 'parson-shaped hole' with a non-stipendiary clergyman has been seen as a cautious and clericalist solution to the problems of rural ministry. In recent years there have been a number of attempts to identify and commission lay people to take responsibility in local churches. A number of dioceses including St Edmundsbury and Ipswich, and Salisbury, have well-developed schemes of lay elders, lay pastors, or pastoral assistants, who are trained and commissioned to take a pastoral and leadership role in the local church; and other dioceses have sought to reinterpret the role of the reader.

In many contemporary discussions of pastoral strategy in the countryside, there is much talk about the significance of the 'focal person' who is the centre and pivot of local church life, and opinions differ as to whether he or she should be ordained or not. This echoes similar discussions in community development work concerning the importance of leadership in voluntary organizations. However, there is a sense in which all these experiments may be regarded as an attempt to maintain the traditional structure of the local church in changed circumstances by filling the 'parson-shaped hole' with a substitute figure. In some instances this has been very successful, but even in these cases it has tended to perpetuate a situation in which the church remains dependent upon the leadership of a single individual.

The pressing need in the country church today is for the local church to take responsibility for its own life and ministry. The church is not a group of people gathered round a minister; but a group of people who together share the ministry. At a time when the number of clergy is declining, and will continue to decline, at least in the immediate future, it is necessary to recapture the historic nature of the local church as an organization which is not wholly dependent upon the availability of stipendiary clergy. The local church needs to see itself again as responsible for its own life, worship and ministry. If the Church is to survive and grow in the modern countryside, the deeply rooted expectation that everything must be initiated and carried out by the incumbent must give place to a view of the church which is locally based. In each parish there is a need to develop a ministerial team of people who will together be the community ministry of the church in that place. Of course, already informally, in many places such a team exists, comprised of people who corporately take responsibility for the many-sided aspects of church life, including its worship and pastoral ministry. This needs to be developed and shaped in a much more purposeful way, so that all parishes in the countryside possess a nucleus of people who pray together and are the community ministry of the church in that place. It is the role of the clergyman to support the ministerial team, to identify and encourage new members; to help the local church define and set its goals; to provide the training; and to animate and invigorate such a ministerial team. Such a team would be comprised of church wardens, readers and other office holders, as well as those who have gifts in leading worship and in pastoral ministry, and those responsible for other aspects of church life such as its youth and children's work. It might encourage one of its members to offer for non-stipendiary ministry. The development of community ministry and maintaining the team's coherence in the centre of the church's ministry in country parishes, is an important part of a stipendiary clergyman's work.

However, no one should minimize the difficulty of persuading people, particularly those who already have considerable responsibilities both to their families and to their jobs, to take on such additional commitments. Many enterprises in the village fail because it is impossible to find people who are willing to provide the necessary leadership, who can sacrifice a sufficient amount of their time, and who are willing to accept the discipline of such an undertaking. At the same time, areas differ considerably in the availability of such leadership. In some cases there seems to be an oversupply, while in others it is hard to find people who will form part of such a team. There will certainly be some areas, particularly the more remote countryside, in which a more clergy-centred style of ministry will remain appropriate. However, it is necessary in the contemporary situation of rural parishes for the Church as a whole to make its life and future growth less dependent on the availability of stipendiary clergymen. By contrast, the clergyman's role becomes that of supporting and serving the local church and developing its community ministry, rather than the more directive and traditional understanding.

Any consideration of the Church in the modern countryside will be dominated by two central questions: What sort of Church is it? and Whose Church is it? Just as it has been noted above that there are two distinct congregations in the country church today, so there are two models of the Church as an institution: the village church model and the gathered church model. Traditionally, the village church has been seen as conterminous with the community and deeply rooted in all aspects of local life, of which it is both the custodian of history and an important focus of activity and identity. The Church, according to the village church model, is seen as conterminous with the village and as an expression of its religious life. Richard Hooker, in his famous statement of this historic Anglican understanding, wrote: 'With us one society is both Church and Commonwealth . . . which people are not part of them the Commonwealth, and part of them the Church of God, but the selfsame people whole and entire.'*

Every villager, whether he attends worship frequently, infrequently, or not at all, is still thought of as in some sense belonging to the Church, and this even extends to members of other Churches, many of whom (particularly in the non-conformist tradition) still refer to the parish church and its incumbent as 'our church' and 'our vicar'. The church represents the spiritual aspect of village life, and whether it is well attended or not, it is still

---

* *Of the Laws of Ecclesiastical Politie* (1597), Book *VII*, ch. 1, par.7.

thought of as 'the villagers' church'. There is a sense in which the few, who form the regular congregation, are there on behalf of and in place of the many who are absent, and represent in a real manner the totality of the village. Threats to the church, such as structural deterioration or pastoral reorganization, are felt by the whole village and a response is looked for and found from the whole community. The idea of membership is foreign to the village church model; it is a church whose frontiers coincide with that of the village and through whose doors all enter, not as intruders, but as those with an acknowledged place. The philosophy of the village church model is that of dissolving the church in the veins of village society so that all village life is baptized and hallowed by the church. Such a church will not attempt to create the multitude of church-based organizations which can be found in a suburban parish, but will encourage members of the congregation to be involved in the activities and organizations of the village. This attitude towards the village is symbolized by the parish magazine, which is not the house journal of the church, but is a community document reflecting the many-sided aspects of village life and containing contributions and announcements from all the various elements of the village.

By contrast, many of those who have recently moved into the village, see its church as a scaled-down version of a suburban or city centre church. A successful church, by this estimation, is one that has a full carpark on Sunday, a host of midweek clubs and meetings, and a successful and growing congregation with many young people. It is in every sense a gathered church, which is seen as a separate organization within the village, with its own membership, organization, leaders, and events. Recent liturgical changes (as have been mentioned above) have served to emphasize the notion of the gathered church as a self-identifying group of people, 'the happy fellowship of the faithful few'.

It can be seen that these two models in large part coincide with the distinction between those who see community in terms of identification, and those who see it in terms of participation (a distinction which was examined in Chapter 6). The significance of this division is magnified by the fact that in any particular village, it tends to be the farmers and the old village community who adhere to the village church model, while many of the commuters and the retired are likely to espouse the gathered church model. There is little doubt that the gathered church model has gained ground in recent years, partly because of the movement into the countryside of people who have previously had experience of urban churches, and partly because the clergy themselves have learned this model of the church during their theological training and early ministerial experience.

Thus, in many villages, there are in effect two understandings of the church which at times relate to one another uneasily. On the one hand the church is seen as comprised of committed and dedicated members, who are regular worshippers and concerned with the church as an organization which has distinct boundaries and an identifiable membership. On the other hand are those who view the church as simply the expression of the village in its spiritual dimension and who do not feel that it is necessary to participate regularly in order to belong. Members of this group, despite the fact that they tend to hold themselves apart from church organizations and representative bodies, none the less regard themselves as belonging to the church by identification rather than by participation. At critical times in the life of the church, they will prove to be among the most vocal, demanding a considerable if not decisive say in how matters should be resolved. At times this can lead to conflict between the two churches, particularly when changes to the building, the churchyard or the pattern or form of services are being contemplated. Thus there is a basic tension between those who see the church as a focus of the village community which attempts to give a Christian understanding and meaning to the whole life of the village, which it in a sense represents, and those who see the church as a gathering of Christians out of the community, to form a distinct, self-contained organization with a degree of self-consciousness and definition. Contemporary rural ministry, for those who adhere to this latter model, often appears to be one of being the chaplain to the gathered community in a cluster of villages. Clearly, such an understanding is fundamentally different from historic notions of the Anglican pastoral ministry.

In any particular village, the church cannot choose to adopt one of these models and to reject the other. Characteristically, some of the time the church will accord with the village church model and, on other occasions, with the gathered church model. On Christmas Day it is the village church model which is in the ascendancy; on Good Friday it is the gathered church model which predominates. In a sense, a clergyman has to be 'bilingual' and to know by instinct how to relate to these two different understandings of the nature of the church and how to interrelate them one to another. Achieving this successfully in the modern village is part of the skill of contemporary rural ministry.

The other basic tension surrounds the question, organizational rather than theological, 'Whose church is it?' — a question which manifests itself in clear terms when a balance has to be struck between the centralist tendencies advocated by the clergy, and the localist preferences of parishioners, mentioned above. Basically, many clergy who are now required to minister to a number of parishes and, in consequence, do the same thing a number of times over in different places, in varying degrees wish to regard their multi-parish ministries as single entities and plan accordingly. By contrast, many of the laity wish to maintain the maximum possible degree of church life in their own village, and even if they do have to share a clergyman, they still expect him to devote time and attention to their village, as if it were a single pastoral responsibility. Initially, quite unrealistic expectations are sometimes demanded of a clergyman, but eventually some accommodation between these two views has to be achieved. This is an area where considerable tension arises in the local rural church, particularly in those places where the limits of church life have been defined by the clergyman, and church life has become reduced to the capacity of that clergyman. In practice, it is important to identify which aspects of church life are appropriately maintained at the local level and which aspects can be centralized. There is much to be said for centralizing some aspects of the financial and administrative life of a multi-parish ministry, and youth and children's work are best done at a level where it is possible to bring a number of people together, rather than in the local parishes where, in each case, the numbers will be few. By contrast, worship and pastoral work are best done at a local level and here the ministerial community has a major contribution to make. Centralized decision-making inevitably involves fewer people, and a situation should not develop where a church in an area is effectively run by a small central committee, an inner group from which the majority of people feel excluded. Each church will want to retain some responsibility for its own life, and this is a way of involving a large number of people in the life and witness of the church. Clearly, a clergyman cannot be expected to attend all the meetings and the appointment of an active vice-chairperson is important.

If the character of the rural church is small and local, so also it is ecumenical. Any country church today will contain a significant proportion of worshippers who were once members of other churches. In many places, especially in the remoter countryside, the commuters, the retired and the second-home owners who come to the village in large numbers, usually attend the parish church irrespective of former denominational allegiances, for in part they see this as an expression of their membership of the village community. In this way the parish church has become an ecumenical church and its worship and its organization need to take account of this factor. At the same time, there are in many villages chapels and churches of other denominations with whom the parish church now works in close co-operation. The old legacy of division between church and chapel, which mirrored deeper divisions in Victorian rural society, has given way to a new era of ecumenical co-operation in the countryside. Although there are relatively few formal ecumenical projects in rural areas, and these are often centred on market towns, none the less there are many church-sharing schemes, a significant number of which involve the Roman Catholic Church. In other villages it is not uncommon to find a degree of co-operation between the Methodist Church and the parish church, whereby certain services are held in winter in the Methodist chapel which is usually much easier to warm, and in the parish church during the summer months. Many villages have recognized that the existence of two places of worship, with small congregations struggling to keep the buildings watertight and heated, is an anachronism. In recent years there has been a steady and encouraging growth of co-operation between different churches, and there is now a great deal of informal sharing in the countryside which often extends to such activities as joint youth clubs and Sunday schools.

The central thrust of Jesus' teaching is that of the Kingdom of

God, and many of his parables begin with the words 'The Kingdom of God is like . . .' The Kingdom is about community and interrelatedness, and has a ready resonance with the particular character of ministry in country parishes. It is the role of the church in the rural community today to be a model of community, a sign of the Kingdom, at the centre of the contemporary village, and to maintain, as has been maintained for generations, the silent and steady witness of the church to the priorities and vision of the Kingdom. In an increasingly fragmented village, comprised of different groups with significantly different understandings, the church needs to be a symbol and model of community and a place of reconciliation, based on the worshipping congregation, in which the focus is Christ in whom people are reconciled and committed to serve their fellows. The church in the village should be characterized by the authentic marks of Christian community: the primacy of love; concern for the disadvantaged; a willingness to bear the cost of community to oneself; an understanding of the discipline of fellowship; and an acknowledgement in humility of our interdependence. The church in the countryside today needs to develop forms of ministry which allow for the affirmation of these marks of the Kingdom, and which are at the same time sensitive to the contours of modern rural society. For the church will survive and grow in the countryside, not by building an alternative community, as it has done in suburban areas, but by developing and sustaining the historic continuity which exists between the church and the village, which allows God's hidden purpose to be made visible, tangible, audible and evident within the village.

Some recent writing has sought to identify a pattern or blueprint of the future of the church in the countryside. Clearly, there will be no single pattern, but the diversity which can be currently observed will, if anything, become more marked. For the church in the countryside will become an increasingly local church, reflecting the nature, the balance and the priorities of a particular village. Local ministry is always a high-risk policy for the church, but the present crisis demands that such risks be taken and they should not be cramped in the name of ecclesiastical uniformity. The future of the rural church will be a time of exciting experiments, a time of much trial and no doubt some error. In some places lay ministerial teams will corporately take responsibility for the life of the parish church; in others non-stipendiary ministers will provide a focus for the development of a community ministry. Everywhere the stipendiary clergy will need to reinterpret their ancient role so that they are ready to enable the ministry of the whole Church to be manifest and exercised according to the needs of the local situation. In every place church people will continue to express their confidence in the future of the village by their deep involvement in the community life of that settlement.

Some commentators have suggested that in many places the rural church will die within a generation. The church in the village will not die, and nothing speaks more eloquently of the determination of country people to preserve the church in their midst than the vast amount of effort and time which has been spent in recent years on raising money, working upon the fabric of the church, and keeping tidy the churchyard (once such an obvious barometer of neglect). Undeniably the church in the countryside, particularly in remoter areas, is experiencing profound problems, but in every area there are unmistakable signs of hope and confidence in the future of the parish church in the village.

13

The Country Clergyman Today

The question which, in a variety of forms, everyone asks of contemporary rural ministry is: 'How can a single clergyman serve so many rural parishes?' The question is simply answered: 'He can, but not in the manner familiar to his predecessors.' In the previous chapters it has been suggested that the countryside in general, and the church in particular, is in the midst of a period of profound change. For generations, though villages changed and altered, they remained essentially farming communities, and rural ministry, for all the changes in church life, remained that of a settled, local and personal ministry in a face-to-face community. Until relatively recently, the ministry of a country clergyman was recognizably similar to that of Chaucer's 'poor clerk', of whom he wrote:

> This noble ensample to his sheep he gaf,
> That first he wroughte and afterwards he taught,
> To drawen folk to hevene by fairnesse
> By good ensample this was his bysynesse.

Such a ministry, like that of George Herbert at Bemerton; Jeremy Taylor at Uppingham, or John Keble at Hursley, was essentially a local, static and stable ministry, in which personal example was of crucial significance. As Jeremy Taylor wrote in a Charge to the clergy of his Ulster diocese, in 1660, 'men will strive to be like you if you be like to God . . .'. George Crabbe wrote in 1810 of his local minister:

> Sober, chaste, devout and just,
> one whom his neighbours could believe and trust.

The ministry of George Herbert may be regarded as the archetype of this 'cure of souls' pattern of pastoral ministry. Although Herbert's actual ministry at Bemerton was relatively short (1630–33), through his poetry, his writing (particularly *A Priest to the Temple*, published in 1652), and the biography of him by Izaak Walton, Herbert became, for generations of Anglican clergy, the symbol of this pattern of ministry. Even if in the eighteenth and early nineteenth centuries it was a pattern of ministry frequently disregarded, none the less it remained the ideal, in Herbert's words, 'a mark to aim at'. At its best it was the drawing of a community to God through the personal example, leadership and care of its priest. Above all it was the personal ministry of a known person in a knowable community, for the cure of souls pattern of ministry inevitably centred church life around the person and personality of the priest. In a real sense, in rural Anglicanism the priest became the church, and people found it difficult to conceive of church life without a resident clergyman whose job it was to run the church and to be the church in the fullest sense of that term. Inevitably, such a view of ministry led to a clericalized understanding of the nature of the church, as Herbert Kelly wrote in 1917: 'For "I believe in the Holy Catholic Church" we are mentally substituting a new clause. "I believe in a holy and energetic clergy".' This close identification of the church with the clergy, which is such a prominent feature of traditional rural Anglicanism, has left an indelible impression on church life in all country villages.

In the late nineteenth century and the early twentieth century, when one or two neighbouring parishes where the population was not large, were placed under the care of a single clergyman, it was still possible to exercise a cure of souls pattern of ministry. However, when a clergyman today is asked to serve anything up to a dozen scattered hamlets, it is clear that he cannot exercise a ministry based on such understandings. At some stage a threshold is crossed, at which point the cure of souls pattern of rural ministry becomes impractical and impossible. What had been a strength in former generations, for it undoubtedly had been, has become a weakness. Tensions have inevitably arisen between traditional expectations of the clergyman's role, shaped over many generations, and what is possible under contemporary conditions. Not surprisingly, the modern country clergyman still finds that many people expect that he will be able to minister to their village in a way which conforms to the traditional understandings of the cure of souls pattern.

The sharp decline in the number of clergy has inevitably meant that today each rural clergyman serves a number of parishes. In some dioceses clergy are not inducted to benefices of less than 2,000; in some areas this means six or eight villages. The constraints imposed by traditional expectations mean that in some cases a clergyman may find that, in serving a large number of country parishes, he is expected to do much of what his predecessors did, but multiplied by the number of parishes he now serves. In a group of six parishes there may be as many parochial church councils; each village has its own church, its own pattern of services, church activities and fund-raising events, as well as the pastoral demands made on the clergyman. The problem of multiplication becomes acute at the major church festivals, when a country clergyman may find himself celebrating Christmas, Easter, Harvest and Remembrance Day six times in different communities.

While, in many parishes, members of the congregation take responsibility for elements of the administrative life of the church, there remain parishes in which much of this work falls to the clergyman (who, in any event, remains legally responsible for many things in the life of the church). The effect of all this is that a clergyman can spend almost all his time performing a contracting range of duties within an expanding number of parishes. Inevitably, he will have less time for that diffuse involvement in the many-sided aspects of village life which characterized the ministry of his predecessors. These and other changes serve to exacerbate the tensions between the expectations of many people and what is realistically possible for the contemporary clergyman. At the same time the clergyman himself can become uneasily aware that his role is being reduced to that of a chaplain and administrator to the churchgoing group rather than that of serving the community as a whole. This tends to accelerate the transition from the village church model to a gathered church model, noted in the previous chapter.

Many of these problems come into focus for a clergyman on Sundays. Parishes vary considerably in what they regard as an appropriate pattern of services, but, as has been mentioned above, most parishes would prefer a service in their own church each Sunday (preferably before lunch, but not too early) with their own clergyman present. Inevitably, a major bottleneck occurs on Sunday mornings, when a clergyman may find himself taking as many as four or five services. In order to do this, in some places the clergyman arrives when the service has already started and leaves before it is completed. Such a pattern of worship denies the clergyman and the congregation the benefit of a reflective and prayerful start to the service and, of particular importance, the time of greeting and conversation when the service is over. The clergyman simply does not get to hear about what is going on in the village, what concerns people, or who may need visiting, because he is already travelling towards another service in a village three miles away. Furthermore, the strain of such a 'tip and run' ministry on the clergyman himself is considerable; inevitably the quality of worship is bound to suffer, for it is not possible to take as many as six or seven services in a day with the degree of attention and concentration which worship demands. In one overseas diocese the bishop has made it a rule that no clergyman should celebrate communion more than twice in one day; some form of limitation has much to recommend it. But the present practice of many multi-parish ministries (confirmed by a recent survey) is for the clergyman to arrive in a hurry, to start the service, which cannot last more than forty-five minutes, in order that he may quickly get into his car and drive to take another service, which begins a quarter of an hour after the last one has finished. The problems of dull duplication and the impossibility of satisfying expectations, which relate to the cure of souls pattern of ministry, are two of the most problematic aspects of contemporary rural ministry.

Thus it is apparent that traditional understandings of rural ministry, associated with George Herbert, cannot be implemented unchanged in the contemporary situation. A clergyman cannot exercise a ministry of that nature when he serves six or eight small villages, each with their own church. In such a situation he cannot be the *persona ecclesiae* at the centre of a coherent community of which he is the representative and embodiment of its spiritual dimension. Nor can he exercise the type of leadership which his nineteenth-century counterpart exercised, and which ramified into every dimension of village life. Today the country clergyman's role is to foster, encourage and develop the life of the local church in the villages which he serves, which must necessarily grow to the point where they are no longer immediately dependent for every aspect of their life on his energy and initiative. Leadership must be shared by the clergyman with members of the congregation who, together, form a ministerial team jointly responsible for the life and witness of the church in that area. The development of a community ministry breaks the ancient dependence of rural church life on the person and personality of the clergyman, which inevitably meant that the life of the church was restricted to the energy and drive of the particular clergyman.

Inevitably, in the past, the traditional village church became a dependent community, but once the resident clergyman was no longer available it frequently became a church community which contracted and in some cases almost died. For, in a real sense, many country churches saw themselves as almost totally dependent upon the leadership of a resident clergyman; when there was no longer a vicar living in the vicarage, the church began to wither. The modern rural church must be a community church responsible for many aspects of its own life and witness. It will need to shake itself free of many traditional understandings which have served the country church well in the past but are no longer possible or practical. At the same time rural clergy will need to appreciate how their own role has changed within this new situation. No longer will the clergyman be the person who initiates and carries through every aspect of church life, but he will be there to support and assist the development and growth of the church in the parishes which he serves.

Such a role inevitably will be significantly different in character from traditional understandings. The modern country clergyman needs to be a person who has the skill, knowledge and ability, as well as the personality, to make a ministerial team function to its best advantage. Such a person needs to possess particular abilities in motivating and enabling the team to achieve its goals. He will need to have the skills to resolve conflicts within the team; to optimize the contribution of team members; to identify the appropriate means and marshal the required resources within the parishes. By its nature, this style of rural ministry is a lower-profile and more self-effacing style of leadership than that exercised by traditional country clergy. Far from inhibiting and discouraging members of the church from sharing in the common task, such a style of ministry should have as one of its principal aims that of encouraging and facilitating church members to become responsible for various aspects of church life. As a consequence of this form and style of leadership, church members will feel able to take their part in the work and life of the parish, with the sense that they are sharing in a common task and without feeling that they are trespassing on the prerogative of the clergyman.

At the centre of each parish there needs to be a team of people who are corporately able to witness and minister in that place. It is in the context of such teams that what is called 'the ministry of the laity', but in all truth is the ministry of the whole church, will develop and grow. The priest, by his skill, his knowledge and his ability must enable the priesthood of the whole Church to be manifest and exercised according to the needs of the local situation. He must be able to animate and invigorate a local team of people to be 'the Church' in that particular village. In many country parishes local church members realize that, just as the local church has become increasingly self-sufficient in financial terms, so it has to become self-sufficient in ministerial terms. In many country churches today services are taken by local people, some of whom have gone forward for training as non-stipendiary ministers or as readers, specifically to meet the situation which faces their local church. Many dioceses run ministerial training courses and people increasingly can be found who will take responsibility, not just for the children's work of the church, but for the overall pastoral involvement of the local church in its village community. As local people become increasingly aware of the needs, so there is, in some areas at least, no shortage of those willing and able to take on these roles.

However, one of the constraints which has to be overcome is the traditional understanding of some clergy that 'running the parish' is solely their responsibility. There is little doubt that the development of this type of shared and corporate ministry involves the clergy in a considerable redefinition of their role. The term 'shared ministry' means what it says: the clergyman has to be prepared to share with the congregation the ministry of the church. Understandably, some clergy feel undermined and diminished, and they look back wistfully to the days of the cure of souls pattern. But changed circumstances demand changed attitudes and the modern rural clergyman's role is significantly different from that of previous generations.

269

The church today is not a group of people gathered round a minister, but a group of people who together share the work and function of ministry in the local community, supported by a clergyman. For it is not the ministry which makes the church; it is the church which validates the ministry. The authority given to the ministry is in reality that conferred on it by the church. However, some recent writing, in seeking to stress the importance of shared and corporate ministry in the church almost inevitably has given the impression of according a much lesser significance to the ordained ministry, and indeed, in some places, of finding almost no place for it, reducing the ministry to one of prayerful anonymity. Such a tendency is exemplified by a recent report, 'A Strategy for the Church's Ministry' (1983), in which the clergy are seen as members of a diocesan team deployed throughout the diocese on the basis of a central strategy with no permanent attachment to a local church. It would seem that such a strategy appears to deny the essential localism of the church, particularly in rural areas. It needs to be affirmed that the stipendiary clergy have a critical and crucial role within the modern rural church. As the Final Report of the Anglican—Roman Catholic International Commission (1982) has said: 'Like any human community the Church requires a focus of leadership and unity, which the Holy Spirit provides in the ordained ministry.' Shared ministry will not just happen; it needs to be fostered and called out by the stipendiary clergy. The country clergyman today is called by his skill, his ability and his knowledge, to enable the priesthood of the whole Church to be manifest and exercised within a group of parishes, according to the needs of the local situation. He represents and epitomizes the corporate priesthood of the Church; he is the enabler of the community ministry; he is the animator of the people of God. By his holiness, humility and good sense, he articulates the priesthood of the people of God, and, in this sense, he activates them to fulfil their calling and vocation of ministry within the local parishes.

It is possible to identify four principal roles which the modern rural clergyman must perform. First, it is his responsibility to call the local ministry of the church into being, to train it and to foster it. There is little to encourage the view that, if the stipendiary clergy were withdrawn from the countryside, a local ministry would appear of its own volition. The local ministry of the church has to be fostered, encouraged and developed by the stipendiary clergyman. In many places this will become a principal part of his role, and identifying and training suitable people will occupy much of his time. In practice it has been found that local ministry teams operate best where there is a clear understanding of who does what, and where there are known boundaries between different areas of responsibility. The setting of these boundaries and the holding together of a team of volunteers is a highly demanding and exacting role. However, as the life of the team develops (some members will leave and others will join and new tasks will have to be addressed), so the clergyman's role will continue to remain important. In small country churches it is easy for one dominant person to move into that central role which the traditional resident clergyman once filled. The modern stipendiary clergyman, who will inevitably be a man from outside, needs to have both the strength and the authority to resist this and to allow the team to function as a team. Inevitably, conflicts will arise within any group of people (and small churches at times can be smallminded) and the priest has an important role in containing and minimizing their disruptive effects, in order that the team may function to the best possible advantage. As a Methodist group once said, 'We need the minister to keep us apart so that we stay together'.

Second, it is the stipendiary clergyman's role to help the local church to define and set its goals; rather, to ensure that the church continues to fulfil its ancient functions as a church. Local churches, like other organizations, frequently need someone to tell them that what they most desire may not be in their best interests and that they are departing from their original goals. A group of people may become content with running an organization for its own sake, and thus they lose sight of its purposes and the direction in which they should be moving. This function of setting the goals is an ancient, priestly and episcopal role in which the priest represents the unity of the church and relates the local congregation to the wider Church outside the village. In local terms, an enthusiastic team of people can occasionally lose sight of the fact that what draws them together is their common service of Christ.

Third, it is the stipendiary priest's task to provide the insight and knowledge which the team needs, for the church is, by definition, a community of insight. Religion is ultimately about goals and ends: 'Seek ye first the Kingdom of God.' The stipendiary clergyman has had the theological education and has the time to continue his studies, and he must act as the resource for the local church. He must be learned, in the sense of having spiritual understanding and biblical knowledge which he is capable of placing at the disposal of the local church. In short, he is its teacher and instructor in these matters, and his stipendiary and full-time status allows him the time to devote to this teaching. The totality of his commitment remains an important sign in an age which finds commitment to anything problematic. In a sense, the distinction between the stipendiary and the non-stipendiary clergy approximates the distinction between the 'religious' and the 'secular' clergy. Perhaps we need the 'religious' stipendiary clergy to be more religious, for they are in the Church for the sake of the world. The 'secular' non-stipendiary clergy need to be more secular, for they are in the world for the sake of the Church. The cautiousness which has rightly guarded the Church of England from speaking of two classes or types of priest, should not obscure the fact that in the Church of the future such clergy will have significantly different functions. The one is not a part-time approximation of the other, but has its own specific nature and function. Conversely, the stipendiary ministry must regard the providing of appropriate spiritual resources and insights, and the ability to communicate them in the local church, as a central part of its role (a fact which should significantly influence recruitment and training).

Fourth, it is the stipendiary clergyman's role to take ultimate responsibility for the work of the Church in that area. This is basically what the parochial system means: that there is one man who is responsible for the life of the Church in any particular area; there is someone who sleeps uneasily if all is not well with the Church. Today, this role is of increasing rather than diminishing importance, for as the Church at the local level becomes increasingly similar to a voluntary associational organization, it could become as fragile and transient as are many such organizations. It is the presence of a person charged with the ultimate care and responsibiliy for the Church in a particular area which prevents this happening. At the same time, in a country parish, people can be persuaded to do almost anything, including becoming members of a ministerial team, but it is only with the greatest difficulty that they can be persuaded to take responsibility for that which they are about to do. To 'help the Vicar' is one thing; to be personally responsible is another. Such people know well the subtle pressures that a small community can exert. It is the priest, as the man from outside, who must lift from them the burden of this responsibility, freeing them to do those things in the village which they would not do without this sense of freedom. By being the 'scapegoat', by being prepared to take responsibility for what others do, the priest is able to free people to do things which, in other circumstances, the burden of responsibility would inhibit and prevent them. The knowledge that the burden of responsibility is ultimately his, frees others to engage in the work of ministry in the village.

For generations, people have tended to look upon the life of a country clergyman as quiet and uneventful, slow-paced and undemanding. Ashley Oxenden wrote in 1857 that 'ministry in the countryside is often looked upon as one of tranquil ease and unruffled calm. And many a man, before ordination, has mapped out for himself a life of light burdens and few trials'. Today churchwardens realistically appreciate that it needs a fit and energetic man to carry out the duties of a modern country clergyman. While, generations ago in Warwickshire, when people wished to denote scarcity, they remarked 'as rare as sweat on a parson's brow'; today it is more common to find a clergyman rushing from one engagement to another in a week of constant activity and to hear him remark ruefully that a course in rally driving would be an appropriate addition to the theological college curriculum. Far from being the Church's least demanding and most generalized ministry, ministry in the countryside has become increasingly specialized and significantly different in many essential points from that of ministry in suburban or urban areas. While urban ministry is largely church-centred and is aimed at building up a strong church community in a particular area, almost as an alternative community, the country church is much more closely related to the local community as a whole. In a town a successful church tends to be judged by the number of playgroups, old people's lunches, and meetings of various organizations which take place in church premises. In the countryside the church building is used for worship alone and all these other activities are part of the life of the village as a whole. Within a village the clergyman will be expected to fulfil an acknowledged role and meet a wide range of expectations; certainly, few jobs can give a person such a breadth of contacts with such a diversity of people. While the urban clergyman may serve a coherent, monochrome housing area, in a village, as previous chapters have outlined, there will be a wide range of people with different expectations and different understandings of the place of the church and the clergyman. Balancing and holding together these differing expectations within a small-scale community is a skilled job, where mistakes can do permanent and long-term damage (which subsequently has to be lived with).

Inevitably, the country clergyman is much more visible to the wider community than is his urban counterpart. Everyone in the village will know where the rectory or the vicarage is and a thick hedge or a high wall cannot insulate the clergyman and his family from the interest and comments of the village. People who live in a village find it difficult to be indifferent about their clergyman, and almost all writers on rural ministry have stressed the significance of a clergyman's personal example in a small community. Villages are very exposed places in which to live; it is difficult to hide there and people naturally tend to know much more about their neighbours than they do in urban areas. Who the clergyman is, as a person, will count for more than all the projects and organizations which he initiates in the community. Many who move to rural ministry find the high visibility of their role a particularly daunting factor (as do the members of their families); anyone who wishes to lead a very private life should not consider country ministry.

Thus, unlike his urban counterpart whose main aim is to create an alternative community within an urban area, the country clergyman's role is that of witnessing to God in the midst of the activities of village life and pointing the village towards God and his Kingdom. Rural ministry does not require people who are experts in anything, but individuals who can communicate the essential mystery of faith to others and build up a team of villagers who can be the Church in that place. The country clergyman must smell of heaven as Esau smelt of the fields; he must communicate, by his person, something of the living reality of God as he goes about his ministry in the villages that he serves.

To minister, in the diversity of a modern rural community, to a cluster of small country parishes, requires skills of a very high order, coupled with a patience and tolerance which do not deteriorate to mere acceptance or apathy. To point a village towards God, to speak a word about the essential mystery of existence, to keep people mindful of God and his purposes, to live a life which is eloquent of that prayerful holiness and pastoral concern which, in every generation, has marked the Anglican rural ministry at its best, is not likely to be easy in the mobile, materialistic rural community of today. But the Church is not called to win the world for Christ; rather, it is to help all to see that the world is already his and that the Kingdom is all about us. To do this in the same place for many years, and to accept with equanimity the trials and limitations of such a community, is a demanding role. A priest in the contemporary countryside needs to have his spiritual life firmly rooted and to have that quiet, deep stability of faith which communicates itself to others. He may wear his faith lightly and unostentatiously but he must believe it implacably and communicate it to others. Although the shape of the modern rural church will be that of a community ministry, the clergyman is still needed to be its representative, enabler and animator, not in the sense of a man who does everything for a passive congregation, but as a man who motivates and enables people to be the Church in the local situation. Such a man, as he goes about the village, must project the deep joy and excitement of Christian believing, if he is to communicate it to others. He must be patient and willing to accept disappointments and rebuffs. But there is no greater calling; no greater joy; no more profound privilege.

Bibliography

The bibliography is divided into five sections and all books are published in the United Kingdom, except where otherwise stated.

I THE COUNTRY PARISH: AN INTRODUCTION (Chapters 1, 2 and 6)

Arensberg, C. M., and Kimball, S. T., *Family and Community In Ireland* (1940).
Arts Council of Great Britain, *Landscape in Britain 1850—1950* (1983).
Barrell, J. *The Idea of Landscape and the Sense of Place* (1972).
Beckinsale, R., and Beckinsale, M., *The English Heartland* (1980).
Bell, C., and Newby H., *Community Studies: an introduction to the sociology of local communities* (1971).
Bell, C., and Newby, H., (eds.), *Sociology of Community; a selection of readings* (1974).
Berger, P. L., *A Rumour of Angels* (1969).
Board of Social Responsibility, *Planning for Community; the planning process and human needs. The report of a working party* (1977).
Briggs, M. S., *Rusticus or the future of the countryside* (1927).
Brogan, H., *Life of Arthur Ransome* (1984).
Cameron, K., *English Place Names* (1961).
Carpenter, H., *Secret Gardens; the Golden Age of Children's Literature* (1985).
Cave, L. F., *Warwickshire Villages* (1976).
Cheatle, J. R. W., *Guide to the English Landscape* (1975).
Church Assembly, *Putting Our House in Order* (1941).
Clark, K., *Ruskin Today* (1964).
Clark, K., *Civilization; a personal view* (1969).
Cohen, A. P., *Belonging: identity and social organisation in British rural culture* (1982).
Coleman, B. I., (ed.) *The Idea of the City in Nineteenth Century Britain* (1973).
Darley, G., *Villages of Vision* (1978).
Davies, E. and Rees, A., (eds.), *Welsh Rural Communities* (1966).
Douglas, M., *Natural Symbols* (1970).
Drabble, M., *A Writer's Britain: Landscape in Literature* (1972).
Eliade, M., *The Myth of the Eternal Return* (1949).
Emmett, I., *A North Wales Village; a social anthropological study* (1964).
Engen, R., *Kate Greenaway; a biography* (1981).
Farjeon, E., *Edward Thomas. The Last Four Years* (1958).
Frankenberg, R., *Village on the Border; a social study of religion, politics and football in a North Wales community* (1957).

Frankenberg, R., *Communities in Britain* (1966).

Galeski, B., *Basic Concepts of Rural Sociology* (1972).

Gardiner, C. H., *Your Village and Mine* (1944).

Goldsmith, W., *The Deserted Village* (1769).

Greenaway, K., *Under the Window* (1879).

Higgs, J., (ed.), *People in the Countryside* (1966).

Hoskins, W. G., *The Making of the English Landscape* (1955).

Hoskins, W. G., *English Landscapes* (1973).

Jefferies, R., *The Life of the Fields* (1884).

Jennings, P., *The Living Village* (1972).

Knoepflmacher, U. C., and Tennyson, G. B., (eds.), *Nature and the Victorian Imagination* (1977).

Kroeber, K., *Romantic Landscape Vision: Constable and Wordsworth* (Wisconsin 1975).

Lerner, L., *The Uses of Nostalgia: studies in pastoral poetry* (1972).

Littlejohn, J., *Westrigg: the sociology of a Cheviot parish* (1964).

Lively, P., *The Presence of the Past* (1975).

Loomis, C. P., and Beagle, J. A., *Rural Sociology: the strategy of change* (1975).

Lowenthal, D., *The Past is a Foreign Country* (1985).

Malmse, E., *English Landscaping and Literature* (1966).

Marsh, J., *Back to the Land: the pastoral impulse in Victorian England from 1880 to 1914* (1982).

Martin, E. W., *The Shearers and the Shorn: a study of life in a Devon community* (1965).

Martin, E. W., (ed.), *Country Life in England* (1966).

Massingham, J. H., *The English Countryman* (1942).

Mitford, M. R., *Our Village* (first published 1824) (1982).

Muir, R., *The English Village* (1980).

Nash, R., *Wilderness and the American Mind* (Yale 1967).

Ordnance Survey, *The Ordnance Survey Atlas of Great Britain* (1982) [articles by R. A. Butlin and M. J. Wise].

Pahl, R. E., 'The urban-rural continuum', *Sociologia Ruralis* vol.VI (1966), reprinted in Pahl R. E. (ed.), *Readings in Urban Sociology* (1968) pp. 263–300.

Philip, N., (ed.), *Between Earth and Sky: poetry and prose of English rural life and work between the Enclosures and the Great War* (1984).

Quennell, P., *John Ruskin: the portrait of a prophet* (1949).

Ravillious, J., and Ravillious, R., *The Heart of the Countryside* (1980).

Redfield, R., *The Folk Culture of Yucatan* (1944).

Redfield, R., *The Little Community: viewpoints for the study of a human whole* (1955).

Redfield, R., *Peasant Society and Culture* (1960).

Rees, A. D., *Life in a Welsh Countryside: a social study of Llanfihangel yng Ngwynfa* (1950).

Robin, J., *Elmdon: community and change in a north-west Essex village 1861–1964* (1980).

Rowse, A. L., *The English Spirit* (1944).
Sanderson, D., *Rural Sociology and Rural Social Organisation* (1942).
Saville, J., *Rural Depopulation in England and Wales 1851—1951* (1957).
Seebohm, F., *The English Village Community* (1883).
Shepard, P., *Man in the Landscape: a historic view of the esthetics of nature* (New York 1967).
Stacey, M., *Tradition and Change: a study of Banbury* (1960).
Tate, W. E., *The English Village Community* (1967).
Thomas, F. C., *The Changing Village* (1938).
Tonnies, F., *Gemeinschaft und Gesellschaft* (1887), tr. C. P. Loomis, *Community and Association* (1955).
Unwins, R., *The Rural Muses* (1954).
Walter, J. A., *The Human Home* (1982).
William, M., *Thomas Hardy and Rural England* (1972).
Williams, R., *The Country and the City* (1975).
Williams, W. M., *The Sociology of an English Village: Gosforth* (1956).
Williams, W. M., *The Country Craftsmen: a study of some rural craftsmen and the rural industries organisation in England* (1959).
Williams, W. M., *A West Country Village: Ashworthy — Family Kinship and Land* (1963).
Willmott, P., and Young, M., *Family and Kinship in East London* (1957).
Willmott, P., and Young, M., *Family and Class in a London Suburb* (1960).
Wirth, L., 'Urbanism as a way of life', *American Journal of Sociology* vol.99 (1938) pp. 1—24.
Wood, J. G., *The Common Objects of the Country* (1885).

2 THE VILLAGE IN THE PAST (Chapters 3 and 4)

Arch, J., *The Story of his Life told by Himself* (1898).
Ashby, M. K., *Joseph Ashby of Tysoe 1858—1919* (1961).
Ashby, M. K., *The Changing English Village 1066—1914* (1974).
Baker, W. P., *The English Village* (1953).
Baring-Gould, S., *Old Country Life* (1913).
Beresford, M., *Lost Villages of England* (1954).
Beresford, M., *History on the Ground* (1957).
Beresford, M. W., and Hirst, J. G., (eds.), *Deserted Medieval Villages* (1971).
Bourne, George, (pseudonym of George Sturt) *Change in the Village* (1912).
Bovill, E. W., *English Country Life 1780—1830* (1962).
Briggs, A., 'City and Countrysides: British and American experience, 1860—1914', University of Leicester H. J. Dyos Memorial Lecture (1981).
Bushaway, B., *By Rite: custom, ceremony and community in England 1700—1880* (1982).
Chambers, D., and Mingay, G. E., *The Agricultural Revolution 1750—1880* (1966).
Chayanov, A. V., *The Theory of Peasant Economy* (Illinois 1966).
Cobbett, W., *Rural Rides* (1829).
Coulton, G. G., *Medieval Village, Manor and Monastery* (1925).
Coulton, G. G., *Medieval Panorama* (1938).

Bibliography

Crabbe, G., *The Village* (1783).
Cunliffe, B., *Iron Age Communities in Britain* (1974).
Darby, H. C., and Terrett, I. M., *The Doomesday Geography of Midland England* (1954).
Darby, H. C., (ed.), *A New Historical Geography of England* (1973).
Dunbabin, J. P. D., *Rural Discontent in Nineteenth Century Britain* (1974).
Elton, Lord, *The Two Villages* (1949).
Evans, G. E., *The Horse in the Furrow* (1960).
Evans, G. E., *Ask the Fellow who Cut the Hay.* (1965).
Evans, G. E., *Where Beards Wag All* (1970).
Firth, M. M., and Hopkinson, A. W., *The Tolpuddle Martyrs* (1974).
Fussell, G. E., *The English Dairy Farmer 1500—1900.* (1966).
Fussell, G. E., *The Old English Farming Books from Fitzherbert to Tull 1523—1730* (1966).
Gibbs, J. A., *A Cotswold Village* (1898).
Gill, R., *Happy Rural Seat* (1972).
Goody, J., Thirk, J., and Thompson E. P., (eds.), *Family and Inheritance: rural society in Western Europe 1200—1800* (1976).
Gough, R., (ed. D. Hey), *The History of Myddle (1701—2)* (1981).
Green, F. E., *The Tyranny of the Countryside* (1913).
Groves, R., *Sharpen the Sickle!* (1948).
Habakkuk, H. J., 'English landownership 1680—1740', *Economic History Review* vol.10 (1940) p. 2f.
Haggard, H. R., *A Farmer's Year* (1899).
Haggard, H. R., *Rural England* (1902).
Hammond, J. L., and Hammond, B., *The Village Labourer, 1760—1882: a study in the Government of England before the Reform Bill* (1911).
Hey, D., *An English Rural Community: Myddle under the Tudors and Stuarts* (1974).
Hilton, R. H., *The English Peasantry in the Later Middle Ages* (1975).
Hobsbawm, E. J., and Rudé, G., *Captain Swing* (1973).
Holt, J. C., *Robin Hood* (1982).
Homans, G. C., *English Villagers of the Thirteenth Century* (1940).
Hopkins, H. *The Long Affray: the poaching wars 1760—1914* (1984).
Horn, P., *Joseph Arch* (1971).
Horn, P., *The Victorian Country Child* (1974).
Horn, P., *Labouring Life in the Victorian Countryside* (1976).
Horn, P., *Education in Rural England 1800—1914* (1978).
Horn, P., *The Rural World 1780—1850: social change in the English countryside* (1980).
Hoskins, W. G., *The Midland Peasant: the economic and social history of a Leicestershire village* (1981).
Howe, M., *The Brackenford Story* (1952).
Howitt, W., *The Rural Life of England* (1838).
Jefferies, R., *The Story of my Heart* (1883).
Jefferies, R., *Hodge and His Master* (1946).
Jessop, A., *Arcady, For Better or Worse* (1887).

Bibliography

Johnson, A. H., *The Disappearance of the Small Landlord* (1909).
Jones, E. L., *The Development of English Agriculture 1815—1873* (1968).
Ketteridge, C., and Mays, C. W., *Five Miles from Bunkum: a village and its crafts* (1972).
Kitchen, F., *Brother to the Ox* (1940).
Kitson Clark, G., *The Making of Victorian England* (1962).
Kosminsky, E. A., (ed. R. H. Hilton), *Studies in the Agrarian History of England in the Thirteenth Century* (1956).
Laskett, P., *The World we have Lost* (1965).
Laskett, P., (ed.), *Household and Family in Past Time* (1972).
Le Roy, L. E., *Montaillou: Carthars and Catholics in a French Village* (1978).
Lukes, S., *Individualism* (1973).
Lyons, J. O., *The Invention of Self: the hinge of consciousness in the eighteenth century* (Illinois 1978).
MacFarlane, A., *The Origins of English Individualism* (1978).
Marshall, J. D., *The Old Poor Law 1795—1834* (1968).
Marshall, S., *Fenland Chronicle* (1967).
Martin, E. W., *The Secret People* (1954).
Martin, E. W., *The Book of the Village* (1962).
Mills, D. R., (ed.), *English Rural Communities: the impact of a specialised economy* (1973).
Mingay, G. E., *English Landed Society in the Eighteenth Century* (1963).
Mingay, G. E., *Enclosure and the Small Farmer in the Age of the Industrial Revolution* (1968).
Mingay, G. E., *Rural Life in Victorian England* (1977).
Moreau, R. E., *The Departed Village* (1968).
Morgan, D. H., *Harvesters and Harvesting. 1840—1900: a study of the rural proletariat* (1982).
Morris, C., *The Discovery of the Individual 1050—1200* (1972).
Morsley, C., *News from the English Countryside 1850—1950* (1983).
Nohl, J., *The Black Death* (1973).
Norfolk Federation of Womens' Institutes, *Within Living Memory: a collection of Norfolk Reminiscences* (1971).
Oakley, W., *Winged Wheels* (1978).
Orwin, C. S., and Whetham, E. H., *History of British Agriculture 1846—1914* (1964).
Oxley, J. W., *Poor Relief in England and Wales 1601—1834* (1974).
Packington, H., *English Villages and Hamlets* (1934).
Parker, R., *Cottage on the Green* (1973).
Parker, R., *The Common Stream* (1975).
Peacock, A. J., *Bread or Blood: a Study of the Agrarian Riots in East Anglia 1816* (1965).
Perry, P. J., *British Agriculture 1875—1914* (1973).
Postan, M. M., *Essays on Medieval Agriculture and General Problems of the Medieval Economy* (1973).
Postan, M. M., *The Medieval Economy and Society* (1975).

Quinault, R., and Stevenson, J., *Popular Protest and Social Order 1790—1820* (1974).

Reaney, P. H., *The Origin of English Place Names* (1960).

Redford, A., *The Economic History of England 1760—1860* (2nd ed. 1960).

Roser, M. E., *The English Poor Law 1780—1930* (1971).

Russell, E. J., *A History of Agricultural Science in Great Britain* (1966).

Samuel, R., (ed.), *Village Life and Labour* (1975).

Saville, J., *Depopulation in England and Wales 1855—1955* (1957).

Sharp, T., *The Anatomy of the Village* (1946).

Slater, G., *The English Peasantry* (1907).

Springall, L. M., *Labouring Life in Norfolk Villages 1834—1914* (1936).

Spufford, M., *Contrasting Communities: English villagers in the sixteenth and seventeenth centuries* (1974).

Stone, L., *The Crisis of the Aristocracy 1558—1641* (1965).

Stone, L., and Stone, J., *An Open Elite? England 1540—1880* (1984).

Taplin, K., *The English Path* (1979).

Tate, W. E., *The English Village Community and the Enclosure Movement* (1967).

Tawney, R. H., *The Agrarian Problem in the Sixteenth Century* (1912).

Thirsk, J., (ed.), *The Agrarian History of England and Wales* vol.IV (1967).

Thomas, E., *Richard Jefferies* (1908).

Thompson, F., *Lark Rise to Candleford* (1945).

Thompson, F., *Still Glides in the Stream* (1948).

Thompson, F. M. L., *English Landed Society in the Nineteenth Century* (1962).

Titow, J. Z., *English Rural Society 1200—1350* (1969).

Trades Union Congress, *The Story of the Dorchester Labourers* (1957).

Trevelyan, G. M., *English Social History* (1944).

Trow-Smith, R., *A History of British Livestock Husbandry 1700—1900* (1956).

Tusser, T., *Five Hundred Points of Good Husbandry* (1557, ed. G. Grigson 1984).

Twigg, G., *The Black Death: a biological reappraisal* (1984).

Tyrrell, S. J., *A Countryman's Tale* (1973).

Warren, C. H., *England is a Village* (1940).

Wolf, E. R., *Peasants* (New Jersey 1966).

Woodforde, J., *The Truth about Cottages* (1969).

Yelling, J. A., *Common Field and Enclosure in England 1450—1850* (1977).

Young, C. M., *Victorian England* (2nd edn. 1953).

Young, F. B., *Portrait of a Village* (1937).

3 THE CONTEMPORARY VILLAGE (Chapters 5, 7, 8 and 9)

Agricultural Economics Research Institute (Oxford), *Country Planning. A Study of Rural Problems* (1944).

Alan, R. H., and Harley, J. B., *Man Made the Land* (1973).

Ambrose, P., *A Quiet Revolution; social change in a Sussex village* (1974).
Ashton, J., and Long, W. H., (eds.), *The Remoter Rural Areas of Britain* (1972).
Association of County Councils, *Rural Deprivation* (1979).
Association of District Councils, *Rural Recovery: Strategy for Survival* (1978).
Baron, S., (ed.), *Country Towns in the Future England* (1944).
Barr, J., 'Durham's Murdered Villages', *New Society* (1969) pp. 23—5.
Beresford, T., *We Plough the Fields. British Farming Today* (1975).
Best, R. H., and Rogers, A. W., *The Urban Countryside* (1973).
Bielckus, C. L., Rogers, A. W., and Wibberly, G. P., *Second Homes in England and Wales.* Wye College Studies in rural land use, No.11 (1972).
Blythe, R., *Akenfield: portrait of an English village* (1969).
Body, R. B., *Agriculture: the triumph and the shame* (1982).
Bonham-Carter, V., *The English Village* (1951).
Bonham-Carter, V., *The Survival of the English Countryside* (1971).
Bracey, H. E., *Social Provision in Rural Wiltshire* (1952).
Bracey, H. E., *English Rural Life: village activities, organisations and institutions* (1959).
Bradley, T., 'Reworking the Quiet Revolutions; Industrial and labour market structuring in village England' *Sociologia Ruralis,* vol.XXV, No.1 (1985), p. 40f.
British Railways Board, *Reshaping British Railways* (Beeching Report, 1963).
Broady, M., (ed.), *Marginal Regions. Essays on Social Planning* (1973).
Broady, M., 'Mid-Wales; a classic case of rural self-help', *The Planner,* vol.66 (1980) pp. 94—5.
Brown, M., and Winyard, S., *Low Pay on the Farm.* (Report of Low Pay Unit, 1975).
Cherry, G. E., (ed.), *Rural Planning Problems* (1976).
Chisholm, M., *Rural Settlement and Land Use* (1962).
Christaller, W., *Die Zentralen Orte in Suddeutschland,* tr. C. W. Baskin, *Central Places in Southern Germany* (1966).
Clark, D., *Rural Housing Initiatives* (1981).
Cloke, P., *Key Settlement in Rural Areas* (1979).
Clout, H. D., *Rural Geography: an introductory survey* (1972).
Constable, M., (ed.), *No Place in the Country. A report on second homes in England and Wales* (1973).
Coppock, J. D., (ed.), *Second Homes: curse or blessing* (1977).
Country Landowners Association, *The Changing Uplands* (1970).
Countryside Review Committee, *Leisure and the Countryside* (1977).
Countryside Review Committee, *Rural Communities* (1977).
Crichton, R. M., *Commuters' Village. A study of Community and Commuters in the Berkshire village of Stratfield Mortimer* (1964).
Cumbria Countryside Conference, *Report on Village School Closures since 1970* (1985).
Dartington Amenity Research Trust, *Second homes in England and Wales, an appraisal* (1973).

Dartington Amenity Research Trust, *Deprived Rural Regions: discussion paper* (1976).

Davidson, J., and Wibberley, G. P., *Planning and the Rural Environment* (1977).

Department of the Environment, *Study of Rural Transport in Devon* (1971).

Department of the Environment, *Study of Rural Transport in West Suffolk* (1971).

Donaldson, J. G. S., and Donaldson, F., *Farming in Britain Today* (1969).

Ernle, Lord, *English Farming, Past and Present.* (6th edition 1961).

Fairbrother, N., *New Lives, New Landscapes* (1970).

Franklin, S. H., *Rural Societies* (1971).

Gasson, R., *Gainful Occupations of Farm Families* (1968).

Gilg, A., *Countryside Planning: the first three decades 1945—1976* (1978).

Gilg, A., (ed.), *Countryside Planning Year Book* (1981) and (1983).

Green, R., *Country Planning: the future of rural regions* (1971).

Grigg, D., *The Dynamics of Agricultural Change* (1982).

Hall, P., (ed.), *The Containment of Urban England* (1973).

Hampshire County Council and Mass Observations Ltd., *Village Life in Hampshire* (1966).

Harris, C., *Hennage: a social structure in miniature* (1974).

Hasbach, W., *A History of the English Agricultural Labourer* (1898).

Havinden, M. A., *Estate Villages: a study of the Berkshire villages of Ardington and Lockinge* (1966).

Jones, G., *Rural Life* (1973).

Losch, A., 'The Nature of Economic Regions', *Southern Economic Journal,* vol. 5 (1938—9) pp. 71—3.

MacConnell, D., *The Tourist. A new theory of the Leisure Class* (New York 1976).

Miller, H. C., *The Ageing Countryman* (1963).

Ministry of Agriculture, Fisheries & Food, *Agricultural Returns for the United Kingdom* (June 1985).

Moseley, M. J., 'A Look at Rural Transport and Accessibility', *The Village,* vol.32 (1977) pp. 33—5.

Mueller, E. W., and Ekola, G. C., *The Silent Struggle for mid-America. The Church in Town and Country Today* (Minneapolis 1963).

National Council of Social Service, *Structure Plans and Rural Communities* (1979).

National Council of Voluntary Organisations, *Country Work: a guide to rural employment initiatives* (1982).

National Council of Voluntary Organisations, *At Your Convenience: report of the Rural Advice and Information Committee* (1984).

Newby, H., *The Deferential Worker: a study of farm workers in East Anglia* (1977).

Newby, H., *Green and Pleasant Land? Social change in rural England* (1979).

Newby, H., Bell, C., Rose, D., and Saunders, P., *Property, Paternalism & Power* (1978).

Nicholson, S., *Out of Town. Out of Mind? A study of rural unemployment.*

Leicester Diocesan Board of Social Responsibility (1985).

Pahl, R. E., *Urbs in Rure: London School of Economics Geographical Paper*. No.2 (1965).

Peel, J., and Sayer, M., *Towards a Rural Policy and its Application to Norfolk*. (1973).

Perry, P. J., *British Agriculture 1875—1914* (1973).

Perry, P. J., *British Farming in the Great Depression* (1973).

Phillips, D., and Williams, A., *Rural Britain. a social geography* (1984).

Radford, E., *The New Villagers: urban pressure on rural areas in Worcestershire* (1970).

Report of the Committee on Land Utilization in Rural Areas (The Scott Report) (1942).

Rodefield, R. D., et al (ed.), *Changes in Rural America — Causes, Consequences and Alternatives* (Saint Louis 1978).

Saville, J., *Rural Depopulation in England and Wales 1851—1951* (1957).

Shelter, *Tied Accommodation* (1974).

Shoard, M., *The Theft of the Countryside* (1981).

South West Economic Planning Council, *Retirement to the South West* (1975).

Springhall, M., *Labouring Life in Norfolk Villages 1834—1914* (1936).

Standing Conference of Rural Community Councils, *The Decline of Rural Services* (1978).

Standing Conference of Rural Community Councils, *Whose Countryside?* (1979).

Stapledon, R. G., *The Land, Now and Tomorrow* (1935).

Thomas, D. St J., *The Rural Transport Problem* (1963).

Thomas, D. St J., *The Country Railway* (1976).

Thorburn, A., *Planning Villages* (1971).

Thorns, D., *Suburbia* (1973).

Tranter, R. B., (ed.), *Strategies for family-worked farms in the UK*. Centre for Agricultural Strategy, paper 15 (1983).

Veblens, T., *The Theory of the Leisure Class* (1899).

Vidich, A. J., and Nensman, J., *Small Town in Mass Society. Class, power and religion in a rural community* (Princeton 1968).

Walker, A., *Rural Poverty: Poverty. deprivation and planning in rural areas* (1978).

Warwickshire Rural Community Council, *Rural Working Options: the report of the Community Rural Enterprise in Warwickshire Project* (1983).

Watson, J. A. S., *The History of the Royal Agricultural Society of England 1839—1939* (1939).

Whitby, M. C., and Willis, K. G., *Rural Resource Development: an economic approach* (1978).

White, D., 'Dying Village', *New Society*. vol.19 (1972) pp. 108—9.

4 THE PARISH CHURCH IN THE PAST (Chapters 10 and 11)

Addison, W., *The English Country Parson* (1947).

Addleshaw, G. W. O., *The Beginnings of the Parochial System*. St Anthony's House Publications No.3 (1953).

Addleshaw, G. W. O., *The Development of the Parochial System from Charlemagne (768–814) to Urban II (1088–1099)*. St Anthony's House Publications No.6 (1964).

Andrews, J. H. B., 'The Country Parson (1969)', *Theology*. vol. LXXII (March 1969) pp. 103ff.

Armstrong, H. B. J., (ed.), *A Norfolk Diary* (1949).

Armstrong, H. B. J., (ed.), *Armstrong's Norfolk Diary* (1963).

Atkinson, J. C., *Forty Years in a Moorland Parish* (1891).

Baring-Gould, S., *The Vicar of Morwenstow* (1913).

Baring-Gould, S., *The Church Revival* (1914).

Barnard, H. C., *A History of English Education from 1760* (1961).

Beresford, J., (ed.), *Diary of a Country Parson. The Rev'd James Woodforde* 5 vols. (1924–1931).

Best, S., *Village Libraries and Reading Rooms* (1854).

Bowker, M., 'The Henrician Reformation and the Parish Clergy', *Bulletin of the Institute of Historical Research*. vol.50 (1977) pp. 32–3.

British Council of Churches, *The Land, the People and the Churches* (1945).

Brown, C. K. F., *The Churches' Part in Education; 1833–1941* (1942).

Brown, C. K. F., *A History of the English Clergy 1800–1900* (1953).

Burgess, H. J., *Enterprise of Education* (1958).

Carpenter, S. C., *Church and People 1789–1889* (1933).

Chadwick, O., *The Victorian Church* 2 vols. (1966 and 1970).

Christmas, F. E., *The Parson in English Literature* (1950).

Christie, O. F., (ed.), *The Diary of the Rev'd William Jones of Broxbourne 1777–1821* (1929).

Clark, G. K., *Churchmen and the Condition of England. 1832–1884* (1973).

Clarke, W. K. L., *Eighteenth Century Piety* (1944).

Coles, B. S. S., *Pastoral Work in Country Districts* (1906).

Colloms, B., *Victorian Country Parsons* (1979).

Coombes, H., and Bax, H. N., (eds.), *Journal of a Somerset Rector* (1930).

Cornish, F. W., *The English Church in the Nineteenth Century* 2 vols. (1910).

Cross, C., *Church and People 1450–1660: the triumph of the laity in the English Church* (1976).

Currie, R., Gilbert, A., and Horsley, L., *Churches and Churchgoers* (1977).

Davies, J., *The Subdivision and Rearrangement of Parishes* (1849).

Deanesly, M., *The Pre-Conquest Church of England* (1961).

Ditchfield, P. H., *The Parish Clerk* (1907).

Ditchfield, P. H., *The Old-time Parson* (1908).

Edwards, D. L., *Christian England. Its Story to the Reformation* vol.1. (1981).

Edwards, D. L., *Christian England. From the Reformation to the Eighteenth Century* vol.2 (1983).

Edwards, D. L., *Christian England from the Eighteenth Century to the First World War* vol.3 (1984).

Ellman, E. B., *Recollections of a Sussex Parson* (1912).

Evans, E. J., 'Some Reasons for the Growth of English Rural Anti-Clericalism 1750–1830', *Past and Present*. vol. LXVI (1975) pp. 84–109.

Fendall, C. P., and Crutchley, E. A., *The Diary of Benjamin Newton 1816—1818.* (1933).

Fletcher, R. *In a Country Churchyard* (1978).

Forbes, G. M., *George Herbert's Country Parson* (1949).

Gibson, D., (ed.), *A Parson in the Vale of White Horse. George Woodward's letters from East Hendred. 1753—1761* (1962).

Gilbert, A. D., *Religion and Society in Industrial England* (1976).

Girdlestone, C., *Seven Sermons. preached during the prevalence of cholera in the parish of Sedgley* (1833).

Girdlestone, C., *Sanitary Reform* (1853).

Goddard, E., *Reminiscences of a Wiltshire Vicar* (1887).

Godfrey, J., *The Church in Anglo-Saxon England* (1962).

Godfrey, J., *The English Parish 600—1300* (1969).

Goodridge, R. M., 'The Religious Condition of the West Country in 1851', *Social Compass,* (1967) p. 285.

Hammond, P., *The Parson and the Victorian Parish* (1971).

Harrison, B., *Drink and the Victorians: the temperance question in England 1815—1872* (1971).

Hart, A. T. and Carpenter, E., *The Nineteenth Century Country Parson* (1954).

Hart, A. T., *The Eighteenth Century Country Parson* (1955).

Hart, A. T., *The Country Priest in English History* (1959).

Hart, A. T., *The Man in the Pew 1558—1660* (1960).

Hartridge, R. A. R., *The History of Vicarages in the Middle Ages* (1930).

Heath, P., *The English Parish Clergy on the Eve of the Reformation* (1969).

Heeney, B., *A Different Kind of Gentleman* (Connecticut, 1976).

Herbert, G., 'A Priest to the Temple or the Country Parson. His Character and Rule of Holy Life. (1652), ed. F. E. Hutchinson'. *The Work of George Herbert* (1941) pp. 223ff.

Higham, F., *Catholic and Reformed; a study of the Anglican Church 1559—1662* (1962).

Horne, P., 'Problems of a Nineteenth Century Vicar 1832—1885', *Oxford Diocesan Magazine* (October 1968) p. 16; (November 1968) p. 18.

Inglis, K. S., *Churches and the Working Classes in Victorian England* (1963).

Jessop, A., *The Trials of a Country Parson* (1890).

Kebbell, T. E., 'The Country Parson as he was and as he is', *Blackwoods Magazine,* vol.142 (Sept. 1887) p. 34f.

Kerr, E., *Hunting Parson. The Life and Times of the Rev'd John Russell* (1963).

Kilvert, F., (ed. W. Plomer), *Kilvert's Diary 1870—1879* (1944).

Lawson, J., *Green and Pleasant Land* (1955).

Legg, J. W., *English Church Life from the Restoration to the Tractarian Movement* (1914).

Linnell, C. D., (ed.), *The Diary of Benjamin Rogers 1720—1771.* Bedfordshire Historical Record Society, vol. XXV (1950).

MacDermott, K. H., *Sussex Church Music in the Past* (1922).

MacDermott, K. H., *The Old Church Gallery Minstrels* (1948).

Marsh, P. T., *The Victorian Church in Decline* (1969).

Matthews, A. G., *Walker Revised, being a revision of John Walker's sufferings of the clergy during the Grand Rebellion 1642—1660* (1948).

McClatchey, D., *Oxfordshire Clergy 1777—1869* (1960).

Molesworth, J. E. N., *Tales from the Scrapbook of a Country Clergyman* (1831).

Monro, E., *Agricultural Colleges and their Working* (1850).

Monro, E., *Parochial Papers for the Clergyman, the Schoolmaster, and the Family* (1856).

Moorman, J. R. H., *A History of the Church of England* (1953).

Moorman, J. R. H., *Church Life in England in the Thirteenth Century* (1955).

More, P. E., and Cross, F. L., *Anglicanism: the thought and practice of the Church of England illustrated from the religious literature of the seventeenth century* (1935).

Moule, H. C. G., *Memories of a Vicarage* (1913).

Newsome, D. H., *Godliness and Good Learning* (1961).

Norman, E. R., *Church and Society in England 1770—1970* (1976).

Obelkevich, J., *Religion and Rural Society, South Lindsey 1825—1875* (1976).

Overton, J. H., and Relton, F., *The English Church 1714—1800* (1906).

Owen, D., *English Philanthropy 1600—1960* (1965).

Pantin, W. A., *The English Church in the Fourteenth Century* (1955).

Platt, C., *The Parish Churches of Medieval England* (1981).

Purcell, W. H., *Onward, Christian Soldier* (autobiography of Sabine Baring-Gould) (1957).

Report from the Clergy of a District in the Diocese of Lincoln, convened for the purpose of considering the state of religion (1800).

Report of the Medical Poor Relief Committee 1844. Parliamentary Papers 1844, vol. IX.

Report of the Poor Law Commissioners (1840).

Report of the Select Committee on the Sale of Beer (1833).

Report of the Special Assistant Poor Law Commisssioners on the Employment of Women and Children in Agriculture (1843).

Robinson, W., *The Magistrate's Pocket Book* (1825).

Robinson, W., *Lex Parochialis* (1827).

Russell, A., *The Clerical Profession* (1980).

Seymour, R., and Mackarness, J. F., *Eighteen Years of a Clerical Meeting; minutes of the Alcester Clerical Association from June 1842 to August 1860* (1862).

Smith, A., *The Established Church and Popular Religion* (1970).

Soloway, R. A., *Prelates and People. Ecclesiastical Social Thought in England 1783—1852* (1969).

Southern, R. W., *The Making of the Middle Ages*, (1953).

Spooner, E., *Parson and People; or incidents in the everyday life of a clergyman* (1964).

Stokes, F. G., (ed.), *The Bletchley Diary of the Rev'd William Cole, M. A., F. S. A., 1765—7* (1931).

Bibliography

Sykes, N., *Church and State in the Eighteenth Century* (1934).

Sykes, N., *The English Religious Tradition* (1953).

Sykes, N., *From Sheldon to Secker* (1959).

Thompson, A. H., *The English Clergy and their Organisation in the Later Middle Ages* (1947).

Thompson, K. A., *Bureaucracy and Church Reform: the organisational response of the Church of England to social change 1800—1965* (1970).

Trotter, E., *Seventeenth Century Life in a Country Parish* (1919).

Twining, R., *Recreations and Studies of a Country Clergyman in the Eighteenth Century* (1882).

Ward, W. R., *Religion and Society in England 1710—1850* (1972).

Ward, W. R., 'The Tithe Question in England in the Early Nineteenth Century', *Journal of Ecclesiastical History*, vol. XVI (1965) p. 67.

Warne, A. A., *Church and Society in Eighteenth Century Devon* (1969).

Watkins, E. I., *Roman Catholicism in England from the Reformation to 1950* (1957).

West, F., *Sparrows of the Spirit* (rev. edn. 1961).

Wilkinson, A., *The Church of England in the First World War* (1979).

Witts, F. E., (ed. D. Verey), *The Diary of a Cotswold Parson 1783—1854* (1978).

Yeo, S., *Religion and Voluntary Organisations in Crisis* (1976).

Young, G. M., *Victorian England. Portrait of an Age* (1936).

5 THE CONTEMPORARY PARISH CHURCH AND ITS MINISTRY (Chapters 12 and 13)

Adair, J., *The Becoming Church* (1977).

Archbishops' Council on Evangelism, *A Workbook on Rural Evangelism*. (1977).

Bath & Wells Diocesan Pastoral Committee, *Working Together. A Report of the Teams and Groups Working Party* (1981).

Beeson, T., (ed.), *Partnership in Ministry* (1964).

Beeson, T., *The Church of England in Crisis* (1973).

Beveridge, W. E., *Managing the Church* (1971).

British Council of Churches, *Handbook for Teams and Groups* (compiled by J. Hammersley 1981).

Browning, W., *A Handbook of the Ministry* (1985).

Byers, D, and Quinn, B., *New Directions for the Rural Church* (New York 1978).

Calvert, I, (ed.), *A Second Workbook on Rural Evangelism* (1984).

Carr, W., *The Priestlike Task* (1985).

Carroll, J. W., (ed.), *Small Churches are Beautiful* (New York 1977).

Church Pastoral Aid Society, *Rural Ministry* (1975).

Clark, J., *Mission in Rural Communities* (1978).

Clarkson, A. G., 'Deadlock in Rural Somerset', *New Fire*. no.7 (1971) pp. 29—34.

Diocese of Canterbury, *Report of the Working Party on Multi-Parish Units* (1981).

Diocese of Oxford, *Report of Bishop's Theological Advisory Group on Ministry* (1984).

Diocese of St Edmundsbury and Ipswich, *Lay Elders Handbook* (n.d.).

Diocese of St Edmundsbury and Ipswich, *Shared Ministry*. Report of Working Party on Ministry (1980).

Donaldson, C., *Rising from the Root: the early Christians and tomorrow's church* (1985).

Dorey, T., *Rural Ministries*. Report of Oxford Institute for Church and Society (1979).

Down, M., 'The Shape of the Rural Church', *Theology*, vol.87 (1984) pp. 164—72.

Dudley, C. C., *Unique Dynamics of the Small Church* (Nashville 1977).

Dudley, C. C., *Making the Small Church Effective* (Nashville 1978).

Dudley, C. C., *Where Have All Our People Gone? New choices for old churches* (New York 1979).

Eaton, D., 'Ministry in Surrey Villages', *New Fire*, vol.8 (1984) pp. 203—8.

Edwards, D. L., *Religion and Change* (1969).

Ferris, P., *The Church of England* (revised edn 1964).

Francis, L. J., *Rural Anglicanism. A future for young Christians?* (1985).

Gill, R., 'Theology of the Non-stipendiary Ministry', *Theology* vol.80 (1977) pp. 410—13.

Green, S. V., 'Blue-print for Rural Deanery', *Prism*, (September 1961) p. 14f.

Habgood, J., *Church and Nation in a Secular Age* (1983).

Hodge, M., *Non-stipendiary Ministry in the Church of England* (1983).

Hopkins, S., *The Rural Ministry* (1970).

Jagger, P. J., *History of the Parish and People Movement* (1978).

Lloyd, R., *The Church of England 1900—1965* (1966).

Luke, R. H., *The Commission of the Church in the Countryside* (1982).

Madsen, P. O., *The Small Church: valid, vital and victorious* (Valley Forge 1975).

Marshall, M., *The Anglican Church Today and Tomorrow* (1984).

Mathieson, M. M., *The Shepherds of the Delectable Mountains. Story of the Washington County Mission Program* (Cincinnati 1979).

Morgan, E. R., *The Church in Country Parishes* (1940).

Newton, C., *Life and Death in the Country Parish*. Board of Mission and Unity (1981).

Nott, P., 'Teams and Groups and their Problems', *Theology*, vol.81 (1978) pp. 14—17.

Paton, D. M., (ed.), *Reform of the Ministry: a study of the work of Roland Allen* (1968).

Paul, L., *The Deployment and Payment of the Clergy* (1964).

Paul, L., *A Church by Daylight* (1973).

Paul, L., Russell, A., and Reading, L., (eds.), *Rural Society and the Church*. Report of the Hereford Conference 1976 (1977).

Pawley, B. C., 'Pastoral Re-organisation and Liturgical Reform in a French Rural Deanery', *Theology*, vol.63 (1960) p. 432.

Poulton, J., *Fresh Air: a vision for the future of the rural church* (1985).

Ransom, S., Bryman, A., and Hinings, B., *Clergy. Ministers and Priests* (1977).

Report of the Commission on the Deployment and Payment of the Clergy, *Partners in Ministry* (1967).

Report of the Lincoln Consultation on Rural Society (ed. I. Beckwith 1979).

Report of the Ministry Co-ordinating Group. *Team and Group Ministries* (1985).

Report of the Oxford Diocesan Board of Social Responsibility. *The Rural Face of the Diocese* (1981).

Rudge, P., *Ministry and Management: studies in ecclesiastical administration* (1968).

Rural Theology Association, *Occasional Papers.*

Russell, A., *The Village in Myth and Reality* (1975).

Russell, A., (ed.), *Groups and Teams in the Countryside* (1975).

Russell, A., *The Clerical Profession* (1980).

Saumarez Smith, W. H., *An Honorary Ministry.* ACCM Occasional Paper no.8 (1977).

Sedgewick, P., (ed.), *A Rural Life Reader* (1984).

Smith, A. C., *The South Ormsby Experiment* (1960).

Smith, A. C., *Team and Group Ministry* (1985).

Tiller, J., *A Strategy for the Church's Ministry* (1983).

Tomorrow's Church Group, *Kingdom and Ministry: A Workbook on Lay Ministry* (1979).

Toon, P., 'Preserving Medieval Churches', *Theology* vol.87 (1984) pp. 110—13.

Towler, R., 'The Changing Status of the Ministry', *Crucible.* (May 1968) p. 73.

Towler, R., and Coxon, A. P. M., *The Fate of the Anglican Clergy* (1979).

Wignall, P., *Taking Custody of the Future* (1982).

Wilson, B., *Religion in Secular Society: a Sociological Comment* (1966).

Wilson, B., *Contemporary Transformations of Religion* (1976).

Wilson, B., *Religion in Sociological Perspective* (1982).

Welsby, P. A., *A History of the Church of England 1945—1980* (1984).

West, F., *The Country Parish Today and Tomorrow* (1960).

Index